Analyzing Character

By Katherine Blackford

INTRODUCTION

"There is one name," says Elbert Hubbard, "that stands out in history like a beacon light after all these twenty-five hundred years have passed, just because the man had the sublime genius of discovering ability. That man is Pericles. Pericles made Athens and to-day the very dust of the street of Athens is being sifted and searched for relics and remnants of the things made by people who were captained by men of ability who were discovered by Pericles."

The remark of Andrew Carnegie that he won his success because he had the knack of picking the right men has become a classic in current speech. Augustus Caesar built up and extended the power of the Roman Empire because he knew men. The careers of Charlemagne, Napoleon, Disraeli, Washington, Lincoln, and all the empire builders and empire saviours hold their places in history because these men knew how to recognize, how to select, and how to develop to the highest degree the abilities of their co-workers. The great editors, Greeley, Dana, James Gordon Bennett, McClure, Gilder and Curtis, attained their high station in the world of letters largely because of their ability to unearth men of genius. Morgan, Rockefeller, Theodore N. Vail, James J. Hill, and other builders of industrial and commercial empires laid strong their foundations by almost infallible wisdom in the selection of lieutenants. Even in the world of sports the names of Connie Mack, McGraw, Chance, Moran, Carrigan and Stallings shine chiefly because of their keen judgment of human nature.

If the glory that was Greece shone forth because Pericles kindled its flame, then Pericles in any time and amongst any people would probably have ushered in a Golden Age. Had Carnegie lived in any other day and sought his industrial giants, he would no doubt have found them. If a supreme judge of latent talent and inspirer of high achievement can thus always find material ready to his hand, it follows that humanity is rich in undiscovered genius--that, in the race, there are, unguessed and undeveloped, possibilities for a millennium of Golden

Ages. Psychologists tell us that only a very small percentage of the real ability and energy of the average man is ever developed or used.

"Poor man!" says a reviewer, speaking of a contemporary, "he never discovered his discoverer." The man who waits for his Pericles usually waits in vain. There has been only one Pericles in all history. Great geniuses in the discovery, development, and management of men are rare. Most men never meet them. And yet every man can discover his discoverer.

Self-knowledge is the first step to self-development. Through an understanding of his own aptitudes and talents one may find fullest expression for the highest possibilities of his intellect and spirit. A man who thus knows himself needs no other discoverer. The key to self-knowledge is intelligent, scientific self-study.

In the year 1792, Mahmoud Effendi, a Turkish archer, hit a mark with an arrow at 482 yards. His bow, arrows, thumb-ring and groove are still on exhibition in London as proof of the feat. His prowess lay in his native gift, trained by years of practice, to guess the power of his bow, the weight and balance of his arrow, and the range and direction of his target; also, the sweep of the wind. This he gained by observations repeated until the information gathered from them amounted to almost exact knowledge. Thousands of gunners to-day hit a mark miles away, with a 16-inch gun, not because they are good guessers, but because, by means of science, they determine accurately all of the factors entering into the flight of their projectiles. Pericles judged men by a shrewd guess--the kind of guess called intuition. But such intuition is only a native gift of keen observation, backed by good judgment, and trained by shrewd study of large numbers of men until it becomes instinctively accurate.

In modern times we are learning not to depend upon mere guesses--no matter how shrewd. Mahmoud Effendi could not pass on to others the art he had acquired. But the science of gunnery can be taught to any man of average intelligence and natural aptitudes. Pericles left posterity not one hint about how to judge men--how to recognize ability. Humanity needs a scientific method of judging men, so that any man of intelligence can discover genius--or just native ability--in himself and others.

As the result of our ignorance, great possibilities lie undeveloped in nearly all men. Self-expression is smothered in uncongenial toil. Parents and teachers, groping in the dark, have long been training natural-born artists to become mechanics, natural-born business men to become musicians, and boys and girls with great aptitudes for agriculture and horticulture to become college professors, lawyers, and doctors. Splendid human talent, amounting in some cases to positive genius, is worse than wasted as a result.

In our experience, covering years of careful investigation and the examination of many thousands of individuals, we have seen so much of the tragedy of the misfit that it seems at times almost universal. The records of one thousand persons taken at random from our files show that 763, or 76.3 per cent, felt that they were in the wrong vocations. Of these 414 were thirty-five years old or older. Most of these, when questioned as to why they had entered upon vocations for which they had so little natural aptitude, stated that they had either drifted along lines of least resistance or had been badly advised by parents, teachers, or employers.

We knew a wealthy father, deaf to all pleas from his children, who spent thousands of dollars upon what he thought was a musical education for his daughter, including several years in Europe. The young lady could not become a musician. The aptitude for music was not in her. But she was unusually talented in mathematics and appreciation of financial values, and could have made a marked success had she been permitted to gratify her constantly reiterated desire for a commercial career. This same father, with the same obstinacy, insisted that his son go into business. The young man was so passionately determined to make a career of music that he was a complete failure in business and finally embezzled several thousand dollars from his employer in the hope of making his escape to Europe and securing a musical education. Here were two human lives of marked talent as completely ruined and wasted as a well-intentioned but ignorant and obstinate parent could accomplish that end.

A few years ago a young man was brought to us by his friends for advice. He had been educated for the law and then inherited from his father a considerable sum of money. Having no taste for the law and a repugnance for anything like office work, he had never even attempted to begin practice. Having nothing to do, he was becoming more and more dissipated, and when we saw him first had lost confidence in himself and was utterly discouraged. "I am useless in the world," he told us. "There is nothing I can do." At our suggestion, he was finally encouraged to purchase land and begin the scientific study and practice of horticulture. The last time we saw him he was erect, ruddy, hard-muscled, and capable looking. Best of all, his old, petulant, dissatisfied expression was gone. In its place was the light of worthy achievement, success, and happiness. He told us there were no finer fruit trees anywhere than his. Such incidents as this are not rare--indeed, they are commonplace. We could recount them from our records in great number. But every observant reader can supply many from his own experience.

Thousands of young men and women are encouraged, every year, to enroll in schools where they will spend time and money preparing themselves for professions already overcrowded and for which a large majority of them have no natural aptitudes. A prominent physician tells us that of the forty-eight who were graduated from medical school with him, he considers only three safe to consult upon medical subjects. Indeed, so great is the need and so increasingly serious is it becoming, as our industrial and commercial life grows more complex and the demand for conservation and efficiency more exacting, that progressive men and women in our universities and schools and elsewhere have undertaken a study of the vocational problem and are earnestly working toward a solution of it in vocational bureaus, vocational schools, and other ways, all together comprising the vocational movement.

Roger W. Babson, in his book, "The Future of the Working Classes: Economic Facts for Employers and Wage Earners," says: "The crowning work of an economic educational system will be vocational guidance. One of the greatest handicaps to all classes to-day is that 90 per cent of the people have entered their present employment blindly and by chance, irrespective of their fitness or opportunities. Of course, the law of supply and demand is continually correcting these errors, but this readjusting causes most of the world's disappointments and losses. Some day the schools of the nation will be organized into a great reporting bureau on employment opportunities and trade conditions, directing the youths of the nation--so far as their qualifications warrant--into lines of work which then offer the greatest opportunity. Only by such a system will each worker receive the greatest income possible for himself, and also the greatest benefits possible from the labors of all, thus continually increasing production and yet avoiding overproduction in any single line." That the main features of the system suggested by Mr. Babson are being made the basis of the vocational movement is one of the most hopeful signs of the times.

Dr. George W. Jacoby, the neurologist, says: "It is scarcely too much to say that the entire future happiness of a child depends upon the successful bringing out of its capabilities. For upon that rests the choice of its life work. A mistake in this choice destroys all the real joy of living--it almost means a lost life."

4

Consider the stone wall against which the misfit batters his head:

He uses only his second rate, his third rate, or even less effective mental and physical equipment. He is thus handicapped at the start in the race against those using their best. He is like an athlete with weak legs, but powerful arms and shoulders, trying to win a foot race instead of a hand-over-hand rope-climbing contest.

Worse than his ineptitude, however, is the waste and atrophy of his best powers through disuse. Thus the early settlers of the Coachela Valley fought hunger and thirst while rivers of water ran away a few feet below the surface of the richly fertile soil.

No wonder, then, that the misfit hates his work. And yet, his hate for it is the real tragedy of his life.

Industry, like health, is normal. All healthy children, even men, are active. Activity means growth and development. Inactivity means decay and death. The man who has no useful work to do sometimes expresses himself in wrong-doing and crime, for he has to do something industriously to live. Even our so-called "idle rich" and leisure classes are strenuously active in their attempts to amuse themselves.

When, therefore, a man hates his work, when he is dissatisfied and discontented in it, when his work arouses him to destructive thoughts and feelings, rather than constructive, there is something wrong, something abnormal, and the abnormality is his attempt to do work for which he is unfitted by natural aptitudes or by training.

The man who is trying to do work for which he is unfitted feels repressed, baffled and defeated. He may not even guess his unfitness, but he does feel its manifold effect. He lacks interest in his work and, therefore, that most vital factor in personal efficiency--incentive. He cannot throw himself into his work with a whole heart.

When Thomas A. Edison is bent upon realizing one of his ideas, his absorption in his work exemplifies Emerson's dictum: "Nothing great was ever accomplished without enthusiasm. The way of life is wonderful--it is by abandonment." He shuts himself away from all interruption in his laboratory; he works for hours oblivious of everything but his idea. Even the demands of his body for food and sleep do not rise above the threshold of consciousness.

Edison himself says that great achievement is a result, not of genius, but of this kind of concentration in work--and, until the mediocre man has worked as has Edison, he cannot prove the contrary. Mr. Edison has results to prove the value of his way of working. Even our most expert statisticians and mathematicians would find it difficult to calculate, accurately, the amount of material wealth this one worker has added to humanity's store. Of the unseen but higher values in culture, in knowledge, in the spread of civilization, and in greater joy of living for millions of people, there are even greater riches. Other men of the past and present, in every phase of activity, have demonstrated that such an utter abandonment to one's tasks is the keynote of efficiency and achievement. But such abandonment is impossible to the man who is doing work into which he cannot throw his best and greatest powers-- which claims only his poorest and weakest.

This man's very failure to achieve increases his unrest and unhappiness. Walter Dill Scott, the psychologist, in his excellent book, "Increasing Human Efficiency in Business," gives loyalty and concentration as two of the important factors in human efficiency. But loyalty pre-supposes the giving of a man's best. Concentration demands interest and enthusiasm. These are products of a love of the work to be done.

The man employed at work for which he is unfit, therefore, finds it not a means of self-expression, but a slow form of self-destruction. All this wretchedness of spirit reacts directly upon the efficiency of the worker. "A successful day is likely to be a restful one," says Professor Scott,-- "an unsuccessful day an exhausting one. The man who is greatly interested in his work and who finds delight in overcoming the difficulties of his calling is not likely to become so tired as the man for whom the work is a burden.

"Victory in intercollegiate athletic events depends on will power and physical endurance. This is particularly apparent in football. Frequently it is not the team with the greater muscular development or speed of foot that wins the victory, but the one with the more grit and perseverance. At the conclusion of a game players are often unable to walk from the field and need to be carried. Occasionally the winning team has actually worked the harder and received the more serious injuries. Regardless of this fact, it is usually true that the victorious team leaves the field less jaded than the conquered team. Furthermore, the winners will report next day refreshed and ready for further training, while the losers may require several days to overcome the shock and exhaustion of their defeat.

"Recently I had a very hard contest at tennis. Some hours after the game I was still too tired to do effective work. I wondered why, until I remembered that I had been thoroughly beaten, and that, too, by an opponent whom I felt I outclassed. I had been in the habit of playing even harder contests and ordinarily with no discomfort--especially when successful in winning the match.

"What I have found so apparent in physical exertion is equally true in intellectual labor. Writing or research work which progresses satisfactorily leaves me relatively fresh; unsuccessful efforts bring their aftermath of weariness.

"_Intellectual work which is pleasant is stimulating and does not fag one, while intellectual work which is uninteresting or displeasing is depressing and exhausting_....

"To restore muscular and nerve cells is a very delicate process. So wonderful is the human organism, however, that the process is carried on perfectly without our consciousness or volition except under abnormal conditions.

"Food and air are the first essentials of this restoration. In-directly the perfect working of all the bodily organs contributes to the process--especially deepened breathing, heightened pulse, and increase of bodily volume due to the expansion of the blood vessels running just beneath the skin.

"Here pleasure enters. Its effect on the expenditure of energy is to make muscle and brain cells more available for consumption, and particularly to hasten the process of restoration or recuperation.

"The deepened breathing supplies more air for the oxidation of body wastes. The heightened pulse carries nourishment more rapidly to the depleted tissues and relieves the tissues more rapidly from the poisonous wastes produced by work. The body, the machine, runs more smoothly, and few stops for repairs are made necessary.

"In addition to these specific functions, *pleasure hastens all the bodily processes which are of advantage to the organism.* The hastening may be so great that recuperation keeps pace with the consumption consequent on efficient labor, with the result that there is little or no exhaustion. This is, in physiological terms, the reason why a person can do more when he 'enjoys' his work or play, and can continue his efforts for a longer period without fatigue. The man who enjoys his work requires less time for recreation and exercise, for his enjoyment recharges the storage battery of energy."

But the misfit can take none of this pleasure in his work. He is unhappy because he cannot do his best; he is wretched because he feels that he is being defeated in the contest of life; he is miserable because he hates the things he has to do; he can take no satisfaction in his work because he feels that it is poorly done; and, finally, all of his joylessness reacts upon him, decreasing his efficiency and making him a more pitiable failure.

So this is the vicious circle:

Misfit; Inefficient; Unhappy; More inefficient.

Rather is it a descending spiral, leading down to poverty, disease, crime and death.

Now, consider the man who has found *his* work. To him the glorious abandonment which is the way to achievement is possible. Such a man does not merely exist--he lives, and lives grandly. His work gives him joy, both in its doing and in its results. It calls out and develops his highest and best talents. He therefore grows in power, in wisdom, in health, in efficiency, and in success. All his life runs in an ascending spiral. No task appalls him. No difficulty daunts him. He may work hard--terribly hard. He may tunnel through mountains of drudgery. He will shun the easy ways and leave the soft jobs to weaker men. But through it all there will be a song in his heart.

Work to such a man is as natural an expression as hunger, or love, or pleasure, or laughter. He returns to it with zest and eagerness. Such a man's work flows out from his soul. It is an expression of the divine in him.

The almost universal cry for leisure is due to the almost universal unfitness of men and women for their tasks. The wise man knows that there is no happiness in leisure. The only happiness is self-expression in useful work. And so we come again to the problem of fitting the man to his work. Every man is a bundle of possibilities. Every man has a right to usefulness, prosperity and happiness. These are possible only through knowledge of self, knowledge of others, knowledge of work, and the ability to make the right combination of self and others and work.

Man has learned much about the material universe. Nearly everything has been analyzed and classified. Man weighs, measures, tests, and in others ways scrupulously determines the fitness of every bit of material that goes into a machine before it is built. There are scientific ways of selecting cattle, horses, and even hogs for particular purposes. Purchasing departments of great commercial and industrial institutions maintain laboratories for the determination, with mathematical exactitude, of the qualifications and fitness to requirements of all kinds of materials, tools and equipment. And yet, when it comes to the choice of his own life work, the guidance of his children in their vocations, or the selection of employees and co-workers, the average man decides the entire matter by almost any other consideration than scientifically determined fitness. He takes counsel with personal prejudices, with customs and traditions, with pride, or with fear--or he leaves the decision to mere guess-work, or even chance.

It is time, therefore, that man should learn about himself and others, and especially about those things which are vital to even a moderate enjoyment of the good things of life.

Two diametrically opposite states of mind have been responsible for this lack of careful study of the aptitudes, characteristics, and qualifications of man and the ways of determining them in advance of actual performance. The first of these has been characterized by loose thinking, unscientific methods, arbitrary and complicated systems--- such as palmistry, astrology, physiognomy, phrenology, and others of the same ilk. In these systems, some truth, patiently learned by sincere and able workers, has been befogged and contaminated by hasty conclusions of the incompetent and clever lies of charlatans. Thus the whole subject has fallen into disrepute with intelligent people. Ever since the earliest days of recorded history there have been attempts at character reading. Many different avenues of approach to the subject have been opened; some by sincere and earnest men of scientific minds and scholarly attainments; some by sincere and earnest but unscientific laymen; and some by mountebanks and charlatans. As the result of all this study, research and empiricism, a great mass of alleged facts about physical characteristics has been accumulated. When we began our research seventeen years ago, we found a very considerable library covering every phase of character interpretation, both scientific and unscientific. A great deal has been added since that time. 'Much of this literature is pseudo-scientific, and some of it is pure quackery.

The second state of mind is a reaction from the first. Some men of science are timid about accepting or stating anything in regard to character analysis. They demand more than conclusive proof; what they insist upon is mathematical accuracy. Until a man can be analyzed in such a way as to leave nothing to common sense or good judgment, they hesitate to acknowledge that he can be analyzed at all. But in the very nature of the case, the science of character analysis cannot be a science in the same sense in which chemistry and mathematics are

9

sciences. So far our studies and experiences do not lead us to expect that it ever can become absolute and exact. Human nature is complicated by too many variables and obscured by too much that is elusive and intangible. We cannot put a man on the scales and determine that he has so many milligrams of common sense, or apply the micrometer to him and say that he has so many millimetres of financial ability. Human traits and human values are relative and can be determined and stated only relatively. We shall, therefore, waste both time and human values if we wait until our knowledge is mathematically exact before we make it useful to ourselves and to others.

The sciences of medicine, agriculture, chemistry and physics are not yet exact. They are in a state of development. We have, however, the good sense to apply them so far as we know them, and to accept new discoveries, new methods, and new ways of applying them, as they come to us. And so, in the study of ourselves, let us throw aside traditions; let us forget the mountebanks and charlatans of the past; let us not wait for the final work of the mathematician; but, with plain common sense, let us apply such knowledge as we have at hand. This knowledge should be the result of careful observation, of a careful and prolonged study of all that science has discovered in regard to man, his origin, his development, his history, his body, and his mind. Every conclusion reached should be verified, not in hundreds, but in thousands of cases, before it is finally accepted.

The perfection of such a science requires the united efforts of many investigators, experimenters, and practical workers, such as teachers, employers, social workers, parents, and men and women everywhere, each in his own way and in the solution of his own problems. Were a uniform method adopted and made a part of the vocational work of our social settlements, our public schools, our colleges and universities, and other institutions, also by private individuals in selecting their own vocations; were uniform records to be made and every subject analyzed followed up, and his career studied, we should, in one generation, have data from which any intelligent, analytical mind could formulate a science of human analysis very nearly approaching exactitude.

As a result of the application of such a uniform method, the principles of human analysis would rapidly become a matter of common knowledge and could be taught in our schools just as we to-day teach the principles of chemical, botanical, or zoological analysis. In the industries, the scientific selection, assignment and management of men have yielded increases in efficiency from one hundred to one thousand per cent. The majority of people that were dealt with were mature, with more or less fixity of character and habits. Many of them were handicapped by iron-clad limitations and restrictions in their affairs and in their environments. What results may be possible when these methods, improved and developed by a wider use, are applied to young people, with their plastic minds and wonderful latent possibilities, we cannot even venture to forecast.

While we are accustomed to thinking of unfitness for our tasks as the one form of maladjustment due to our ignorance of human nature in general and individual traits in particular, there are other forms which, in their own way, cause much trouble and the remedying of which leads to desirable results. These are many and varied, but may be grouped, perhaps, most conveniently under two or three general headings.

First, there is the relationship between employers and employees. The disturbances and inharmony which mark this relationship, and have marked it throughout human history, are due as much, perhaps, to misunderstanding of human nature as to any one other cause. When employers select men unfitted for their tasks, assign them to work in environments where they are handicapped from the start, and associate them together and with executives in combinations which are inherently inharmonious, it is inevitable that trouble should follow.

The larger aspects of the employment problem are treated in the second part of this book. Inasmuch, however, as the subject has been more fully discussed in another volume,[1] no attempt is made to go into details.

Adjustment to environment means very largely the ability successfully to associate with, cooperate with, and secure one's way among one's fellow men. In order to be successful in life, we must first live on terms of mutual cooperation with our parents; second, secure the best instruction possible from our teachers; third, make social progress; fourth, secure gainful employment, either from one employer, as in the case of the laborer and the executive, or from several, as in the cases of professional men. Having secured employment, our progress depends upon our ability to attain promotion, to increase our business or our practice, to add to our patrons. Salesmen must sell more, and more advantageously. Attorneys must convince judges and juries, as well as obtain desired testimony from witnesses. Preachers and other public speakers of all classes must entertain, interest, arouse, and convince their audiences. Writers must each appeal successfully to his particular public as well as to his publisher. Engineers must establish and sustain successful relationship with clients, employers, and employees.

In the third part of this book, therefore, we deal more or less at length with the psychological processes of persuasion and their application in various forms and to the varied personalities of those whom we wish to persuade.

Finally, in the fourth part, we devote three chapters to a consideration of the Science of Character Analysis by the Observational Method, the principles of which underlie all of the observations and suggestions appearing in the first three parts.

In presenting the material in this volume, our aim has been not to propound a theory, but merely to make practical, for the use of our readers, so far as possible, the results of our own experiences in this field.

[Footnote 1: The Job, The Man, The Boss, by Katherine M.H. Blackford, M.D., and Arthur Newcomb.]

PART ONE

ANALYZING CHARACTER IN VOCATIONAL GUIDANCE

CHAPTER I

CAUSES OF MISFITS

"Blessed is the man who has found his work."--Carlyle.

Only the rarest kind of soul has a clear call to his vocation. Still rarer is he who, knowing his work, can create circumstances which will permit him to do it. Of the thousands of young people who have sought us for counsel, only a very small percentage have had even a vague idea of what they are fitted to do, or even what they wished to do. Strange to say, this lack of definite knowledge as to vocation holds true of those who have just graduated from college or university. Many a college graduate has said to us: "Why, I shall teach for a few years until I have fully made up my mind just what I wish to do. Then I shall take my post-graduate course in preparation for my life work." Even so late a decision as this often proves unsatisfactory.

IGNORANCE AND PURPOSELESSNESS

The causes for uncertainty as to work are many and varied. And yet all the many causes can be traced to two fundamental deficiencies in human nature which are but poorly supplied in our traditional systems of training and education. The first of these is, of course, ignorance-- ignorance of self, ignorance of work, ignorance on the part of parents, teachers, and other advisors; ignorance on the part of employers. As a race, we do not know human nature; we do not know how to determine, in advance of actual, painful and costly experience, the aptitudes of any individual. We blunder a good deal even in trying to learn from experience. We do not know work; we do not know its requirements, its conditions, its opportunities, its emoluments. And so, in our ignorance, we go astray; we lead others astray. We neglect important and vital factors in human success and happiness because we do not know how important and how vital they are. Our ignorance of their importance is due to our ignorance of human nature and of work.

A second cause for our uncertainty lies in the almost universal human habit of purposelessness. Drifting, not steering, is the way of nearly all lives. It is hard mental work to plan, to consider, to study, to analyze; in short, to think. Someone has said that the average man would rather lie down and die than to take the trouble really to think. It is easier to await the knock of opportunity than to study her ways and then go out and capture her. She treads paths which may be known. She has a schedule which may be learned. She may thus be met as certainly as by appointment. Those who await her knock at the door may be far from where she passes.

We in America, especially, place altogether too high a value on our ingeniousness, our resourcefulness. We therefore put off the evil day. We say to ourselves: "There is plenty of time. I'll manage somehow or other when the time comes for action." We are rather proud of our ability to meet emergencies. So we do not plan and take precautions, that emergencies may not arise. It is too easy to drift through school and college, taking the traditional, conventional studies that others take, following the lines of least resistance, electing "snap courses," going with the crowd. It is too easy to take the attitude: "First I will get my education and develop myself, and then I will know better what I am fitted to do for a life work." And so we drift, driven by the winds of circumstance, tossed about by the waves of tradition and custom. Eventually, most men find they must be satisfied with "any port in a storm." Sailors who select a port because they are driven to it have scarcely one chance in a thousand of dropping anchor in the right one.

In our ignorance, we do not know how fatal to success and happiness is

13

this lack of purpose. We fail to impress it upon our youth. And, when one demands chart and compass, we cannot supply them. No wonder belief in luck, fate, stars, or a meddling, unreasonable Providence is almost universal!

Ignorance and lack of definite purpose, the two prime causes of misfits, have many different ways of bungling people into the wrong job and keeping them there.

IMMATURE JUDGMENT

The first of these is immaturity of judgment on the part of young people. There is a popular fallacy that the thing which a young man or a young woman wants most to do must be the thing for which he or she is preeminently fitted. "Let him follow his bent," say some advisors, "and he will find his niche." This does not happen often. The average young man is immature. His tastes are not formed. He is undeveloped. His very best talents may have never been discovered by himself or others. It is well known to those who study children that a boy's earliest ambitions are to do something he thinks spectacular and romantic. Boys long to be cab drivers, locomotive engineers, policemen, cowboys, soldiers and aviators.

A little nephew of ours said he wanted to be a ditch-digger. Asked why, he said: "So I can wear dirty clothes, smoke a pipe, and spit tobacco juice in the street." The little fellow is really endowed with an inheritance of great natural refinement and a splendid intellect. As he grows older, his ideals will change and he will discover there is much to ditch-digging besides wearing dirty clothes, smoking a pipe, and expectorating on the public highways. He will also learn that there are things in life far more desirable than these glorious privileges. Of course, these are mere boyish exuberances, and most people do not take them seriously. On the other hand, they illustrate the unwisdom of trusting to the unguided preferences of a youthful mind. The average young man of twenty is only a little more mature than a boy of ten. He still lacks experience and balance.

Those of us who have passed the two-score mark well know how tastes change, judgments grow more mature, ideas develop, and experience softens, ripens or hardens sentiment as the years go by. It is unquestionably true that if children were given full opportunity to develop their tastes and to express themselves in various ways and then given freedom of choice of their vocations, they would choose more wisely than they do under ignorant, prejudiced, or mistaken judgments of parent or teacher. Yet the tragedy of thousands of lives shows how unscientific it is to leave the choice of vocation to the unguided instincts of an immature mind.

INFLUENCE OF ASSOCIATION

Boys and girls often choose their careers because some popular friend or associate exerts an undue influence upon them. George is going to be a doctor. Therefore Joseph decides he, too, will be a doctor. Mary looks forward to being a teacher. Mary is the very intimate chum of Josephine. Then Josephine decides, also, that she is going to be a teacher. We knew one earnest and popular young man in college who persuaded about three dozen of his associates to join him in preparation for the foreign mission field. In one class in college a fad caused several young men to lose good opportunities because they decided to take up the practice of medicine. In one high school class, several young men became railroad employees because the most popular of their number yearned to drive a locomotive. And this enterprising youth, with parental guidance and assistance, became a lawyer.

POOR JUDGMENT OF PARENTS

Parental bad judgment is one of the most frequent causes of misfits. Even when parents are sincere and try to be wise, choice of a child's life work is very difficult for them. In the first place, they either underestimate or overestimate their children. What parent, worthy of the high privilege, can be absolutely impartial in judging the talents of his child? Arthur Brisbane says that Nature makes every baby look like a genius in his mother's eyes, so that she will gladly sacrifice her life, if necessary, for her child. It may be a wise provision, but it does not tend to make parents reliable guides to vocations for their offspring.

Then, many parents do not know work. They do not understand the demands of the different professions. Their point of view is narrowed by their own experiences, which have been, perhaps too harsh, perhaps too easy. Many parents have a narrow, selfish, rather jealous feeling that their children cannot be any more intelligent than they are. "The old farm was good enough for me; it is good enough for my son"; "the old business was good enough for me; it is good enough for my son." This is the attitude. This is why many parents either refuse their children the advantages of an education and insist upon their going to work at an early age, or compel them to take a hated schooling.

On the other hand, there are parents who consider their children prodigies, geniuses, intended to occupy some great and magnificent position in the world. Most frequently they hold their judgment entirely apart from any real talents on the part of the child. Few human woes are more bitter than the disappointment and heartache of both parent and son when a young man who might have been a successful and happy farmer or merchant fails utterly as an artist or writer.

Parents often persuade their children to enter vocations upon the flimsiest possible pretexts. Almost every child takes a pencil and tries to draw, yet there are many parents who spend thousands of dollars in trying to make great artists of children who have only the most mediocre artistic ability. Mere purposeless drawing of faces and figures is an entirely different thing from the drudgery necessary to become a great artist. The mere writing of little essays and compositions is quite a different thing from the long, hard training necessary to become a writer of any acceptability. Merely because a child finds it easier to dawdle away the hours with a pencil or a brush than to go into the harvest field or into the kitchen is not a good reason for supposing that this preference is an indication of either talent or genius.

A parent's judgment of the requirements of a profession is oftentimes most amusingly erroneous. We remember a father who told us that he was quite certain that his son was born to be a ruler of men. When we asked why, he told us in all seriousness that from early childhood his boy's blood boiled with indignation against people who had committed indignities upon kings and princes. Of course, in one sense of the word, this parent was insane, and yet his bad judgment was scarcely more ridiculous than that of many other parents. We have met parents who seemed to think that success in the practice of law depended wholly upon the ability to make speeches. We have seen other parents who thought that success in banking depended upon the ability to count money and hold on to it. Even intelligent people have the false idea that an architect needs only to be a good draughtsman. The number of people who imagine that success in business is won by shrewdness and sharp practice is very large.

PARENTAL PREJUDICES

Parents are often influenced by the most irrelevant of prejudices in counseling their children as to vocation. A man who has had an unfortunate experience with a lawyer is very likely to oppose strenuously any move on the part of his son to study and practice law. Many practical men have intense prejudices against art, music, literature, and other such professions for their sons. The number of parents who are prejudiced against a college education is legion. On the other hand, there are a goodly number of men who are prejudiced against any vocation for their sons which does not involve a college education.

Many parents who have worked hard and toiled unremittingly at any particular profession oftentimes feel that they want their children to do something easier, something requiring less drudgery, and so bitterly oppose their following in their fathers' footsteps. On the other hand, many fathers are domineering in their determination that their sons shall follow the same vocation in which they made their success.

Parents are often prejudiced in favor of vocations followed by dear friends or by men whom they greatly admire. A successful lawyer, preacher, engineer, or business man will influence the choice of vocations for the children of many of his admiring friends and acquaintances.

Multitudes of parents have foolish prejudices against any kind of work which soils the hands or clothing--even against the dinner-pail. On the other hand, hard-fisted parents may have prejudices against any vocation which keeps the hands soft and white, and the clothing clean and fine.

Thus, in many ways do the prejudices of parents, based upon ignorance, work tragedy in the lives of children. Either through a sense of duty and loyalty or because they have not sufficient solid masonry in their backbones, children follow the wishes of their parents and many all but ruin their lives as a result.

"THE LEARNED PROFESSIONS"

One of the most disastrous prejudices upon the part of parents is that in favor of what are called "the learned professions." To make a lawyer, a physician, or a minister of one's son is held to be the highest ambition on the part of large numbers of otherwise intelligent fathers and mothers. The result of this kind of prejudice on the part of so many parents is that the so-called learned professions are over-crowded--and overcrowded with men and women unfitted for their tasks, both by natural inheritance and by education and training. There follows mediocre Work, poor service, low pay, poverty, disease, and misery.

FAMILY TRADITIONS

There are traditions in some families which carry their curse along with them down through the generations. There are families of preachers, families of soldiers, families of lawyers, families of physicians, families of teachers. Many a young man who would have otherwise

17

been a success in the world has toiled along at a poor, dying rate, trying to live up to the family tradition and make a success of himself as a teacher, or lawyer, when he ought to have been a mechanic, an actor, or a banker.

Another form of parental prejudice is a father's desire to have his son become a success in the vocation which he himself longed to enter, but could not. "My father is a successful business man," said a young man to us not long ago. "When he was a young man he wanted to enter law school and practice law, but because of lack of funds and because he had to support his widowed mother's family, he did not have the opportunity. All his life he has regretted that he was unable to realize his ambition. From my earliest years he has talked to me about becoming a great lawyer; he spent thousands of dollars in sending me through high school, college and law school; he has given me years of post-graduate work in law. I have now been trying to practice law for two years and have made a complete failure of it. Yet, so intense is his desire that I shall realize his ambition, that he is willing to finance me, in the hope that, eventually, I may be able to succeed in the practice of law. And yet I hate it. I hate it so that it seems to me I cannot drive myself ever to enter a law office for another day."

POOR JUDGMENT OF TEACHERS

When bad judgment and prejudice of parents do not interfere with a child's development and his selection of a vocation, he is often turned into wrong channels by the bad judgment of his teacher or teachers. It is natural for many teachers to try to influence their favorite pupils to enter the teaching profession in the same special branch to which the teachers themselves are attached. We once knew a professor of Latin who was an enthusiast on the subject. As the result of his influence, many of his students became teachers of Latin. Teachers, like parents, also frequently fail to see the indications of aptitude where it is very great.

Like parents, teachers also are oftentimes ignorant of the requirements of work. They are frequently narrow in their training and experience, and therefore do not understand much about practical life, practical work, and practical requirements. Many teachers, even college professors, seem to be obsessed with the idea that a student who learns a subject easily will be successful in making a practical application of it. Not long ago a student in engineering in one of our most prominent universities came to us for consultation. He told us that his professors all agreed that he was well fitted to succeed as an engineer. He, however, had no liking for the profession and did not believe that he would either enjoy it or be successful in it. Our observations confirmed his opinions. It turned out that his instructors thought him qualified for engineering merely from the fact that he learned easily the theoretical principles underlying the practice.

ECONOMIC NECESSITY

Perhaps one of the most potent causes of misfits in vocation is economic necessity. The time comes in the life of most boys when they must earn their own living or, perhaps, help support the parental family. In such a case, a search is made for a job. Local conditions, friendship, associations, chance vacancies--almost any consideration but that of personal fitness governs in the choice of the job. Once a boy is in a vocation, he is more than likely to remain in it--or, because of unfitness, to drift aimlessly into another, for which he is even less adapted. An entertaining writer in the "Saturday Evening Post" has shown how the boy who accidentally enters upon his career as a day laborer soon finds it impossible to graduate into the ranks of skilled labor. He remains not only a day laborer, but an occasional laborer, his periods of work interspersed with longer and longer periods of unemployment. Unemployment means bad food, unwholesome sanitary conditions and, worst of all, bad mental and moral states. These are followed by disease, incompetency, inefficiency, weakness, and, in time, the man becomes one of the unemployed and unemployable wrecks of humanity. Crime then becomes practically the only avenue of escape from starvation or pauperism.

Thousands of young men taking a job, no matter how they may dislike the work, feel compelled to remain in it because it is their one hope of income. The longer they remain in it the harder it is for them to make a change. Sad, indeed, is the case of the boy or girl who is compelled, in order to make a living or to help support father, mother, brothers and sisters, to drop into the first vacancy which offers itself.

RESTLESSNESS

The restlessness of many a boy and girl results in his or her choice of an utterly wrong vocation. Boys whose parents would be glad to see them through college or technical school cannot wait to begin their careers. Impatient and restless, they undertake the work which will yield quick results rather than develop their real talents or seek opportunities for advancement of which they are by nature capable. Over and over again those who come to us for consultation say: "Father would have been willing to have put me through school, but I couldn't

19

wait; I simply had to get out and have my own way. I have never ceased to regret it. Now I have to work hard with my hands; with a proper education, and in my right job, I could have used my head." The reader has doubtless heard many such stories from friends and acquaintances. The world is full of misfits who failed of their great opportunity because they were too restless, too impatient, to make proper preparations for their life work. This restlessness, unfortunately, is a characteristic of many of the most energetic, most capable, and most intelligent young people, to whom an education would be worth much, to whom proper training and preparation would bring unusual self-development. It is, therefore, of the highest importance that the young man or young woman and his or her parents or guardian should be especially cautious when there is this feeling of intense eagerness to begin work.

VERSATILITY

Perhaps one of the most difficult causes of misfits to overcome is versatility. He who can do many things well seems always to have great difficulty in fixing upon any one thing and doing that supremely well. The versatile man is usually fond of variety, changeable, fickle; he loves to have many irons in the fire; he likes to turn from one kind of work to another. It is his great failing that he seldom sticks at any one thing long enough to make a marked success of it. Because of his great versatility, too, he is often a serious problem, even for those who can study his case scientifically. It is difficult to give him counsel and it is even more difficult for him to give heed to that counsel when it has been given. The one hope of the exceedingly versatile individual is to find for himself some vocation which has within it an opportunity for the exercise of many different kinds of talents, and for turning quickly from one kind of work to another. Routine, monotony, detail work, and work which is confining in its character and presents a continual sameness of environment, should be avoided by this type of individual.

MEDIOCRITY AND UNGUESSED TALENTS

The inability to do any one thing particularly well is, in its way, as serious a handicap in the selection of a vocation as great versatility. One who can do nothing well finds it just as hard to decide upon a vocation as one who can do everything well. Perhaps the large majority of those who come to us for consultation do so because they feel that they have no particular talent. Oftentimes this is the case. But frequently there are undeniable talents which have simply never been discovered and never developed. Even in the case of those with no particular talent, there is always some combination of aptitudes, characteristics, disposition, and other circumstances which makes one particular vocation far more desirable than any other. It is most important that the individual with only a moderate inheritance of intelligence and ability should learn to invest his little in the most profitable manner possible.

Those who escape wrong choice of vocation on account of their own bad judgment and errors in selection; who are not turned aside into the wrong path by the bad judgment, prejudices, and other errors of parents; who escape from the clutches of sincere and well-meaning, but unwise, teachers; who are not thrown into the nearest possible vacancies by economic necessity; who do not fall short of their full opportunities because of restlessness; who do not have their problems complicated by too great versatility or too little ability, still have many a rock and shoal to avoid.

BLUNDERS OF EMPLOYERS

One very frequent cause of misfits in vocation is the bad judgment of employers. This bad judgment, like that of parents and teachers, arises from ignorance--ignorance of human nature, of the particular individual, and, strange to say, of the requirements of the work to be done. Whole volumes could be written on the bad judgment of employers in selecting, assigning, and handling their employees. This, however, is not the place for them. Neither is this the place for the discussion of the remedies to be applied.

Even after the young man has entered a vocation and found that he does not fit in it, there is plenty of opportunity for him to make a change if he is made of the right stuff and can secure the right kind of counsel and guidance. But this "IF" is a tremendously big one.

Many causes--both inside and outside of himself--tend to prevent the average man from changing from a vocation for which he is not fit to one in which he is fit. Perhaps a brief consideration of some of these factors in the problem may be of assistance to you.

SOCIAL AMBITION

One reason for continuing in the wrong vocation is social ambition. Rightly or wrongly--probably wrongly--there are certain vocations which entitle one to social recognition. There are others which seem, at least, to make it difficult for one to secure social recognition. Social ambition, therefore, causes many a man to cling desperately to the outskirts of some profession for which he is unfitted, in the everlasting

21

hope of making a success of it and thus winning the social recognition which is his supreme desire.

Poor, short-sighted, and even blind, victims of their own folly!

They do not see that any work which is human service is honorable. They miss the big truth that the man who delivers better goods or renders better service than other men is not only entitled to profit, but also has, by divine right, unassailable social standing.

LAZINESS

One of the most potent causes of failure is laziness. And the worst form of the malady is mental laziness. Once a man is in any line of work, he simply remains there by following the lines of least resistance. It requires, in the first place, hard mental effort to decide upon a new line of work. It requires analysis of work, analysis of one's self, of conditions, and of environment, in order to make an intelligent and worthy change. Not only this, but an advantageous change in vocation usually involves additional study, additional training, hard, grinding work in preparation for the new task. And it is altogether too easy for the lazy man to drift along, mediocre and obscure, in some vocation for which he is poorly fitted than to go through the grueling, hard work of preparing himself for one in which he will find an opportunity for the use and development of his highest and best talents.

LACK OF OPPORTUNITY

Many men do not change their vocations, when they find that they are misfits, because of lack of opportunity. There may be no real chance for them in the locality where they live and conditions may make it almost impossible for them to leave. Of course, the strong, courageous soul can *make* its own opportunities. Theoretically, perhaps, everyone can create circumstances. But, in real life, there are comparatively few strong, courageous souls--few who can mould conditions to their will. Probably, however, the average man could do much more than he does to improve his opportunities were it not for inertia, lack of self-confidence, and lack of courage, all of which he could overcome if he would.

It is oftentimes the case that the man who desires to make a change feels that the only work which would appeal to him is in a profession or trade already overcrowded. This may be true in the locality where he lives, but there is always room for every competent man in any truly useful kind of work. For the man who is well qualified, by natural aptitudes and training, no profession is overcrowded.

LACK OF EDUCATION AND TRAINING

Many men of intelligence, who, perhaps, know what their calling should be, are compelled to continue in work which is uncongenial and for which they are poorly fitted because of their lack of education and training. Hundreds of men and women come to us, only to find that they have started in the wrong work and have remained in it so long that a change to their true vocation is practically impossible. They have assumed responsibilities which they cannot shirk. The education and training needed would take too long and would cost too much. Yet many have toiled away at night and in odd moments on correspondence courses or in night schools, and have thus, finally, won their way to their rightful places in the work of the world. But at what a cost!

It is of the highest importance that every individual should learn as early as possible in life what career he is best fitted to undertake. Every year spent in mistaken preparation or uncongenial employment makes proper training more expensive and more difficult. There are many arts which, perhaps, cannot be learned properly after one has reached maturity. It is said that no one has ever become a great violinist who did not begin his study of the instrument before the age of twelve. However that may be, psychologists and anatomists agree in informing us that the brain of a human being is exceedingly plastic in childhood, and that it gradually grows more and more impervious to impressions and changes as the individual matures. Sad, indeed, is the case, therefore, of the individual who waits to learn what his vocational fitness is until he is fully mature and is, perhaps, loaded up with the cares and responsibilities of a family, and cannot take either the time or the money to secure an education which his natural aptitude and his opportunities demand.

DEFICIENT SELF-CONFIDENCE

Many men remain in uncongenial occupations because they lack confidence in themselves. This is distressingly common. Everywhere we find men and women occupying humble positions, doing some obscure work, perhaps actually frittering away their time upon trifles and mere details, doing something which does not require accuracy, care, responsibility, or talent, merely for fear they may not be able to succeed in a career for which they are eminently fitted.

On one occasion a young man of the most undoubted dramatic talent and oratorical ability sought us for counsel. "I have always felt," he said, "a strong inner urge, sometimes almost irresistible, to go upon the platform or the stage. But, because I have lacked confidence in myself,

23

I have always, at the last moment, drawn back. The result is that to-day I am dissatisfied and unhappy in the work I am doing. I do it poorly. I long constantly for an opportunity to express myself in public. Years are going by, I have not developed my talent as I should, and I am beginning to feel that my case is hopeless." This lack of self-confidence is more common by far than many people would imagine. Arthur Frederick Sheldon has said: "Most men accomplish too little because they attempt too little." Our observations incline us to believe that this is the truth. Taking humanity as a whole, far more men fail because they try to do too little than because they try to do too much. Humanity is a great mine of undiscovered and undeveloped talents. It follows that we fall far short of our best because we do not expect and demand enough of ourselves.

CONSERVATISM

A man came to us for consultation in regard to his vocation. Just why he had come, it afterward turned out, it was hard to see. Perhaps he only wanted to settle matters in his own mind without taking definite action upon them. He was engaged in mercantile business, a business left to him by his father. He hated it. After a careful analysis, we informed him that he had undoubted scientific talents, and that, with training, he could make a name for himself in research and discovery. He was overjoyed at this information, but he manifested no disposition to change his vocation. He said: "Much as I dislike the mercantile business, I hate to change. A change will mean selling out, upsetting my whole mode of life and activity, removing into a different community, beginning a new life in many of its phases. I cannot look forward to such a complete revolution with any degree of pleasure, so I guess I will have to keep along in the old store, much as I would like to devote the rest of my life to test-tubes, crucibles, and scales."

There are many such men. Change is more hateful to them than unloved work. They fall into grooves and ruts. They would rather continue in their well-worn ways than to go through the mental anguish of breaking old ties, remaking methods of life and work, moving away from friends and relatives, and otherwise changing environment, conditions, and employment.

LACK OF COURAGE

Many men have self-confidence and yet lack courage. That may seem to be a paradoxical statement, but if the reader will study carefully

24

some of the men he knows, he will understand that this is the truth. Men may have plenty of confidence in themselves, but they may lack the courage to face difficulties, to overcome obstacles, to meet hard conditions, to pass through disagreeable experiences. Such are the men who lack the initiative, the push, the aggressiveness, to do as well as they know how, to do as much as they can, to undertake the high achievement for which they have the ability. The cases of such men would be hopeless were it not for the fact that some powerful incentive, like an emergency or necessity, some tremendous enthusiasm, some strong determination, some deep conviction, urges them on to the expression of the fulness of their powers. Lacking even any of these, it is possible for the man who lacks courage to develop it.

Courage is developed by doing courageous acts. The man who feels that he lacks courage, who knows that he needs to forget his fears and his anxieties, has half won his battle. Knowing his deficiencies, he can by the very power of his will compel himself to courageous words and acts, thus increasing and developing his courage and, as a result, his efficiency.

LACK OF AMBITION

Finally, people do not undertake work in their proper vocations because of a lack of ambition. This is, indeed, a fundamental deficiency. Perhaps it underlies many of those we have already described. Certain it is that we usually obtain what we most earnestly and ardently desire. Someone has said that when a man knows definitely and in detail just exactly what he desires, he is halfway toward attainment. Now, a man does not know definitely and in detail what he wants unless he wants it so intensely that it is always in his mind; he thinks about it, dreams of it, and paints mental pictures of himself enjoying it; perhaps spends hours in working out the detail of it. When a man has an ambition which drives him on to this kind of mental exercise, he usually has one which overcomes his inertia, burns out his laziness, triumphs over his lack of confidence in himself, urges him out of grooves and ruts, and enables him to overcome deficiencies in education and training, is an incentive to him for the creating of opportunities where none exist, gives him courage for anything, and kindles ever afresh his enthusiasm and determination. There is no obstacle so great that it will not dissolve and vanish away into thin air in the heat of such an overwhelming desire and ambition as this.

We need to remind ourselves, however, that even the most ardent ambition goes astray unless it is guided by accurate knowledge. Many a man has attacked his problem with great courage and high ambition, only to meet defeat because, through lack of knowledge, he has chosen a career for which he was unfitted.

These, then, are some of the reasons people go into and remain in vocations where they do not fit. They are the reasons, also, why so many men are failures or near-failures. Any man is a failure in just the degree in which he falls short of developing and using his best and highest talents and powers.

William James, the psychologist, has said that most men use only a very small percentage of their real abilities. Harrington Emerson, efficiency engineer, says that the average man is only twenty-five per cent efficient and that his inefficiency is due to unfitness for the work he is trying to do. Students of economics say that only ten per cent of all men are truly successful. In this chapter we have presented many of the reasons for the misfit and failure. Some of them are chargeable to parents, teachers, and employers. But the most serious belong rightfully at the door of the individual himself. "The fault, dear Brutus," says Cassius, "is not in our stars, but in ourselves, that we are underlings."

It is highly desirable that parents, teachers, and other guides and advisors of the young should fully inform themselves about human nature and about work. They ought to rid their minds of prejudice and thus free themselves from unwise tradition and useless conventionality. Above all, they need to arouse themselves to the vital importance of ideals--of a clear, definite purpose, based upon accurate knowledge and sound judgment--in other words, upon common sense. This is the vocational problem.

FACTORS OF THE VOCATIONAL PROBLEM

The vocational problem consists, first, of the need of accurate vocational analysis; second, of the need of wise vocational counsel; third, of the need of adequate vocational training; fourth, of the need of correct vocational placement.

It is obvious that the vocational problem cannot be adequately solved by dealing with pupils or clients in groups or classes. It is a definite, specific, and individual problem. Group study is interesting and instructive, but, alone, does not give sufficient knowledge of individual peculiarities and aptitudes. It is obvious from the foregoing analysis of the vocational problem that it is practically identical at all points with the problem of scientific employment. Just as the highest efficiency of the employment department depends upon accurate analysis of the job and of the man, so the highest usefulness of the vocational bureau or vocational counsellor depends upon complete and exact knowledge of the requirements in different lines of endeavor, and the ability to analyze human nature accurately. It is obvious that wise counsel cannot be given, adequate training cannot be prescribed, and correct placement is impossible until these analyses have been properly made.

The child or adult of unusual ability, with well-marked inclinations and strong in the fundamentals of character, is never difficult to analyze, counsel, train, or place. If given an opportunity to gain knowledge, and freedom in the exercise of choice, he will almost surely gravitate into his natural line of work. He is not the real problem of the vocational expert. But the vast majority of children are average, or even mediocre. They show little inclination toward any study or any work. They have weaknesses of character that will inevitably handicap them, no matter what vocation they enter. They are the real problem. There is another class, almost equally distressing. They are the people who are brilliant, who learn easily, and who are so adaptable that they can turn their hands to almost anything. They are usually so unstable in temperament that it is difficult for them to persist in any one kind of endeavor long enough to score a success.

METHODS OF ANALYSIS IN USE

The need, in dealing with these problems, for some more reliable guide than the young person's inclinations and preferences has deeply impressed itself upon those engaged in vocational study and vocational work. They are earnestly seeking to find some better way. To this end, we have the questionaire, by which is brought out between the lines, as it were, the particular aptitudes and disposition of the subject. And this method is not without its advantages. We have also psychological tests. These are of fascinating interest and have yielded some valuable results. Some vocational workers use the psychological tests and some do not. Even those who are most enthusiastic for them admit that they are complicated, that they require expensive apparatus and specially trained examiners, and that even the best results obtainable cover a very narrow field in the character and aptitudes of the subject.

UNIFORM METHOD NEEDED

The present need is for some uniform, readily applicable, inexpensive, and comprehensive method of analysis. The advantages of such a method are immediately apparent. First, its uniformity would permit the making of records for comparison, covering a very wide range of subjects, environment, and vocations. Second, even the simplest classifications, which are readily learned and easily applied by the inexpert, would yield tangible and measurable results and would be far better than the present unstandardized and wholly unscientific methods. Third, were such a uniform method adopted and made a part of the vocational work of our institutions; were uniform records to be made and wisely used, we should soon have a body of useful knowledge on this subject. Fourth, as the result of the application of such a uniform method, text books and charts could be prepared which would form the basis of popular education in vocational guidance.

But this book will find its way into the hands of many whose own vocational problems cry out for solution. Such need first to know themselves, to know their aptitudes and talents, whether developed or undeveloped. They need to study vocations--to know everything about the kinds of work they might do, from their requirements to their possibilities twenty, thirty, or forty years in the future. Finally, they need the courage, self-confidence, industry, progressiveness, and ambition to throw off the shackles of circumstance and, in the light of scientific truth, to press forward to the achievement, success, fulness of life, and happiness possible through development and use of all their powers.

CHAPTER II

ELEMENTS OF FITNESS

In our study are two small pieces of clear white marble. Each of them is decorated with a beautifully designed little flower in natural color. This flower is depicted by the skillful inlaying of semi-precious stones. These marbles came from Agra, India. They are samples of the handiwork which makes the Taj Mahal one of the most beautiful structures in the world. In the fitting of this inlay work the stones-- some of them almost as hard as diamonds--are cut and polished to nearly mathematical accuracy of size and shape. But the more carefully and exactly these are made, the more badly they fit and the worse failure is the whole design, unless the spaces intended for them in the marble are likewise cut and prepared with nicety and accuracy. In the selecting of a life work, similarly, the same care must be taken in learning accurately the requirements of work--the exact size and shape, as it were, of each vocation--as is spent upon learning the exact qualifications of each individual. Both require common sense and intelligent judgment.

We measure a man's height in centimeters or inches. Pounds and ounces or grams and centigrams offer us exact standards of measuring his weight. But there are no absolute standards for measuring the man himself, and probably there never can be. Human values, therefore, can be standardized only relatively. By the study of large groups we can, however, ascertain approximately the average or normal. In this way, physical standards have been set up as to pulse rate, temperature, respiration, etc. Chemical analysis determines norms of blood composition, and microscopic investigation determines the average number of blood corpuscles per cubic centimeter. The Binet-Simon mental tests are based upon certain approximate averages of intelligence and mental development established in the same way. The Münsterberg associated-word test of intelligence and other psychological experiments are among the efforts made to establish such standards. These are valuable as far as they go and probably yield all the information that their originators claim for them, which, unfortunately, is not a great deal. By time and motion studies, we are enabled to set up standards of efficiency that work out well in practice. All these, however, still leave us in the dark as to the man himself--his honesty, his loyalty, his highest and best values.

ELEMENTS OF THE VOCATIONAL PROBLEM

But, granted for the moment that we could devise and successfully apply exact and accurate standards of measurement for human beings, our work would be only partially done. Any mechanic knows that it is a sad waste of time and pains to standardize tenons, with micrometer and emery paper, to a thousandth of an inch, so long as the mortises are left unstandardized. A valuable man makes an unusual record on the staff of some employer. Other employers immediately begin to lay plans to entice him away. Transferred to another organization, he may prove mediocre, or even undesirable, in his services. Hiring "stars" away from other employers has proved disastrous so many times that the practice is no longer common. Many a flourishing and fruitful tree has been transplanted, only to wither and die--a tragedy involving the tree itself and both orchards. Measured by every known standard, a man thus enticed away may be close to 100 per cent efficient, but the man is only one ingredient in the compound from which results are expected. To know and to rate his aptitudes, abilities, personality, and possibilities is of the highest importance, but these cannot be rated except in relation to his work and to his environment. These are the other two ingredients in the compound. It is quite obvious that all standards for judging men-

-and for self-analysis--must vary with relation to the work they are to do and the environment in which they are placed.

The important factors of any vocation may be classified very broadly under three heads, namely, nature, position, and requirements. Chart I gives a classification of work, with a few suggestive subdivisions, under each of these three general heads. The meanings of the subdivisions listed under "Nature" and "Position" are clear.

CHART I /Physical |Mental |Combination of Physical and Mental |Professional /Nature..........|Commercial | |Industrial | |Fine | |Coarse | |Light | \Heavy, etc. | Work....| /Executive |Position........|Subordinate | \Staff | | /Physical | |Moral | |Intellectual \Requirements....|Emotional |Volitional |Aptitudes |Experience \Training, etc.

PHYSICAL REQUIREMENTS

Work has its physical requirements as to size, build, strength, endurance, freedom from tendencies to disease, agility, and inherent capacity for manual and digital skill. It may also have certain requirements as to eyesight, hearing, reaction time, muscular co-ordination, sense of touch, and even, in some particular places, sense of smell and sense of taste. Moral requirements may vary from those of a hired gunman to those of a Y.M.C.A. secretary or a bank cashier.

INTELLECTUAL REQUIREMENTS

Intellectual requirements and requirements in aptitudes, experience, and training vary, of course, with every kind of work, and almost with every particular job. One most valuable division of people intellectually is as to capacity of intellect. Some people have fine intellects, capable of great accomplishments in the way of education and training. They are particularly fitted for intellectual work; they have mental grasp; they comprehend; they reason; they have good judgment; they learn easily; they remember well. In every way their intellects are active, energetic, capable. Other people have only moderate intellectual capacity. They express themselves best in physical activity or in the direct, man-to-man handling of others. Their few intellectual activities may be exceedingly keen and accurate--or slow, dull, and vague. People with small intellectual capacity sometimes have remarkable vigor and clearness of mind in some one direction--such as finance, promotion, commerce; judgment of people, horses, cattle, or other living beings; mechanics, invention, music, art, poetry, or some other narrow specialty. Some intellects, in other words, are simply incompetent--others, merely narrow.

People can also be divided, intellectually, into two other classes, the theoretical and the practical. The man with a theoretical intellect is thoughtful, meditative, reflective. His mind works slowly; it is interested in philosophy, in theories, in abstractions, and is capable of dealing with them. On the other hand, it is not particularly well qualified for observing practical things, and for making a practical application of the theories it learns so easily and in which it takes so great an interest. This is the intellect of the philosopher, the dreamer, the educator, the preacher, the writer, the reformer, the poet. This is particularly the intellect of reason, of logic, of ideas and ideals. Whether found amongst the world's leaders or in the lowliest walks of life, its function is always that of dealing with theory, finding out reasons, putting together logical arguments, teaching others and dealing with abstractions. Oftentimes this type of intellect is so impractical that its possessor never possesses anything else. Literature abounds in the tragic tales of philosophers, poets, reformers, and dreamers who starved beautifully and nobly. Every-day life sees thousands more blundering along, either cursing their luck or wondering why Providence withholds its material gifts from people so deserving as they.

Over against this is the practical, matter-of-fact, analytical intellect--the intellect which demands facts and demands them quickly; the intellect which is quick in its operations, impatient, keen, penetrating, intolerant of mere theories and abstractions, not particularly strong in reason and logic, but exceedingly keen and discriminating in regard to the facts. This is the intellect which deals with things, with the material universe, with laws and principles, based upon accurately determined facts. This is the intellect of the preeminently practical man.

Some intellects are particularly fine in critical powers; some have splendid financial ability; some are artistic and musical; some have almost miraculous instinct in mechanical affairs; some are scientific; others are mechanical; still others are inventive. There are many intellects, of course, which combine two or more of these qualities, as, for instance, an intellect blessed with both financial and organizing ability. This is the intellect of the captain of industry, of the multi-millionaire. Then there is the intellect which combines financial, inventive, and organizing ability. This is the intellect of Edison, of Westinghouse, of Curtis, of the Wright brothers, of Marconi, and of Cyrus McCormick. Herbert Spencer was blessed with an intellect capable of both philosophic and scientific thought, both theoretical and practical. Spencer had also great organizing ability, but he devoted it to

31

the organizing of a system of philosophy based upon his scientific researches.

EMOTIONAL REQUIREMENTS

Emotional requirements are many and varied; even more numerous and of greater variety than intellectual requirements, perhaps. Some vocations require great courage, others not; some require a great deal of sympathy; others demand a certain hardness and control of the sympathies. There are vocations which require a keen sense of justice; others in which the presence or absence of a sense of justice is not essential. And so, there must be taken into consideration requirements for honor, for love, for loyalty, for dependableness, for enthusiasm, for unselfishness, for caution, for prudence, for religion, for faith, for hope, for optimism, for cheerfulness, for contentment, for earnestness, and for reverence.

THE COMPLEXITY OF HONESTY

Honesty is laid down by all authorities on employment as absolutely essential to success in any vocation, but there are many kinds of honesty and many standards of honesty. As a matter of fact, each man has his own standard of honesty. After all, it is, perhaps, not so much a question of what a man's standards are as how well he lives up to them. We recall, especially, the cases of two men associated together in business. One man set his standards high. Intellectually, he knew the value of ethics in conduct. He truly wished to make practical in his dealings the high principles he admired. But his cupidity was strong and his will and courage were weak, so he oftentimes argued himself, by specious casuistry, into words and acts which were untruthful and dishonest. Oftentimes, indeed, they came dangerously near to actual crimes against the laws of the State. The other man had rather limited standards of honesty. His motto was, "Let the buyer beware!" If those with whom he dealt were as strong and intelligent as he, and he was clever enough to take advantage of them, he regarded the spoils as rightfully his. It was all in the game. "I don't squeal when they catch me napping," he said, "and why should I look out for their interests?" But he never took advantage of the weak, the ignorant, the inexperienced, or the too credulous. His word was as good as gold. His principles were few and intensely practical, and he would willingly lose thousands of dollars rather than violate one of them.

Honesty is a complex virtue. It means, fundamentally, just and honorable intentions. But it involves, also, knowledge of what is right, a keen and discriminating sense of justice, a true sense of values,

32

courage and will-power to carry out honest intentions, and, finally, sufficient earning power to meet all righteous obligations. Dishonest acts result far more often from ignorance, warped sense of justice, inability to appreciate values, cowardice, weak will, or incompetence, than from wrong intent. Whether or not any individual is endowed with the necessary honesty for success in any particular vocation is, therefore, a problem which can be settled only by careful analysis of all its requirements. Law and banking both require a high *degree* of honesty, but the *kinds* are different.

THE HIGH QUALITY OF COURAGE

Next to honesty, perhaps, courage is most important. The individual who lacks courage shows no initiative; he has no ability to fight his own battles, to stand by his guns, to assert and maintain his convictions and his rights. He is, therefore, always a misfit in any vocation where he is required to take the initiative, to step out and assume responsibilities, to guide and direct the work of others, to meet others in, competition, to discipline others, to defend himself against the attack of others, to defend the rights of those depending upon him as employees, or stockholders, or partners. He may be excellently qualified as a research worker, an experimenter, an administrator of affairs, a teacher, a writer, a lecturer, an artist, or in almost any kind of work where initiative, aggressiveness, and fighting ability are not prime essentials.

PRUDENCE

Almost as important in its bearing upon vocational fitness as honesty and courage is prudence. This is the quality which causes men to bear responsibility faithfully; it is that which makes effective in them a sense of duty. It is the emotional quality which leads men to take precautions, to provide against the future. It is that which prevents them from recklessness in expenditure or speculation, from carelessness, from irresponsibility. It is an absolutely essential quality wherever dependability is required; where one is expected to assume and to carry responsibility, to see that things are done accurately that necessities are provided, that emergencies are prevented.

On the other hand, there are many vocations in which too great prudence, too great caution, is a handicap instead of an advantage. The man who is too cautious, who bears responsibility too heavily, is not fitted for positions and vocations which involve a certain amount of personal danger. He is also likely to be too conservative to enter upon vocations in which a considerable element of speculation is involved.

He is not disposed to take chances; he is too apprehensive and too much given to anxiety to be involved in any vocation where there is uncertainty as to outcome. Many vocations also require a fine blending of prudence with a willingness to take chances and a certain degree of recklessness.

THE ELEMENTS OF ENVIRONMENT

Such is any kind of work in which the results are not tangible and immediately and constantly measurable. In our practice we meet many who grow impatient, apprehensive, and even discouraged when knowledge of success of their efforts is deferred--or is even problematical. These people would far rather work in a subordinate position at a small salary, *certain* to be paid every pay day, than to make twice as much money on a commission basis but not be certain just how much they would be paid on pay day. Thus it is clear that a salesman on a commission basis must have a dash of recklessness in him, and yet, if he is selling high priced goods and wishes to build a permanent business, must be careful and prudent in handling his trade.

The essential elements of environment and their subdivisions are shown in Chart 2. A brief discussion of some of these may clarify the subject.

CHART 2

|Policy of House | |Moral | |Physical |Standards.............< Commercial | |Artistic | |Etc. | | |In Place of Business |Physical Surroundings.< In Locality | |In Home | | |Personal Preference |Management............< | |Personality | | |Personal Preference Environment...< Superior Executive....< Personality | |Methods | | |In Business |Associates............< In Locality | |Socially | | |Hours of Labor | |Periods of Rest | |Temperature | |Compensation |Working Conditions....< Opportunities | |Underground | |Elevation | |Danger | |Etc.

POLICY AND STANDARDS

For a man faithfully and loyally to live up to and represent the policy of the house is obviously necessary. But oftentimes it takes rather definite characteristics to do this.

Every business institution has, or should have, its moral, commercial, financial, artistic, and other standards with reference to personnel, according to the character of the business and other important considerations. And the man who contemplates work with any firm will examine himself to see whether he can harmonize happily with these standards. In like manner, every profession and art has its traditional standards and ethics, which should be considered.

PHYSICAL SURROUNDINGS

In selecting his vocation, the wise man ascertains his fitness for its physical surroundings. Some men cannot work permanently indoors, underground, in a high altitude, in a hot or cold climate, in a damp or a dry climate, in high or low artificial temperature, in the midst of noise or dust or chemical fumes, or by artificial light, or in a locality where certain social advantages do not exist or where satisfactory homes cannot be rented or purchased. Some men are not fitted for city life; others are not fitted for country life. All these and other facts should be taken into consideration with reference to surroundings.

MANAGEMENT AND SUPERIORS

The management of every place has its personal preferences, not based on efficiency. We once knew a manager who was so distressed by impediments of speech that he could not endure persons with these peculiarities in his organization, although their manner of speech had nothing to do with the quality of their work. Every manager has some more or less marked idiosyncrasies, and these must be known and studied by prospective employees. The personality of the management and its effect upon the worker under its direction and leadership are other important factors. The manager who is a keen, positive driver will get good results with a certain type of people in his organization, but only with a certain type. The efficiency of every man in the organization is also conditioned very largely upon the personal preferences, personality, and methods of his immediate superior--his foreman, gang-boss, or chief. Certain types of men harmonize and work well together. Other types are antagonistic and discordant. By their very nature they cannot work in the harmony which is essential to efficiency. In making choice of work, the man with good judgment scrutinizes all these important elements.

ASSOCIATES AND SOCIAL ADVANTAGES

Every vocation has its social environment. There are fellow employees, or professional associates, inevitable in the work itself; also the particular class of society fixed by locality, income, or the standing of the vocation.

This chart may seem, at first sight, to be complex. It must necessarily be so, since it is arranged to cover all professions and trades and all industrial and commercial positions, from the presidency of a corporation, general managership of a railroad, sales management of a factory, or cashiership of a bank, as well as less exalted jobs, down to those requiring little, if anything, more than brute strength. Obviously, not all of these facts need to be considered by every aspirant, but only those which have a bearing upon his particular case. The tendency, however, is to neglect important factors rather than to waste time over those which are unimportant.

PERSONAL ELEMENTS OF THE PROBLEM

Having determined, in the manner indicated, the standards of work and of the environment, the man is ready to examine himself to determine where he fits. There are six headings under which he may classify the various items of information needed in fitting himself to work and environment. These are health, character, intelligence, disposition to industry, natural aptitudes, and experience, as shown in Chart 3. This chart does not, of course, present a complete and detailed list, but it is suggestive.[2] It would not be true to say that any one of these is absolutely more important than the other. They are all important. Their relative importance may be determined by the vocation to be considered.

[Footnote 2: See more detailed lists in appendix.]

HEALTH

Consider the question of health. We include all a man's physical attributes under health. The classification is somewhat arbitrary, but it will be understood. A man must consider himself as to his size, as to his strength, as to his endurance, as to his condition of body (which shows habits), as to his predisposition to health, as to disease, as to his moral health, as to his sobriety, as to his sanity, etc.

CHART 3

|Size |Endurance |Condition of Body In other words, what Health........< Predispositions his physical value is for |Morality a given work in a |Sobriety given environment |Sanity |Etc.

|Honesty |Truthfulness |Loyalty |Discretion   and   Prudence Character.....< Enthusiasm |Courage |Steadfastness |Dependability |Etc., etc

|Ability to Learn |Ability to Understand and Follow Instructions |Judgment |Memory |Observation   Intelligence..< |Speaking |Expression...< | |Writing |Imagination |Reason |Etc., etc.

36

|Energy |Love of Work Disposition to Industry < Willingness |Perseverance |Decision |Etc., etc.

|Financial |Commercial |Mechanical |Artistic |Judicial |Executive |Selling |Advertising |Agriculture Natural Aptitudes.......< Medical |Educational |Legal |Engineering |Floricultural |Horticultural |Stock Breeding |Speed |Accuracy |Patience |Attention to Detail

|Education Experience..............< Training |Previous Record

Without at least fair physical fitness for his work and for his environment, no man can do efficient work in any position.

CHARACTER

The second element is character. A man may rate well in all the six fundamentals with the exception of one, honesty, and he is not worth heat and light and floor space, to say nothing of wages. Dishonest men do not do honest work. The man who is deficient in honesty, in truthfulness, in loyalty, is not really fit for any kind of work in a world where men are interdependent--where the law of compensation is rigidly enforced. We have chosen just a few qualities under the head of character: honesty, truthfulness, loyalty, discretion, prudence, enthusiasm, courage, steadfastness, and dependability. We might go on and on, adding initiative, justice, kindness, good nature, courtesy, punctuality, etc.

INTELLIGENCE

The third criterion is intelligence. Intelligence, of course, relates to mental ability--ability to learn and to understand and follow instructions. Employers are slowly reaching the conclusion that unintelligent labor is the most expensive kind of labor. The man who is unintelligent cannot be taught. Employers cannot give him instructions and feel absolutely sure that he understands them, or, even if he understands them, that he will carry them out properly. Among the qualities which are included under intelligence are judgment and memory, the powers of observation, expression in speaking or in writing, imagination, reasoning power, and all other qualities which are purely intellectual. Most unintelligent people are merely mentally asleep. They need to awaken, to be on the alert, really to take the trouble to think. Many people have capacity for thought who do not use it.

INDUSTRY

The fourth element is disposition to industry. Some wag once said: "All men are lazy, but some are lazier than others." It might sound better to say that all men are industrious, but some men are more industrious than others. There is such a quality of body and mind as the quality of predisposition to action and industry. Industry is very largely dependent upon energy. Energy depends upon oxygen. If one sits in a room that is stuffy and not well ventilated, one soon becomes stupid, sleepy, and not particularly acute mentally. In other words, he is partly starved for oxygen. Now, let him go out into the open air and breathe plenty of oxygen into his lungs. In a little while he raises his chest and brings up the crown of his head and takes the positive physical attitude. He is more energetic. He is eager for activity--for work. Some people are naturally deficient in depth, activity, and quality of lung power. They do not breathe in or use much oxygen, so they are lacking in energy. Such people are not predisposed to industry. Love of work--love of the game that causes a man to be interested in every phase of his work--is not, however, wholly dependent upon energy. It is something in the very heart and fiber of the man. Willingness to work, perseverance in work, and decision come under disposition to industry.

[Illustration: _Photo by F. Gutekunst, Phila_. FIG. 1. Jacob A. Riis, Journalist, Author and Philanthropist. A man of unusual intellectual power, observation, reason, memory, logic, and analysis, with high ideals, great love for humanity, especially the weak and helpless; good powers of expression, sense of humor, courage, and determination. Note large development of upper part of head; fairly well developed brows; high dome over temples; height and width of forehead, especially across center; full lips; well developed nose; strong chin; and alert, poised, kindly expression.]

[Illustration: _Copyright by Underwood & Underwood. New York_. FIG. 2. Dr. Booker T. Washington. Very ambitious, practical, energetic, self-reliant, persistent, determined, capable of rule. Note high head; high, sloping forehead, prominent at the brows; large nose, high in the bridge; and long, straight upper lip.]

[Illustration: FIG. 3. James H. Collins, Author. A splendid example of intellectual type with good bone and muscle. Has excellent balance of mechanical and commercial understanding, keen judgment of men, practical sense, and fine determination, with sentiment, sympathy, friendliness, and faith. Note high, medium-wide head, especially high in center above temples and wide and full through center of forehead; prominence of brows; width between eyes; full, cleanly modeled lips; strong nose and chin; and keen, pleasant, friendly, spirited expression.]

[Illustration: FIG. 4. H.G. Wells, Novelist and Economist. A man of physically frail type, with natural mechanical leanings. Inventive, creative, industrious, humanitarian. Because of his mechanical ability, he uses his creativeness for constructing novels dealing with mechanical invention. Because of his humanitarian instincts, he writes of social and economic world problems. Note large upper portion of head, especially from center of forehead to sides of head; also prominence of brows; large nose, and long head.]

[Illustration: *Copyright American Press Association.* FIG. 5. Mr. Henry Ford, Automobile Manufacturer and Philanthropist. Mr. Ford is of the physically frail type, with a goodly admixture of the bony and muscular element. His natural mechanical bent, therefore, took the intellectual form of invention and organization. His sentiment, responsiveness, sympathy, and idealism are shown by high, rather narrow head, fine texture, height of head just above temples, and gentle, kindly, genial expression.]

[Illustration: FIG. 6. Hugo de Vries, Botanist. An example of physically frail type. Very careful, accurate, painstaking, and patient in mental work. Also very thoughtful, mild in disposition, but determined and persistent. Note large development of upper part of head; long, narrow face; long nose; narrowness of head just above ears; slight squareness of chin, and serious, thoughtful expression.]

[Illustration: _Copyright by B.F. McMann_ FIG. 7. Dr. Henry Van Dyke, United States Minister to Holland, Author, Scholar, and Poet. A good example of physically frail type, with slight tendency to bone and muscle. Refined, intellectual, sensitive, responsive, optimistic, but well-balanced, poised, and keenly discriminating. Dr. Van Dyke shows his tendency to physical activity in his love for the out-of-doors. Note large development of upper portion of head; slight squareness of jaw; height of head above temples, especially in center; fine texture; excellent balance of features, and calm, poised, thoughtful, but kindly expression.]

[Illustration: *Photo by American Press Association.* FIG. 8. Dr. Beverly T. Galloway, Assistant Secretary of Agriculture. Physically frail, but mentally very active. Said to be one of the greatest living authorities on plant culture. Slight squareness of build indicates tendency to interest in out-of-door matters, which, on account of large development of mental qualities, he expresses in an intellectual way.]

NATURAL APTITUDE

The fifth criterion is natural aptitude. Everyone has observed that some people are naturally commercial. We have seen a boy take a penny to school, buy a slate pencil or a lead pencil with that penny, and trade that for an old pocket knife, the knife for something else, and keep on swapping until he had a gun, a set of chess, a bag of marbles, and several other important boys' acquisitions, all from that one penny. Another boy takes penny after penny to school and he never has anything to show for it You know such boys--and grown people, too. Every individual has some such aptitudes--either latent or developed, either mediocre or marked--and his aptitudes fit him better for some one vocation than for any other.

EXPERIENCE

The sixth point to be considered is experience. One might be fitted for a vocation with all of the five points that we have enumerated, and yet not have either the education or the training for it. What shall he do? Theoretically and ideally, every individual should be carefully and thoroughly trained, from his earliest childhood, for the vocation for which he is physically, mentally, and morally fitted. But this seldom happens--and can happen but seldom so long as parents and teachers remain ignorant of human nature and of work. A hard problem, then, confronts the young man or young woman past school days and not trained for the right calling. He or she must decide whether to compromise upon work as nearly right as possible or to make the necessary sacrifices to obtain education, training, and experience. There is much evidence in favor of choosing either horn of the dilemma. A most successful manufacturer called upon us recently. We told him that, with proper training, he would have been even more successful and far better satisfied in the legal profession. "I know you are right," he said. "I have always regretted that circumstances prevented my taking a law course as a young man. However, I have an extensive law library, do practically all the legal work for my firm, and am often consulted on obscure legal points relative to the manufacturing business by lawyers of some renown."

Abraham Lincoln, the farmhand and flatboatman, began the study of grammar at twenty-two and of law still later. Elihu Burritt, "The Learned Blacksmith," who lectured in both England and America, taught himself languages and sciences while working eleven hours a day at the forge.

We enjoy the acquaintance of a woman physician of considerable prominence who did not enter medical college until she was more than fifty years of age. Henry George was a printer who studied economics after he was twenty-seven years old. Frederick Douglass was a slave until he was twenty-one, yet secured a liberal education, so that he became a noted speaker and writer. The following from "Up from Slavery,"[3] by the late Booker T. Washington, shows what can be done by even a poor black boy, without money or influence, to win an education:

[Footnote 3: Doubleday, Page & Company, Garden City, New York.]

BOOKER T. WASHINGTON'S STORY

I determined when quite a small child that, if I accomplished nothing else in life, I would in some way get enough education to enable me to read common books and newspapers. Soon after we got settled in some manner in our new cabin in West Virginia, I induced my mother to get hold of a book for me. How or where she got it I do not know, but in some way she procured an old copy of 'Webster's Blue-back Spelling-book,' which contained the alphabet, followed by such meaningless words as 'ab,' 'ba,' 'ca,' and 'da.' I began at once to devour this book, and I think that it was the first one I ever had in my hands. I had learned from somebody that the way to begin to read was to learn the alphabet, so I tried in all the ways I could think of to learn it--all, of course, without a teacher, for I could find no one to teach me. At that time there was not a single member of my race anywhere near us who could read, and I was too timid to approach any of the white people. In some way, within a few weeks, I mastered the greater portion of the alphabet. In all my efforts to learn to read my mother shared fully my ambition and sympathized with me and aided me in every way that she could. Though she was totally ignorant so far as mere book knowledge was concerned, she had high ambitions for her children, and a large fund of good hard common sense, which seemed to enable her to meet and master every situation. If I have done anything in life worth attention, I feel sure that I inherited the disposition from my mother.

The opening of the school in the Kanawha Valley brought to me one of the keenest disappointments that I ever experienced. I had been working in a salt-furnace for several months, and my stepfather had discovered that I had a financial value, and so, when the school opened, he decided that he could not spare me from my work. This decision seemed to cloud my every ambition. The disappointment was made all the more severe by reason of the fact that my place of work was where

41

I could see the happy children passing to and from school morning and afternoon. Despite this disappointment, however, I determined that I would learn something anyway. I applied myself with greater earnestness than ever to the mastering of what was in the blue-back speller.

My mother sympathized with me in my disappointment and sought to comfort me in all the ways she could and to help me find a way to learn. After a while I succeeded in making arrangements with the teacher to give me some lessons at night, after the day's work was done. These night lessons were so welcome that I think I learned more at night than the other children did during the day. My own experiences in the night-school gave me faith in the night-school idea, with which, in after years, I had to do both at Hampton and Tuskegee. But my boyish heart was still set upon going to day-school and I let no opportunity slip to push my case. Finally I won, and was permitted to go to the school in the day for a few months, with the understanding that I was to rise early in the morning and work in the furnace till nine o'clock, and return immediately after school closed in the afternoon for at least two hours more of work.

The schoolhouse was some distance from the furnace, and as I had to work till nine o'clock, and the school opened at nine, I found myself in a difficulty. School would always be begun before I reached it, and sometimes my class had recited. To get around this difficulty I yielded to a temptation for which most people, I suppose, will condemn me; but since it is a fact, I might as well state it. I have great faith in the power and influence of facts. It is seldom that anything is permanently gained by holding back a fact. There was a large clock in a little office in the furnace. This clock, of course, all the hundred or more workmen depended upon to regulate their hours of beginning and ending the day's work. I got the idea that the way for me to reach school on time was to move the hands from half-past eight up to the nine o'clock mark. This I found myself doing morning after morning, till the furnace 'boss' discovered that something was wrong, and locked the clock in a case. I did not mean to inconvenience anybody. I simply meant to reach that schoolhouse on time.

When, however, I found myself at the school for the first time, I also found myself confronted with two other difficulties. In the first place, I found that all of the other children wore hats or caps on their heads, and I had neither hat nor cap. In fact, I do not remember that, up to the time of going to school, I had ever worn any kind of covering upon my head, nor do I recall that either I or anybody else had even thought anything about the need of covering for my head. But, of course, when I saw how all the other boys were dressed, I began to feel quite uncomfortable. As usual, I put the case before my mother, and she explained to me that she had no money with which to buy a 'store hat,' which was a rather new institution at that time among the members of my race and was considered quite the thing for young and old to own, but that she would find a way to help me out of the difficulty. She accordingly got two pieces of 'homespun' (jeans) and sewed them together, and I was soon the proud possessor of my first cap.

My second difficulty was with regard to my name, or rather, a name. From the time when I could remember anything I had been called simply 'Booker.' Before going to school it had never occurred to me that it was needful or appropriate to have an additional name. When I heard the school roll called, I noticed that all of the children had at least two names, and some of them indulged in what seemed to me the extravagance of having three. I was in deep perplexity, because I knew the teacher would demand of me at least two names, and I had only one. By the time the occasion came for the enrolling of my name, an idea occurred to me which I thought would make me equal to the situation; and so, when the teacher asked me what my full name was, I calmly told him 'Booker Washington,' as if I had been called by that name all my life; and by that name I have since been known. Later in my life I found that my mother had given me the name of 'Booker Taliaferro' soon after I was born, but in some way that part of my name seemed to disappear and for a long while was forgotten, but as soon as I found out about it I revived it, and made my full name, 'Booker Taliaferro Washington.' I think there are not many men in our country who have had the privilege of naming themselves in the way that I have.

The time that I was permitted to attend school during the day was short, and my attendance was irregular. It was not long before I had to stop attending day-school altogether, and devote all of my time again to work. I resorted to the night-school again. In fact, the greater part of the education I secured in my boyhood was gathered through the night-school after my day's work was done. I had difficulty often in securing a satisfactory teacher. Sometimes, after I had secured someone to teach me at night, I would find, much to my disappointment, that the teacher knew but little more than I did. Often I would have to walk several miles at night in order to recite my night-school lessons. There was never a time in my youth, no matter how dark and discouraging the days might be, when one resolve did not continually remain with me, and that was a determination to secure an education at any cost....

After I had worked in the salt-furnace for some time, work was secured for me in a coal mine, which was operated mainly for the purpose of securing fuel for the salt-furnace.

In those days, and later, as a young man, I used to try to picture in my imagination the feelings and ambitions of a white boy with absolutely no limit placed upon his aspirations and activities. I used to envy the white boy who had no obstacle placed in the way of his becoming a Congressman, Governor, Bishop, or President by reason of the accident of his birth or race. I used to picture the way that I would act under such circumstances; how I would begin at the bottom and keep rising until I reached the highest round of success.

One day, while at work in the coal mine, I happened to overhear two miners talking about a great school for colored people somewhere in Virginia. This was the first time that I had ever heard anything about any kind of school or college that was more pretentious than the little colored school in our town.

In the darkness of the mine I noiselessly crept as close as I could to the two men talking. I heard one tell the other that not only was the school established for the members of my race, but that opportunities were provided by which poor but worthy students could work out all or a part of the cost of board, and at the same time be taught some trade or industry.

As they went on describing the school, it seemed to me that it must be the greatest place on earth, and not even Heaven presented more attractions for me at that time than did the Hampton Normal and Agricultural Institute of Virginia, about which these men were talking. I resolved at once to go to that school, although I had no idea where it was, or how many miles away, or how I was going to reach it; I remembered only that I was on fire constantly with one ambition, and that was to go to Hampton. This thought was with me day and night.

In the fall of 1872, I determined to make an effort to get there, although, as I have stated, I had no definite idea of the direction in which Hampton was, or of what it would cost to go there. I do not think that anyone thoroughly sympathized with me in my ambition to go to Hampton, unless it was my mother, and she was troubled with a grave fear that I was starting out on a wild-goose chase. At any rate, I got only a half-hearted consent from her that I might start. The small amount of money that I had earned had been consumed by my step-father and the remainder of the family, with the exception of a very few dollars, and so I had very little with which to buy clothes and pay my traveling expenses.

Finally, the great day came and I started for Hampton. I had only a small, cheap satchel that contained what few articles of clothing I could get. My mother, at the time, was rather weak and broken in health. I hardly expected to see her again, and thus our parting was all the more sad. She, however, was very brave through it all. At that time there were no through trains connecting that part of West Virginia with eastern Virginia. Trains ran only a portion of the way, and the remainder of the distance was traveled by stage-coaches.

The distance from Malden to Hampton is about five hundred miles. I had not been away from home many hours before it began to grow painfully evident that I did not have enough money to pay my fare to Hampton.

By walking, begging rides, both in wagons and in the cars, in some way, after a number of days, I reached the city of Richmond, Virginia, about eighty-two miles from Hampton. When I reached there, tired, hungry, and dirty, it was late in the night. I had never been in a large city before, and this rather added to my misery. When I reached Richmond I was completely out of money. I had not a single acquaintance in the place, and, being unused to city ways, I did not know where to go. I applied at several places for lodging, but they all wanted money, and that was what I did not have. Knowing nothing else better to do, I walked the streets. In doing this I passed by many food-stands, where fried chicken and half-moon apple pies were piled high and made to present a most tempting appearance. At that time it seemed to me that I would have promised all that I expected to possess in the future to have gotten hold of one of those chicken legs or one of those pies. But I could not get either of these, nor anything else to eat.

I must have walked the streets till after midnight. At last I became so exhausted that I could walk no longer. I was tired; I was hungry; I was everything but discouraged. Just about the time when I reached extreme physical exhaustion, I came upon a portion of a street where the board sidewalk was considerably elevated. I waited for a few minutes, till I was sure that no passers-by could see me, and then crept under the sidewalk and lay for the night upon the ground, with my satchel of clothing for a pillow. Nearly all night I could hear the tramp of feet above my head. The next morning I found myself somewhat refreshed, but I was extremely hungry, because it had been a long time since I had had sufficient food. As soon as it became light enough for me to see my surroundings I noticed that I was near a large ship, and that this ship seemed to be unloading a cargo of pig iron. I went at once to the vessel and asked the captain to permit me to help unload the vessel in order to get money for food. The captain, a white man, who seemed to be kind-hearted, consented. I worked long enough to earn money for my breakfast, and it seems to me, as I remember it now, to have been about the best breakfast that I have ever eaten.

"My work pleased the captain so well that he told me if I desired, I could continue working for a small amount per day. This I was very glad to do. I continued working on this vessel for a number of days. After buying food with the small wages I received there was not much left to add to the amount I must get to pay my way to Hampton. In order to economize in every way possible, so as to be sure to reach Hampton in a reasonable time, I continued to sleep under the same sidewalk that gave me shelter the first night I was in Richmond.

"When I had saved what I considered enough money with which to reach Hampton, I thanked the captain of the vessel for his kindness and started again. Without any unusual occurrence I reached Hampton, with a surplus of exactly fifty cents with which to begin my education. To me it had been a long, eventful journey, but the first sight of the large, three-story, brick school building seemed to have rewarded me for all that I had undergone in order to reach the place.

"It seemed to me to be the largest and most beautiful building I had ever seen. The sight of it seemed to give me new life. I felt that a new kind of existence had now begun--that life would now have a new meaning. I felt that I had reached the promised land, and I resolved to let no obstacle prevent me from putting forth the highest effort to fit myself to accomplish the most good in the world.

"As soon as possible after reaching the grounds of the Hampton Institute, I presented myself before the head teacher for assignment to a class. Having been so long without proper food, a bath, and change of clothing, I did not, of course, make a very favorable impression upon her, and I could see at once that there were doubts in her mind about the wisdom of admitting me as a student. I felt that I could hardly blame her if she got the idea that I was a worthless loafer or tramp. For some time she did not refuse to admit me; neither did she decide in my favor, and I continued to linger about her, and to impress her in all the ways I could with my worthiness. In the meantime, I saw her admitting other students, and that added greatly to my discomfort, for I felt, deep down in my heart, that I could do as well as they, if I could only get a chance to show her what was in me.

46

"After some hours had passed, the head teacher said to me: 'The adjoining recitation room needs sweeping. Take the broom and sweep it,'

"It occurred to me at once that here was my chance. Never did I receive an order with more delight. I knew that I could sweep, for Mrs. Ruffner had thoroughly taught me how to do that when I lived with her.

"*I* swept the recitation room three times. Then I got a dusting cloth and I dusted it four times. All the woodwork around the walls, every bench, table, and desk, I went over four times with my dusting cloth. Besides, every piece of furniture had been moved and every closet and corner of the room had been thoroughly cleaned. I had the feeling that, in a large measure, my future depended upon the impression I made upon the teacher in the cleaning of that room. When I was through, I reported to the head teacher. She was a Yankee woman, who knew just where to look for dirt. She went into the room and inspected the floor and closets; then she took her handkerchief and rubbed it on the woodwork, about the walls, and over the table and benches. When she was unable to find one bit of dirt on the floor, or a particle of dust on any of the furniture, she quietly remarked: 'I guess you will do to enter this institution.'

"I was one of the happiest souls on earth. The sweeping of that room was my college examination, and never did any youth pass an examination for entrance into Harvard or Yale that gave him more genuine satisfaction. I have passed several examinations since then, but I have always felt that this was the best one I ever passed."

If Lincoln, Burritt, Booker T. Washington, and thousands of others, with all their handicaps, could secure needed education for their life work, why should any man remain in an uncongenial calling? There is danger that we may give our boys and girls too much help; that life be made too easy for them; that their moral backbones may grow flabby by reason of too much support. Normal young people do not need aid and support. They need guidance and direction--and the majority of them, either the sharp spur of necessity or the relentless urge of an ambition which will not be denied. Almost without exception we have found that the only difference between genius or millionaire and dunce or tramp is a willingness to pay the price.

THE PRICE OF SUCCESS

From an unknown author comes the all-important question to every seeker for success:

"You want success. Are you willing to pay the price for it?

"How much discouragement can you stand?

"How much bruising can you take?

"How long can you hang on in the face of obstacles?

"Have you the grit to try to do what others have failed to do?

"Have you the nerve to attempt things that the average man would never dream of tackling?

"Have you the persistence to keep on trying after repeated failures?

"Can you cut out luxuries? Can you do without things that others consider necessities?

"Can you go up against skepticism, ridicule, friendly advice to quit, without flinching?

"Can you keep your mind steadily on the single object you are pursuing, resisting all temptations to divide your attention?

"Have you the patience to plan all the work you attempt; the energy to wade through masses of detail; the accuracy to overlook no point, however small, in planning or executing?

"Are you strong on the finish as well as quick at the start?

"Success is sold in the open market. You can buy it--I can buy it--any man can buy it who is willing to pay the price for it."

CHAPTER III

CLASSES OF MISFITS

To the casual observer, humanity seems to be divided into countless different kinds of people. In fact, it is often said that of all the millions of people on the earth, no two are just alike. Some writers on vocational guidance, indeed, express discouragement. They see humanity in such infinite variety that it is impossible ever to classify types. Therefore, they mourn, the vocational expert cannot judge of aptitudes except by trial in various kinds of work until, finally, real native talents appear in actual accomplishment. The anthropologist, however, easily divides mankind by means of several broad classifications, A few distinct variations, easily recognizable by the anthropological expert, put every one of the billion and one-half people on the face of the earth in his particular class.

In the same way, to the casual observer, it no doubt seems that the number and kind of misfits is so great that any attempt to analyze them and classify them must meet with failure. Those, however, who have studied the problem and have met and talked with thousands of those struggling against the handicap of unloved and difficult work, find a few classes which include nearly all of them. Just as there are two fundamental reasons why men and women select wrong vocations, and a few common variations upon these two reasons, so there are just a few general ways in which people select the wrong vocations. An examination of some of these will be illuminating to the reader.

THE PHYSICALLY FRAIL

In the beginning of the life of the race all men hunted, fished, fought, danced, sang, and loafed. These were the only manly vocations. There were no clerks, no doctors, and, perhaps, no priests. In some races and under some conditions to-day, all of the men are hunters and fishers, or shepherds and stock-raisers, or all the men till the field. Some years ago, in our country, practically all the male population worked at the trade of agriculture, there being only a few preachers, doctors, lawyers, merchants, and clerks.

In the nations of Europe to-day people are born to certain professions or born to a certain narrow circle of vocations; some people are born to manual labor, and, having once performed manual labor, are thereby firmly fixed in the class of those who earn their living by their hands; others are born in a class above that, and will suffer almost any privation rather than earn their living by manual labor. In the United States this same feeling is becoming more and more prevalent. Our physical work is nearly all of it done by those who came to us from across the sea, and native-born Americans seek vocations in some other sphere.

The common school is everywhere, and education is compulsory. The high school is also to be found in all parts of the country. There are also business colleges, technical schools, academies, universities, colleges, professional schools, correspondence schools, and other educational institutions of every possible kind. These are patronized by the native-born population as well as by many of those who come to us from foreign lands. The result is that, of the first great class which we shall treat, there are comparatively few in relation to the whole population. Even though this is true, there are all too many.

The first class of misfits is composed of those who are too frail for physical labor and who are not well enough educated to take their places amongst clerical or professional workers. These unfortunates do not like hard, manual work; they cannot do it well; they are outclassed in it. They do not hold any position long; they are frequently unemployed; and they are often compelled to live by their wits. As a general rule, those in this class are well equipped intellectually by nature, and would have responded splendidly to educative efforts if they had been given an opportunity. People of this class lack physical courage. They shrink from hardship and will do almost anything to escape physical suffering. It is this lack of courage, as well as their inability to make a decent living out of their hands and muscles, that leads them, in so many cases, to unlawful means.

As a general rule, people of this type have considerable natural refinement, and refinement is always expensive. They are the kind of people of whom it is often said that they have "champagne tastes and beer incomes." It is difficult for them to finance themselves, with any degree of frugality or economy, upon the small and precarious income they earn at manual labor. This is the class of people who sometimes become counterfeiters, sneak thieves, pickpockets, forgers, gamblers, stool pigeons, second-story workers, and petty criminals along other lines which do not require physical courage, strength, and force. Of course, the great majority of these misfits do not enter upon a life of crime. They are, however, poor, often in need, sometimes pauperized, and, as a general rule, their lives are short and miserable. There are those, also, whose cases are not so extreme. Unfitness for manual labor results merely in bare living, a life of comparative poverty, and general lack of success.

THE FAT MAN

Another class of those who are physically unfit for hard, manual labor are those who are too stout. The fat man is, by nature, fitted to sit in a large, luxurious chair and direct the work of others. He is too heavy on his feet for physical work, as a general rule, and is also too much disinclined to physical effort. It is a well-known fact that, almost without exception, fat men are physically lazy. The natural work, therefore, of the stout man is executive work, banking, finance, merchandising, handling of food products, and the arbitration of differences between his fellow men. Fat men are natural bankers, financiers, lawyers, judges, politicians, managers, bakers, butchers, grocers, restaurant owners, preachers, and orators. If, however, the man of this type does not secure sufficient education and training to enable him to undertake one of these professions, but grows up with no other ways to satisfy his wants than by the exercise of his muscles, he is greatly handicapped in the race for success. It is not usual, however, to find a man of this type amongst the ranks of the poor. Most of them are fairly well supplied with means, and usually have plenty to eat, plenty to wear, and a good place to sleep.

In order to obtain the things he desires, the man who has no aptitude for physical labor on account of his great bulk sometimes turns his attention to crime. This type of man may be a gambler, a grafting politician, a confidence man, a promoter of wild-cat stocks or bonds, the man who sits behind the scenes and directs a band of criminals or, perhaps, a whole community of them, or in some other way preys upon the gullibility of the public.

Naturally, there are fat men, also, who are honest and high-principled in their intentions and who still have not fitted themselves for their true vocation in life. Such men, like those who are physically frail and honest, drag through a miserable existence, never fully realizing their possibilities, or expressing themselves; never finding an outlet for their real talents; never making the success of life which they might have made with sufficient training and in their true vocations.

THE MAN OF BONE AND MUSCLE

Just as there were, doubtless, thousands of men too frail or too corpulent for physical work who were compelled to do it in the days when practically all men were either farmers or carpenters and builders, so to-day there are thousands of men far too active for clerical work who are compelled to do it because certain circles in society have a prejudice against manual labor. There is a type of man whose bony and muscular system predominates in his organization. This type of man loves the out-of-doors; freedom is to him a physical and moral necessity. He hates, and even grows irritable under, restraint. He demands physical activity; his muscles call for exercise; his whole physical being is keen for life in the open, with plenty of activity. Yet this type of man, by thousands, is sentenced to spend his life behind the counter or chained to a desk. He is as unhappy there, and almost as badly placed, as if he were, indeed, in prison. Look around the parks, the roads, the athletic fields, the lakes and streams, the woods, and all out-of-door places in this country and you will find this man taking a brief rest from his prison cell, engaged in strenuous forms of muscular activity--tennis, golf, baseball, football, lacrosse, cross-country running, boating, swimming, yachting, motoring, horseback riding, hunting, fishing, exploring, mountain climbing, ranching--in many ways seeking to find an outlet for his stored-up physical energy.

WORK FOR THE ACTIVE MAN

There is plenty of room for the mental capacity, the executive ability, and the splendid organizing genius of this type of man in outdoor work. Our great forests and fields are not producing twenty-five per cent of the amount of wealth that they should produce, under even such scientific methods as are known at present. But these are only the beginning. There is an opportunity for those with both mental and physical aptitudes to undertake the solution of the problem. The resources of the universe are infinite. There is no parsimony in Nature. There is plenty and to spare for all.

Recently there has been a great deal said about the fact that all of the land on the surface of the earth has now been occupied by mankind; that hereafter, food products will become higher and higher in price; that each of us will have to be satisfied with a little less wealth than formerly; that rents will be higher; that the price of land will steadily increase--that, already, there is not enough of the bare necessities of life to go around. This is cited as the cause of pauperism and given as an excuse for war. May not this attitude be mistaken? We have not yet scratched the surface of the possibilities. These out-of-door men are fitted by nature to take the scientific truths discovered by those better fitted to sit indoors, and make practical application of them to the problems of increasing the wealth of the race. If a boy in Alabama can grow 232 bushels of corn on one acre of ground, then farmers all over the country can grow at least 100 bushels of corn on an acre which now yields an average of 25 to 30 bushels. By scientific methods, Eugene Grubb has grown a thousand bushels of potatoes upon an acre of Wyoming land. A considerable addition will be made to the wealth of the race when a thousand other Eugene Grubbs arise and increase the productivity of thousands of other acres of potatoes.

THE BORN LEADER OF MEN

In his excellent little book, "The Art of Handling Men,"[4] Mr. James H. Collins says:

Broadly speaking, the personal equation is that Something in a man that makes him effective in managing other men.

It is the difference between the fellow who lets a political club, a military company or a factory force go all to pieces, and some other fellow who can put the pieces together again, or rather, draw them together instantly. For the man who reorganizes without this Something is like the chap who cleans his own clock--he usually has a few pieces of the organization left over because they wouldn't fit in anywhere. The personal equation is magnetic. It comes along and acts, and every part falls into place, and the organization is capable of performing a lot of new functions.

Not one person in five hundred possesses the faculty. Those who don't, like to comfort themselves with the assurance that it is a gift which Providence forgot to hand out to them. Innumerable stories grow up around the man who does possess it. One glance from his eagle eye, people say, and he reads you through. One word, and he enforces instant obedience. Thus the personal equation is glorified and mystified. But men who really have this valuable Something seldom make much mystery about it. They insist it is largely a matter of common sense, which everyone ought to have at their disposal.

[Footnote 4: Henry Altemus Company, Philadelphia.]

The personal equation has an interesting way of raising moral issues.

One morning in August, 1863, a young clergyman was called out of bed in a hotel at Lawrence, Kansas. The man who called him was one of Quantrell's guerrillas, and he wanted him to hurry downstairs, and be shot. All over the border town that morning people were being murdered. A band of raiders had ridden in early to perpetrate the Lawrence massacre.

The guerrilla who called the clergyman was impatient. The latter, when fully awake, was horrified by what he saw going on through his window. As he came downstairs the guerrilla demanded his watch and money, and then wanted to know if he was an abolitionist. The clergyman was trembling. But he decided that if he was to die then and there, it would not be with a lie on his lips. So he said, yes, he was, and followed up the admission with a remark that immediately turned the whole affair into another channel.

He and the guerrilla sat down on the porch, while people were being killed through the town, and had a long talk. It lasted until the raiders were ready to leave. When the clergyman's guerrilla mounted to join his confederates he was strictly on the defensive. He handed back the New Englander's valuables and apologized for disturbing him, and asked to be thought well of.

That clergyman lived many years after the Lawrence massacre. What did he say to the guerrilla? What was there in his personality that led the latter to sit down and talk? What did they talk about?

'Are you a Yankee abolitionist?' the guerrilla had asked.

'Yes--I am,' was the reply, 'and you know very well that you ought to be ashamed of what you're doing.'

This drew the matter directly to a moral issue. It brought the guerrilla up roundly. The clergyman was only a stripling beside this seasoned border ruffian. But he threw a burden of moral proof on to the raider, and in a moment the latter was trying to demonstrate that he might be a better fellow than circumstances would seem to indicate.

After waking this New Englander to kill him on account of his politics, he spent twenty minutes on the witness stand trying to prove an alibi. He went into his personal history at length. He explained matters from the time when he had been a tough little kid who wouldn't say his prayers, and became quite sentimental in recalling how one thing had led to another, and that to something worse, and so on, until--well, here he was, and a mighty bad business to be in, pardner. His last request, in riding away, was: 'Now, pardner, don't think too hard of me, will you?'

The personal equation is eternally throwing the burden of proof on the people it controls, and forever raising moral issues. The man who has it may operate by no definite plan, just as this clergyman had none for saving his own life. But he will be a confidence man of the most subtle character. His capacity for expecting things of those under him will be tremendous. Subordinates may never have demanded much of themselves. But for him they will accomplish wonders, just because he expects them to.

Three men were placed at the foreman's desk of a growing factory. Each had technical knowledge enough to run a plant three times the size. But all failed. The first was an autocrat, who tried to boss from a pedestal, and the men didn't like him. The next was a politician, whom the men liked thoroughly--which was his shortcoming, for he tried to run the place as they thought it should be run. As for the third, he tried to run it on nerves, to do everything himself, to be everywhere at once. He didn't fail, really--he snapped like a fiddle-string. By that time working tension was relaxed and production wabbling on the down-peak. Nobody knew who was in charge, or what would happen.

Then along came a fourth candidate, with an abnormally developed bump of expectation. He knew how to approve and encourage. Sometimes he said pleasantly: 'I knew you could do that, Bill,' Again, he put it ironically: 'I didn't think you had it in you.' But his strong point was expectation. With apparent recklessness he gave out work two sizes too large for everybody. If a subordinate was a No. 7 man he handed him a No. 9 job as a matter of course, and usually the latter grew up to it. The politician had tried this same scheme, but introduced it backward. Taking a No. 7 man into a corner, he told him impressively that he was a No. 9 and promoted him on the spot, and warned him to say nothing about it to anybody else. Then the man tried to swell to fit the office instead of growing to fit the work. But this fourth candidate made everybody see that doing No. 9 was more creditable than just being it. So everybody became interested in the work, and nothing else.

There was another suggestive point. Taking charge after three foremen had failed, the factory was naturally full of nasty cliques, each with its unhealthy private interest. The new man broke up these cliques by introducing a new interest so big that it swallowed all the little interests, like Aaron's rod. That interest was to turn out work of such quality and in such quantities that the factory could get contracts in competition with an older rival, and provide steady employment.

That this faculty for putting people under obligation is more the man than a method, however, is shown in one of Daudet's delightful little sketches, the story of a head clerk in a French Government bureau who, on getting a fine promotion, wrote home to his father describing his new chief's homely appearance with light-hearted raillery. Next morning on his desk lay his own letter, initialed by his chief. It had been intercepted by the secret service. The chief allowed him to suffer in apprehension one day, and then told him that his indiscretion should rest between themselves. 'Try to make me forget it,' he said, and the incident hung like a dagger over the clerk's head.

Some time after, the latter caught one of his own subordinates stealing from the cash box, and repeated his superior's tactics, even to the formula, 'Try to make me forget it.' With tears in his eyes the subordinate thanked him for his clemency--and a few days later, rifled the safe and fled! The moral of which seems to be that, if the clerk had been enough of a judge of men to use his chief's method effectively, he would never have fallen into the asininity of writing such a letter.

"Those who complain that it is impossible to win the confidence of subordinates might observe the extremely simple fashion in which the man with this Something does the trick--by giving people his own confidence first.

"He has the knack, not only of interesting others, but of keeping up his own interest; in fact, he is often so absorbed in his existence, his work, and the people around him that he is not aware that there is such a malady as lack of interest.

"He has a heartiness and vitality and geniality quite characteristic, or a misanthropy that is hearty, vital, and optimistic--geniality inside out. The milk of human kindness sometimes comes in a dry form."

THE MAN OF SUPREME ABILITY

In his valuable treatise on "The Twelve Principles of Efficiency,"[5] Mr. Harrington Emerson says:

Industrial plants remind me of automobiles. The plants themselves may be more or less good, but on what kind of roads are they running? The philosophy of efficiency is for an industrial plant--for any enterprise, activity, or undertaking--what a network of good roads is for automobiles. Undoubtedly, even on poor roads, automobiles may make some progress, but the worse the road, the more elementary must be the means of locomotion.

[Footnote 5: The Engineering Magazine Company, New York.]

Railroads, high-roads, by-roads, bridle-paths, footpaths, mountain climbs! The unlettered mountaineer of all countries is the best man for the last, and it takes the best kind of trained climbing expert to emulate him; but as the road is improved shoes are exchanged for horses, horses for bicycles, a change from one kind of muscular effort to another; bicycles for automobiles, automobiles for railroad trains, both these latter using incarnate energy instead of muscular or incarnate energy. The all-round skill of the mountaineer becomes the subdivided, specialized skill of many different men, who are supplemented with increasingly complex equipment.

The philosophy of efficiency is to be used to build roads along which any organization can travel with the least friction and the greatest advantage, and the more ramified and involved the business, the more is the philosophy needed.

However, no highly complex automobile, even with the best network of roads, can make any great progress unless in the hands of a skilled directing intelligence; no highly complex human enterprise, though it uses all the principles of efficiency, can make any great progress unless guided by a skilled intelligence.

On personality, on the wisdom of the individual, whether locomotive engineer or von Moltke, whether the manager of a plant employing ten

56

men or Judge Gary, chairman of the board of the gigantic Steel Corporation, will depend the ultimate value of all that creative physical or philosophical ability has brought together.

Recently there was submitted to me in the office of one of Chicago's greatest businesses the draft of its organization. No man can pass on the merits of the details of a complicated organization without long and intimate acquaintance with its workings. Seeing the plan of the Chicago plant, pressed for a suggestion, I said: 'Your chart is upside down; the president belongs at the bottom, sustaining and carrying, through his organization, all the operations of the plant. Because he is in supreme authority he has the responsibility of making available for everyone, down to the tool, all the wisdom in the universe in order that each may fulfil perfectly its special duty and task.'

Whether on the grounds of Long Branch, on the desert trail, in a section, department, division, or plant of a great manufacturing concern or railroad; whether on the deck of a battleship or on a battlefield, what is wanted is a leader who can swing and manage what has been entrusted to him.

It has become the fashion in history to decry the strong-man theory, to turn for understanding to evolution, to explain the strong man as the inevitable accident of the moment. There is evolution; there comes, at last, opportunity, but only rarely does the strong man arise; hence we have England, not Norway or Sweden or Holland; hence we have Prussia, not Saxony; Germany, not Russia; Italy, not Portugal; France, not Spain; Japan, not Siam or Korea.

In 1536 was born in Japan an undersized, monkey-faced boy of good but poor parentage, who, at the age of thirteen, resolved to make himself the chief power in the distracted kingdom. For 200 years the militant barons had warred against each other, each trying to grab, annex, and hold what he could.

The boy, Hideyoshi, deliberately visited the different courts, picked out the baron he thought most endowed with suitable character, succeeded with great difficulty in entering his service in the humblest position, and then steadily and inevitably rose, firstly because he could read human character and always knew almost as soon as they did themselves what his and his lord's enemies were plotting, and secondly, because he was always prepared in advance for any undertaking and skilled in carrying out. Thus, when scarcely more than a child, he reduced the cost of firewood used in the palace to less than one-half; a little later he rebuilt the castle walls in three days, a task estimated as requiring sixty days; again, single-handed, he secured provinces that armies had failed to conquer.

By gifts of tact, of insight, of diligence, of readiness, that each one of us thinks he possesses, that any one of Nippon's 30,000,000 inhabitants might have possessed and exercised, Hideyoshi rose, step by step, until he directed and guided the whole country, his general, Iyeyasu, becoming the first of the Tokugawa dynasty, which lasted from 1603 to 1867, with headquarters at Yeddo (Tokyo).

Temuchin, Jenghis Khan, born in a tent in 1162, son of a petty Mongolian chieftain, succeeded his father when only thirteen years old. Many of the tribes immediately rebelled, but Temuchin held his own in battle and in counsel against open enemies and insidious traitors, until his empire extended from the China Sea to the frontier of Poland--an empire larger than modern Russia, the largest the world has ever seen.

The man of supreme ability is the one who has supernal ideals, who recognizes and uses those underlying principles without which human effort is futile, its results ephemeral. The man of supreme ability is the one who can create and control an organization founded on and using principles to attain and maintain ideals, who then is able to assemble for the use of his organization the incidentals of land, of men and money (Labor and Capital), of buildings and equipment, of methods and devices. All these incidentals make for volume, for quantity, for man's work instead of woman's work, but they do not make for the spirit, nor for the quality, nor for the excellence of work.

THE ELEMENTS OF EXECUTIVE ABILITY

We have quoted thus at length from Mr. Collins and Mr. Emerson to show the inbornness, so to speak, of real executive ability. The art of handling men depends upon certain inherent aptitudes plus a certain amount of the right kind of training. A very large class of executives lacks the aptitude; a still larger class lacks the right kind of training. It is possible, of course, to give training to those who have the aptitude. It is impossible to give training which will make efficient executives of those who are deficient in the natural aptitudes. The result of all this is that we have a very large class of misfits; men who, for some reason or other, have been promoted into executive positions and who do not have the proper qualifications. These men suffer; those under them suffer; those who employ them suffer.

Some men are too active themselves ever to be good directors of the activities of other men. They cannot sit back quietly and direct others.

They demand expression in action. They are, therefore, always thrusting aside their subordinates and doing the thing themselves, because they lack the ability to teach others to do the work and to do it correctly. When such men are compelled to wait for others to accomplish things, they grow irritable, impatient, and lose control of themselves and, therefore, of the situation. They are not ideal executives and do not, as a general rule, rise to very high executive positions. They ought not to attempt to do executive work.

There are others who are too easy-going to command men. They permit their men to get too close to them, and they feel too sympathetic toward them. They are likely, also, to be partial, not to demand or exact enough, and, therefore, their departments are always behind, never quite coming up to quota.

TWO TYPES OF EXECUTIVES

There are two distinct types of executives. There is the impatient, driving, quick, keen, positive, irritable type. This man can get good results from a certain type of worker, but he only irritates, frightens, and drives to sullen resistance other types. The other is the mild, kindly, persuasive, patient, enduring, persistent, determined type of executive, who wins his success by attracting to himself the intense loyalty and devotion of his men. Both types are successful, but they are successful with different kinds of men. The employer who selects executives, therefore, needs to bear this in mind, and to select the right type of men to work under his various lieutenants. On the other hand, men who take executive positions should see that they secure for themselves the type of workers from whom they can secure results. This will not be easy, because, as a general rule, an executive tends to surround himself with men of his own type, which is usually a mistake. Men, in selecting positions, should also bear this truth in mind. They should know the kind of executive under whom they can do their best work, and, if at all possible, work under this kind of superior officer.

SLAVES TO MACHINERY

In an earlier chapter of this book we referred to the type of boy or girl who is too restless to study, to continue in school; who is eager to begin his life work; who therefore leaves school at an early age and takes up some work for which he is then fitted, but which, in after life, he finds to be uncongenial and unprofitable. As a general rule, such individuals are ambitious--oftentimes exceedingly ambitious. They find, as they grow older, however, that they have not sufficient education and training to enable them to realize their ambitions. Thousands upon thousands of these condemn themselves to mere unskilled manual labor.

It is not to be wondered at that these boys and girls leave school, because in school they are compelled to sit quietly and to try to learn things in which they are not interested out of dry, unprofitable books. Such pupils need to spend a great part of their time out-of-doors. They can be thus taught far more easily, will take a greater interest in their studies, and can gain both knowledge and skill which will be more valuable to them in the world of work. They also need to be taught indoors manual training, domestic science, printing, laundry work, scientific horticulture, scientific agriculture, dairying, and many other such branches. The recently projected vocational schools, continuation schools, half-time schools, and other such contrivances for giving the boy or the girl an opportunity to learn a useful trade while he is mastering the three R's, are a very important and valuable step in the right direction; With an opportunity thus to find expression for his mechanical ability and his great activity, the boy will be encouraged to remain longer in school.

Those who have left school at an early age on account of restlessness should take very seriously to heart the fates of tens of thousands of men and women before them who have done the same thing and who have made a failure of their lives, because they did not have sufficient education and training with which to realize their aspirations.

THE IMPRACTICAL

It has been frequently remarked that this is a commercial age. Our great captains of industry, our multi-millionaires, have, most of them, made their fortunes in commerce. This is an age, perhaps--especially in the United States--which rather makes a hero of the business man. For this reason there are many who are ambitious for commercial success. Every year thousands upon thousands of young men and women leave school in order to enter business. By a very natural psychological paradox, there seems to be a fascination about commerce and finance for many young people who have little aptitude for these vocations. Many people, feeling their deficiencies, yearn to convince themselves and others that they are not deficient. It is only another phase of the fatality with which a Venus longs to be a Diana and a Minerva a Psyche. Thousands enter business who have no commercial or financial ability. They cannot know the requirements; they cannot understand the fundamental principles of business. Commercially they are babes in the woods. Therefore they go down to bankruptcy and insolvency, to their

60

great detriment and to the injury of many thousands of others.

These young people are too impractical for business. They may have a theoretical understanding of it, and an intellectual desire to succeed. But, as a result of their impractical type of mind, they neglect details, they overlook important precautions, they are, oftentimes, too credulous, too easily influenced. They usually make poor financiers; they do not make collections well; they are incautious in extending credit and in maintaining their own credit; often they are inefficient and wasteful in management; they do not take proper account of all the costs in fixing prices; they enter into foolish contracts; make promises which they are unable to keep, and oftentimes, as a result of too great optimism, undertake far more than is commercially feasible.

HUNGRY FOR FAME

The same strange quirk in human nature which takes the impractical into the marts, takes many ambitious but inherently unfit into art and literature. The stage-struck girl who has not one scintilla of dramatic ability is so common as to be a joke--to all but herself and her friends. Every editor is wearied with his never-ending task of extinguishing lights which glow brightly with ambition but have no gleam of the divine fire. Teachers of art and music, both in this country and abroad, are threatened with insanity because of the hordes of young men and women who come to them with money in their hands, demanding to be made into famous artists and musicians, not having been born with genius. Some of these unfortunates spend years of time and thousands of dollars in money attempting to fit themselves for careers, only to end in utter failure. Some, even after they have made a comparative failure of their education, eke out a tortured existence, hoping against hope for the golden crown of fame and fortune.

In sober truth the fatal lack in most of these disappointed seekers is not that they have no talent, but that they are too lazy mentally to make a real success of the natural aptitudes they have. They lack "the infinite capacity for taking pains." They are deluded by the idea that success depends upon inspiration--that there is no perspiration. Yet every great writer, every great musician, every great actor, every great author, knows that there is no fame, there is no possibility of success, except through the most prolonged and painstaking drudgery.

"LIFE IS BRIEF--ART IS LONG"

Perhaps no actor of modern times had greater dramatic talents inborn than Richard Mansfield, yet here is the story of how Richard

Mansfield[6] worked, toiled, starved and suffered in achieving success in his art:

His friends crowded St. George's Hall for his first appearance. It was observed, as he uttered the few lines of the Beadle, that he was excessively nervous. When, later in the evening, he sat down at the piano and struck a preliminary chord, he fainted dead away.

[Footnote 6: From "Richard Mansfield," by Paul Wilstach. Charles Scribner's Sons, New York.]

Mr. Reed relieved him of his position at once. In discharging him, he said: 'You are the most nervous man I have ever seen,' It was not all nervousness, however. Mansfield had not eaten for three days. He had fainted from hunger.

"Mansfield was now on evil days, indeed. He moved into obscure quarters and fought the hard fight. It was years before he would speak of these experiences. In fact, he rarely ruminated on the past in the confidences of either conversation or correspondence. Memory troubled him little and by the universal quotation it withheld its pleasures. He dwelt in the present, with his eyes and hopes on the future. It was always the future with him. No pleasure or attainment brought complete satisfaction. He looked to the past only in relation to the future; for experience, for example, for what to avoid.

"Once, when at the meridian of his fame, he was asked to lecture before the faculty and students of the University of Chicago. For his subject he chose, 'On Going on the Stage.' That he might exploit to those before him the reality of the actor's struggle, he lifted for the first time a corner of that veil of mystery which hung between his public and his past, and told of these early London days:

"For years I went home to my little room, if, fortunately, I had one,' he said, 'and perhaps a tallow dip was stuck in the neck of a bottle, and I was fortunate if I had something to cook for myself over a fire, if I had a fire. That was my life. When night came I wandered about the streets of London, and if I had a penny I invested it in a baked potato from the baked-potato man on the corner. I would put these hot potatoes in my pockets, and after I had warmed my hands, I would swallow the potato. That is the truth.'

"At length, his wardrobe became so reduced that attendance at any but the most informal entertainments became out of the question, and finally he had to give up these. Soon he was inking the seams of his coat, and wandered about shunning friends, for fear they would learn to what a condition he was reduced.

"'Often,' he admitted, 'I stayed in bed and slept because when I was awake I was hungry. Footsore, I would gaze into the windows of restaurants, bakeries, and fruit shops, thinking the food displayed in them the most tempting and beautiful sight in the world. There were times when I literally dined on sights and smells,'

"He did every species of dramatic and musical hack work in drawing rooms, in clubs, and in special performances in theatres. Sometimes he got into an obscure provincial company, but he said that his very cleverness was a kind of curse, since the harder he worked and the better the audiences liked him, the quicker he was discharged. The established favorites of these little companies always struck when a newcomer made a hit.

"Richard Barker was the stage manager and Mansfield could never please him. After trying again and again, he once cried: 'Please, Barker, do let me alone. I shall be all right. I have acted the part.' 'Not you,' declared Barker. 'Act? You act, man? You will never act as long as you live!'

"The recollection of the rebuffs, poverty, starvation, inability to find sympathy, because, possibly, of the pride which repelled it, the ill-fortune which snatched the extended opportunity just as he was about to grasp it, the jealousy of established favorites of the encroaching popularity of newcomers, the hardships of provincial travel and life in a part of the country and at a time when the play-actor was still regarded as a kind of vagabond and was paid as such, the severity of the discipline he encountered from the despots over him--all painted pictures on his memory and fed a fire under the furnace of his nature which tempered the steel in his composition to inflexibility. The stern rod of discipline was held over him every moment and often fell with unforgetable severity. He was trained by autocrats in a school of experience more autocratic than anything known to the younger actors of this generation.

"When the part of Chevrial was given to him, Mansfield was fascinated with his opportunity, but he kept his counsel. He applied every resource of his ability to the composition of his performance of the decrepit old rake. He sought specialists on the infirmities of roués; he studied specimens in clubs, on the avenue, and in hospitals; and in the privacy of his own room he practiced make-ups for the part every spare moment. The rehearsals themselves were sufficiently uneventful. He gave evidence of a careful, workmanlike performance, but promise of nothing more.

"While he was working out the part Mansfield scarcely ate or slept. He had a habit of dining with a group of young Bohemians at a table d'hôte in Sixth Avenue. The means of none of them made regularity at these forty-cent banquets possible, so his absence was meaningless. One evening, however, he dropped into his accustomed chair, but tasted nothing.

"'What's the matter, Mansfield?' asked one of the others.

"'To-morrow night I shall be famous,' he said. 'Come and see the play,'

"His friends were accustomed to lofty talk from him. His prophecy was answered with a light laugh and it had passed out of their memories as they drifted into the night. This was one of those intuitions to which he often confessed, and it told him that the years of apprenticeship were behind him and the artist in him was on the eve of acknowledgment.

"On the night of January 11, 1883, the theatre was radiant with an expectant audience--half convinced in advance by the record of the Union Square's past, but by the same token exacting to a merciless degree--to see their old friends in the first performance in America of 'A Parisian Romance.'

"Mansfield made his entrance as the Baron Chevrial within a few moments after the rise of the curtain. It was effected in an unconcerned silence on the part of the audience.

"There were, on the other hand, the deserved receptions of old favorites by old friends, as Miss Jewett, Miss Vernon, Miss Carey, Mr. DeBelleville, Mr. Parselle and Mr. Whiting came upon the scene.

"When Chevrial, finding himself alone with Tirandel and Laubaniere, exposed his amusingly cynical views of life and society, some attention was paid to a remarkable portrait of a polished, but coarse, gay, though aging, voluptuary. The scene was short and he was soon off, though not without a little impudent touch, in passing the maid in the doorway, that did not slip unnoticed. The dramatic disclosures which followed brought the act to a close with applause that augured well. Henri, Marcelle, and Mme. De Targy were called forward enthusiastically.

"The second act revealed the Baron's chambers. With the exception of two minutes, he was on the stage until the curtain fell. The Baron's effort, so precisely detailed, to reach and raise the dumb-bells from the floor; the inveterate libertine's interview with shrewd Rosa, the danseuse, who took the tips he expected would impoverish her and thus

64

put her in his power, for the purpose of playing them the other way: the biting deliberation of his interview with his good Baroness and Henri, who comes to ruin himself to save his family's honor--all held the audience with a new sensation. As he pushed his palsied arms into his coat and pulled himself fairly off his feeble feet in his effort to button it, turned up to his door humming like a preying bumble-bee, faced slowly about again, his piercing little pink eyes darting with anticipation, and off the trembling old lips droned the telling speech: 'I wonder how his pretty little wife will bear poverty. H'm! We shall see'--the curtain fell to applause which was for the newcomer alone. He had interested the audience and was talked about between the acts.

"Mr. Palmer rushed back to his dressing-room and found him studiously adding new touches to his make-up for the next act. 'Young man,' exclaimed the manager, 'do you know you're making a hit?' 'That's what I'm paid for,' replied Mansfield, without lowering the rabbit's foot.

"The third act was largely Marcelle's. The Baron was on for an episodic interval, but succeeded, in that he did not destroy the impression already created.

"The fourth act revealed a magnificent banquet hall with a huge table laden with crystal, silver, snowy linens, flowers, and lights. At the top of a short stairway at the back was a gallery and an arched window through which one looked up the green aisle of the Champs-Elysee to the Arc de Triomphe, dimly visible in the moonlight. The Baron entered for one last glance over the preparations for his *petit souper* for Rosa and her sister of the ballet at the Opera.

"The effectiveness of his entrance was helped by his appearance behind a colonnade, and there he stood, only half revealed, swaying unsteadily while his palsied hand adjusted his monocle to survey the scene. There was a flutter of applause from the audience but, appreciatively, it quickly hushed itself. He dragged himself forward. The cosmetic could not hide the growing pallor of the parchment drawn over the old reprobate's skull. He crept around the table and, with a marvellous piece of 'business' by which he held his wobbly legs while he slowly swung a chair under him, collapsed. The picture was terrible, but fascinating. People who would, could not turn their heads. His valet was quick with water and held the glass in place on the salver while he directed it to the groping arm. The crystal clinked on Chevrial's teeth as he sucked the water.

"Presently he found his legs again and tottered up to the staircase. The picture of the black, shrivelled little man dragging his lifeless legs up to the gallery step by step was never forgotten by anyone who saw it. At the top he turned and said in ominous tones: 'I do not wish to be disturbed in the morning. I shall need a long sleep'; and dragged himself out of sight. He had been on the stage five minutes and had said scarcely fifty words. The picture and the effect were unmistakable. The audience capitulated. There was a roar of applause which lasted several minutes.

"The whispered discussion of this scene was such that scarcely any attention was paid to the stage until the Baron returned. Almost immediately afterward the ballet girls pirouetted into the hall in a flutter of gauze, and the places at the tables were filled. No one listened to the lines; all eyes in the house were focussed on the withered, shrunken, flaccid little old Baron, who sat at Rosa's right, ignored by everyone about him as they gorged on his food and drank his wines.

"Soon he drew himself up on his feet and, raising his glass, said: 'Here's to the god from whom our pleasures come. Here's to Plutus and a million!'"

"The gay throng about the table echoed the toast: To Plutus and a million!' and Chevrial continued:

"'While I am up I will give a second toast: 'Here's to Rosa! The most splendid incarnation that I know!'

"Placing the glass to her lips for a first sip, the lecherous old pagan's own lips sought the spot, sipped, and he sank back into his chair.

"What else went on till he rose again no one knew or minded. No eye in the house could wander from the haggard, evil, smiling, but sinister, old face. Presently he was up once more and, with his raised goblet brimming with champagne, he offered a third toast:

"'Here's to material Nature, the prolific mother of all we know, see, or hear. Here's to the matter that sparkles in our glasses, and runs through our veins as a river of youth; here's to the matter that our eyes caress as they dwell on the bloom of those young cheeks. Here's to the matter that--here's to--here's--the matter--the matter that--here's--'

"The attack had seized him. Terrible and unforgetable was the picture of the dissolution. The lips twitched, the eyes rolled white, the raised hand trembled, the wine sputtered like the broken syllables which the shattered memory would not send and the swollen tongue suddenly could not utter. For one moment of writhing agony he held the trembling glass aloft; then his arm dropped with a swiftness that shattered the crystal. Instinctively he groped up to the stairs for light and air. He reeled as if every step would be his last. Rosa helped him up to the window, but recoiled from him with a shriek. Again his hand flew up, but there was neither glass, wine, nor words. He rolled helplessly and fell to the floor, dead. The curtain fell.

"It was probably the most realistically detailed figure of refined moral and physical depravity, searched to its inevitable end, the stage has ever seen. For a moment after the curtain fell there was a hush of awe and surprise. Then the audience found itself and called Mansfield to the footlights a dozen times. But neither then nor thereafter would he appear until he had removed the wig and make-up of the dead Baron. There was no occasion to change his clothes; he wore the conventional evening suit. The effect of shrivelled undersizedness was purely a muscular effect of the actor. The contrast between the figure that fell at the head of the stairs and the athletic young gentleman who acknowledged the applause was no anti-climax.

"Mansfield had come into his own. The superb art of his performance had dwarfed all about it; the play was killed, but he was from that moment a figure to be reckoned with in the history of the theatre."

It is said that when Paderewsky played before Queen Victoria, she said to him: "Mr. Paderewsky, you are a genius." "Ah, your Majesty," he replied, "perhaps. But before I was a genius, I was a drudge." And this is true. It is said that Paderewsky spent hours every day, even after achieving his fame, practising the scale, improving his technique, and keeping himself in prime condition.

Study the life and achievement of any great man of genius. His genius has consisted principally in his wonderful capacity to labor for perfection in the most minute detail. And yet most ambitious misfits are unwilling to work hard. Their products always show lack of finish due to slipshod methods, unwillingness to spend time, to take pains to bring what they do up to a standard of beautiful perfection, so far as perfection is humanly possible. Those who are mentally lazy do not belong in an artistic vocation. There are probably many things that they can do and do well in some less spectacular lines, some calling that does not require such mental effort.

MISFITS IN THE PROFESSIONS

In the traditional educational system the common school is not particularly adapted to prepare its pupils for life, but rather to prepare them for either a high school or a preparatory school. Passing on to the high school, the same condition prevails. The whole question in every high school and every preparatory school is whether the training will accredit one to certain colleges and universities. So the traditional high school graduate is not prepared for life; he is prepared for college or the university. He goes on to the university. There he finds that he is being prepared chiefly for four or five learned professions--the law, the ministry, medicine, engineering, and teaching. In the beginning, the university was supposed to train a man, not for work, but for leisure. The very word scholar means a man of leisure. People were trained, therefore, not for usefulness, but for show; not to earn their living in the world, but rather, their living having been provided for them by a thoughtful government or a kind-hearted parent, to present evidences of the fact. One of the chief of such evidences was the ability to go to a college or university and to take the time to learn a great deal of useless knowledge about dead languages, philosophies, and dry-as-dust sciences. While this is not true to so great an extent to-day, there is still much of the old tradition clinging about colleges and universities, and we are training men and women, not for commercial or industrial or agricultural lines, but rather, for the learned professions.

THE "WHITE COLLAR MAN"

In England and other European countries no man is held to be a gentleman who has ever earned his living by the work of his hands. No one is accredited with standing as an amateur athlete who has ever "lost caste" in this way. While this caste feeling is not so strong in America as it is abroad, it still has a considerable influence upon parents and their children in the selection of a vocation. While one does not lose caste by doing manual labor, temporarily or as a makeshift, he suffers socially, in certain circles, who chooses deliberately a vocation which requires him to wear soiled clothing, to carry a plebeian dinner-pail, and to work hard with his hands. Because of this, many bricklayers, carpenters, blacksmiths, shoemakers, plasterers, plumbers, and other workers, ambitious socially for their sons, instead of teaching them trades in which they might excel and in which there might be an unrestricted future for them, train them for clerical and office work. Having felt the social handicap themselves, these men and their wives determine that their children shall belong to the class which wears good clothes, has soft, white hands, and eats luncheon at a cafeteria--or from a paper parcel which can be respectably hidden in an inside coat pocket. And so there are armies of "white collar men" who would be healthier, wealthier, more useful, and happier if they wore overalls and jumpers.

68

The "typical" bank clerk is a good illustration. Pallid from long hours indoors, stooped from his concentration upon interminable columns of figures, dissatisfied, discontented, moving along painfully in a narrow groove, out of which there seems to be no way, underpaid, he is one of the tragedies of our commercial and financial age. While the section-hand may become a section boss, a roadmaster, a division superintendent, a general superintendent, a general manager, and, finally, the president of a railroad; while the stock boy becomes, eventually, a salesman, then a sales manager, and, finally, the head of the corporation; while apprentices to carpenters, bricklayers, and plumbers may become journeymen, and then contractors, and, finally, owners of big buildings; while the farmhand may become a farm owner, then a landlord, and, finally, perhaps, the president of a bank; while a workman in a factory handling a wheelbarrow may afterward become the president of the greatest corporation in the world, the clerk, toiling over his papers and his books, is almost inevitably sentenced to a lifetime of similar toil, with small opportunities for advancement before him.

There are men fitted by inheritance and training for clerical work and what lies beyond and above it. They are so constituted that they have the ability to take advantage of opportunities, to forge to the front from such a beginning, and to rise to commanding positions. But this is not true of the men who have aptitudes which would make them successful in active work with their hands, and afterward with hand and brain. These men of inherent activity and skill of hand, men whose bones and muscles were made for work, whose whole nature calls for the out-of-doors, are doomed to stagnate, grow discontented, and finally lose hope, if compelled by pride or bad judgment to undertake the "white collar man's" job.

SOCIAL VALUE OF THE "WHITE COLLAR MAN"

Regarding the social deficiency of this class of worker Martha Brensley Bruere and Robert W. Bruere, in their excellent book, "Increasing Home Efficiency," have the following to say:

"The output of their domestic factory so far is two sons able to earn living salaries, who are useful to the community undoubtedly, but as easy to replace if damaged as any other standard products that come a dozen to the box. They themselves didn't like the upper reaches of the artisan class where they had spent their lives, so they boosted their sons till they could make a living by the sweat of their brains instead of the sweat of their brows. Society can use the Shaw boys, but is it profitable

69

to produce them at the price? The money that made these boys into a clerk and a stenographer cost twenty years of their parents' brain and muscle. Mrs. Shaw has bred the habit of saving into her own bones till now, when she might shift the flatiron, the cook stove and the sewing machine from her shoulders, she can't let go the $10 a month her 'help' eats and wastes long enough to straighten up her spine. These two boys and a daughter still in the making have cost their father and mother twenty years, which Mr. Shaw sums up by saying:

"'So, you see, the final result of making up your mind to do a thing, including the great trouble of bringing up a family, is just getting down to the ground and grinding.'

"Isn't it just possible that society has lost as much in the parents as it has gained in the children? Couldn't we have got the same product some cheaper way? Or a better product by more efficient home management?"

WOMEN'S WORK

Perhaps the saddest of all the misfits are to be found amongst women, or it may be that their cases seem to us to be saddest because there are so many of them. Under the old-time regime there was but one vocation open to women--that of wife and mother. Regardless of aptitudes, physical strength or weakness, personal likes or dislikes, all women were expected to marry and bear children, and to qualify successfully for a vocation which combined the duties of nursemaid, waitress, laundress, seamstress, baker, cook, governess, purchasing agent, dietitian, accountant, and confectioner. In the early days of this country, in addition to these duties, women were also called upon to be butchers, sausage-makers, tailors, spinners, weavers, shoemakers, candle-makers, cheese-makers, soap-makers, dyers, gardeners, florists, shepherds, bee-keepers, poultry-keepers, brewers, picklers, bottlers, butter-makers, mil-liners, dressmakers, hatters, and first-aid physicians, surgeons and nurses. In more modern times, women have entered nearly all vocations. But even yet there is much prejudice against the woman who "descends" out of her traditional "sphere." The woman who is not a wife, mother, and house-keeper--or a domestic parasite, housekeeping by proxy--loses caste among the patricians. Many men and, on their behalf, their mothers and sisters, shudder at the sordid thought of marrying a girl who has been so base as to "work for her living." And so stenographers, clerks, accountants, saleswomen, factory workers, telephone operators, and all other women in the business world are about 99 per cent temporary workers. Even in executive positions and in the professions, most women look upon wages and salaries as favoring breezes, necessary until they drop anchor in the haven of matrimony. And even those who most sincerely proclaim themselves wedded to their careers, in many instances, exercise their ancient privilege, change their minds, and give up all else for husband and home.

Every normal woman was intended by nature to marry. It is right that she should marry. She does not truly and fully live unless she does marry. She misses deep and true joy who is not happily married--and usually feels cheated. But the same may be said of every normal man. The difference is that, according to tradition, marriage is woman's career, while man may choose a life work according to his aptitudes. Because of prejudice, however, it is rarely that the happily married woman makes a business or professional career. Husbands, except those who do so through necessity or those who are unafraid of convention, do not permit their wives to work outside of the home. Because of false pride, many men say: "I am the bread-winner. If I cannot support my wife as she should be supported, then I do not wish to marry." And so thousands of women sigh away their lives at work they hate while a hungry, sad world suffers for what they would love to do.

The waste of these misfits is threefold: First, the women lose the opportunity for service, profit, and enjoyment which should be theirs. Second, the world loses the excellent services which they might render. Third, oftentimes these women are very poor housekeepers. They simply have not the aptitudes. Their husbands and their families suffer.

WOMEN WITHOUT HOMES

Another very large class of misfits, and, perhaps, even more to be pitied than any other, is composed of the women who are compelled to earn a living in the business world, in the professional world, or elsewhere, whose true place is in the home. Many of these are unmarried, either because the right man has not presented himself, or because there are not enough really desirable men in the community to go around. Others are widows. Still others are women who have been deserted by their mates. Some of them are compelled to support their parents, brothers, and sisters, or even their husbands.

If traditional methods and courses of education miss the needs of many of our young men, what shall we say of conventional education for girls? Well, to tell the truth, we do not know what to say. Educational experts, reformers, philosophers, investigators, and editors have spoken and written volumes on the subject. Women upon whom the different kinds of educational formulae have been tried have also written about it. Some of them have told tragic stories. There has been, and is, much controversy. Some say one thing--some another--but what shall common sense say? After all, education is rather a simple problem--in its essentials. It means development--development of inborn talents. And education ought especially to develop the natural aptitude of most of our girls for efficiency in home-making and child-rearing. Most young women enter upon the vocation of wifehood and motherhood practically without any training for these duties.

It is as unscientific to expect all women to be successful wives and mothers as it would be to expect all men to be successful farmers. It is as tragic to expect an untrained girl to be a successful wife and mother as it would be to expect an untrained boy to be a successful physician and surgeon.

EXECUTIVES AND DETAIL WORKERS

A very broad division of misfits is into those who are fitted to do detail work, trying to do executive work, and those who are natural-born executives compelled to do detail work. This is a very common cause of unfitness.

Some men love detail and can do it well. They naturally see the little things. Their minds are readily occupied with accuracy in what seem to others to be trifles, but which, taken together, make perfection. They are careful; they are dependable; they can be relied upon. Such people, however, do not have a ready grasp for large affairs. They cannot see things in their broader aspect. They are not qualified by nature to outline plans in general for other people to work out in detail. They are the men upon whom the world must depend for the careful working out of the little things so essential if the larger plans are to go through successfully.

On the other hand, there are some people who have no patience with details. They do not like them. They cannot attend to them. If depended upon for exactitude and accuracy, they are broken reeds. They forget detail.

There are many executives holding important positions and making a sad failure of them because they are, by natural aptitudes, excellent detail men but poor planners and executives. The following story illustrates, perhaps, as well as anything we could present, the qualities of these overworked, busy, busy executives who have no right to be

72

executives, but ought to be carrying out the plans of someone else:

HOW SOCRATIC HELPED BRAINERD BUILD BUSINESS

People sometimes bring their business troubles to a friend whom we shall call Socratic. And Socratic helps them out for a consideration. His time is valuable and he bought his wisdom at a high price.

Some months ago a pompous fellow dropped in. We recognized him as Brainerd, one of the leading business men of a small city. His story was this: He had built up a big enterprise during the pioneer boom days of easy money and negligible competition. Now, when margins were closer, the pace hotter, and a half dozen keen fellows were scrambling for their shares of a trade he had formerly controlled jointly with one other conservative house, he found sales falling off and his profits dwindling to a minus quantity.

Socratic heard him through; then said: "I'll look your business over, tell you the troubles, and show you how to remedy them for one hundred dollars."

"Oh, I couldn't afford to pay that much, the way business is now," Brainerd objected.

"How much, then, do you figure it would be worth to you to have your sales and profits climb back to high-water mark?"

"Oh, that would be worth thousands of dollars, of course. But can you guarantee me any such results?"

KEEPING THE APPOINTMENT

"Well, if you carefully study over what I tell you, and faithfully follow my advice, and the results are not satisfactory, you need pay me nothing. Is that agreeable?"

"Sure! If you can show me how to bring my profits back to normal, I'll gladly pay you two hundred."

"It's a go!" said Socratic. "Have the contract drawn up ready to sign when I call to begin my examination. When shall that be?"

"Well, let's see. I'm so all-fired busy it's hard to find time for anything. Say early next week sometime."

"All right. What day?"

"Oh, Tuesday or Wednesday."

"Tuesday will be satisfactory. What hour?"

"Well, some time in the forenoon, I guess."

"Ten o'clock be all right?"

"Yes, ten o'clock will do."

"Very well, I'll be there at ten sharp."

Tuesday morning, at ten sharp, Socratic stood by Brainerd's desk. Brainerd was working away like a busy little high-pressure hoisting-engine. He looked up with a bright smile.

"Oh, it's you, is it? Sorry, but I can't do anything for you to-day. I'm awfully up against it for time. Can't you drop in a little later in the week?"

"What day?" Socratic asked.

"Oh, Thursday or Friday," a little impatiently.

"Thursday is all right. What hour? Ten o'clock do?"

"Yes, yes, that will do," sighed the busy, busy business man, his nose deep in his work.

Socratic turned on his heel and walked out.

THE HEAD CLERK'S SALARY

Thursday morning he was again beside Brainerd's desk. It was easy to see that this little buzz-fly was a mile up in the air. Hi$ coat was off, his cuffs turned back, his collar unbuttoned, his hair mussed, and he had a streak of soot across his nose. He hardly looked up. Just kept chugging away like a motor-cycle going up-grade at fifty miles an hour.

Oh, but he was the busy man!

"Sorry to disappoint you again, Socratic," he jerked out, "but I haven't got time to breathe. You'll have to come in again."

"Making stacks of money with all this strenuous activity, I suppose?" asked Socratic.

"Oh, no! It keeps me on the jump like a toad under a harrow to pay expenses."

"Call that a profitable way to spend time and nervous energy so prodigally?"

"It may not be--I suppose it isn't, but I can't help it."

"Your head clerk draws pretty good pay, doesn't he?" asked Socratic.

"Why, yes," answered Brainerd, staring.

"Probably has a bigger income to handle, personally, than you have?"

"Oh, I guess so" You'll have to excuse me, Socratic. I'm too busy to talk to-day."

"Queer, but your head clerk and cashier seem to have plenty of time for conversation. They have been scrapping for fifteen minutes about chances of the Pirates and the Cubs. You feel happy to pay people big salaries for talking baseball?"

"No; of course not; but how can I help it? A man can't hire reliable help for love or money in this town, and I haven't got time to watch all of 'em."

"How would it do to have the bookkeeper check up those sales-slips you are tearing your hair over, instead of manicuring her pretty paddies and tucking in her scolding locks?"

"Well, she was doing something else when I began. Excuse me a minute."

SOME FOOL EXCUSES

And Brainerd dashed away to the front of the store to wait on a nicely dressed lady who had just come in. When he returned he said: "I'll tell you, Mr. Socratic, I've been thinking over the matter of our contract, and I don't believe I'm prepared to go into that thing at present. Times are so hard and I am so rushed for time, and you would probably recommend a lot of things I couldn't afford, and likely couldn't work in with my present system. I guess I'll have to let it go for the present. It would be a good thing, no doubt, but I guess I'll have to do the best I can without it. Some time later, perhaps, I'll take it up with you. Why, I don't even get time to read the papers, and I certainly wouldn't have time to go into that examination with you."

"I've completed my examination," remarked Socratic.

"Why, how's that?" gasped Brainerd. "When did you do it?"

"The day you were in my office. What I have seen and heard on my two visits here only confirms the diagnosis of your case I made then. But the real purpose of the two calls was to endeavor to make you see your troubles as I see them."

"I don't know what you mean, sir," said Brainerd, piqued by the unmistakable trend of Socratic's remarks.

75

"I rather think you do, but I'll take no chances. Your business is desperately ill, isn't it?"

"Yes, I guess it is," reluctantly.

"Then it needs a heroic remedy, doesn't it?"

"Possibly."

"And that remedy must be applied to the source of the trouble. Not so?"

"Yes."

And that source is none other than Mr. James H. Brainerd. No, don't blow up with a loud report. Listen to me. You are really too good a business man to go to the wall for the want of a little teachableness. You have foresight, initiative, energy, and perseverance. These are success-qualities of a high order. But you have fallen into some very costly bad habits.

Let me give you the names of six old-fashioned virtues that you are going to start right in to cultivate. When you have developed them, your profits will take care of themselves.

THE REMEDY

The first is Order. You waste seventy-five per cent of your time and nervous energy because you let your work push you instead of planning your work and then pushing your plan.

The second is Punctuality. You lose time, money, friends, temper, and will-power because you are vague and careless about making appointments and slipshod about keeping them.

The third is Courtesy. This has its source in consideration for others and is closely allied to tact. When you ask me to come and help you, and then tell me you are sorry you can do nothing for me, or sorry to disappoint me, that's patronizing. When you ignore a caller and go to reading papers on your desk, that's rudeness. And you can't afford them in your business.

The fourth is Economy. Your time is worth more to this business than that of all the help put together. And when you spend it doing what a ten-dollar-a-week girl could do just as well, it is sinful extravagance. It wastes not only your time, but hers. Worst of all, it undermines your self-respect and her respect for you.

The fifth is Honesty. When you rush away to wait on some customer yourself because that customer has connived with you for some special cut rates, you may not intend it, but you are dishonest. Business must be done at a profit and all those who share in the privileges of buying from this store should share proportionately in paying you your profit. If anyone doesn't pay his share, the others have to make up for it Give everybody a square, equal deal. That will build confidence and increase trade. And then you can leave your salespeople to wait on all customers, giving you more time for real management--generalship.

The sixth is Courage. It's easy enough to see obstacles, to make excuses, to procrastinate. When a hard task has to be done, you will find it no help to begin to catalog the difficulties. Just fear not, and do it.

Now, you are going to cultivate these virtues, Brainerd, because you see that I am right and because, after all, you are a man of good judgment and reason.

"Never mind the contract. When you think my advice has proved its value, send me what you think it is worth."

And he walked out, leaving Brainerd purple in the face with a number of varied emotions, chief among which were outraged dignity and warm gratitude.

While you and we know many Brainerds, there are men capable of handling large affairs who, through lack of training, lack of opportunity, or a choice of a wrong vocation, are sentenced to sit, year after year, working away in an inefficient, fumbling manner, with a mass of details which they hate and which they are not fitted to take care of properly. Such people are often conscientious; they have a great desire to do their work thoroughly and well, and the fact that they so frequently neglect little details, forget things that they ought to do, overlook necessary precautions, and otherwise fail to perform their duties, is a matter not only of supreme regret and humiliation to them, but of great distress to those who depend upon them.

CAREFULNESS AND RECKLESSNESS

Carefulness and prudence are natural aptitudes. The careless man is not wilfully careless. He is careless because he has not the aptitudes which make a man careful. The imprudent man is not wilfully imprudent, but because he does not have the inherent qualifications for prudence, the taking of precautions, the wise and careful scrutinizing of all the elements entering into success. For some work men are required who have the natural aptitudes of carefulness and prudence. The great tragedy is that this kind of work is often entrusted to men who are so constituted that it is very easy for them to take chances. The person who is naturally optimistic and hopeful and always looks on the bright side cheerfully expects whatever he does to "come out all right," as he expresses it. He therefore neglects to take sufficient precautions; he does not exercise care as he should; he takes unnecessary and unwise risks. The result is that oftentimes his optimism turns out to be very poorly justified. When things do go wrong on account of their carelessness, such people may feel distressed about it for a time, but they soon recover. They hope for "better luck next time." They expect, by their ingenuity and resourcefulness, to more than make up for the troubles which have come as the result of their carelessness. On the other hand, those who are naturally careful and dependable do not have much hope of things coming out right without eternal vigilance and foresight. They are inherently somewhat apprehensive. They take precautions, are on their guard, and leave no stone unturned whose turning may insure success.

But there are certain classes of work which require a willingness to take chances. Such enterprises are speculative. In order to be happy in them, one must have a certain amount of optimism and hopefulness. He must accept temporary failure without discouragement. The heart to look on the bright side of every cloud must be born in one. He must believe always that the future will bring more desirable results. The careless person delights in this kind of work. The element of chance in it appeals to his sporting blood. The danger gives him needed excitement and thrill. The anxious, apprehensive person has no place in such enterprises. Their uncertainties are a drain upon his nervous system. He worries. He makes himself ill with his anxieties and apprehensions. He is unhappy. When disaster does happen, he takes it seriously, feels discouraged, thinks his efforts have been of no avail, can see nothing in the future but black ruin, and otherwise destroys not only his joy in his work, but his efficiency and usefulness in it.

In actual practice we find both prudent and reckless misfits. Such people are unhappy, inefficient, and usually unsuccessful. It is strange that men do not understand, before undertaking a vocation, so elemental and fundamental a thing as the question of carelessness and carefulness. Yet, somehow or other, they do not. We find thousands of men worrying, anxious, distrait, because of the uncertainties of their businesses and the chances they have to take. We find other thousands of men blundering, careless, optimistic, always hopeful for better things in the future, and yet attempting to succeed in a business which requires care, infinite pains and precautions. Thoughtless, impulsive, frivolous people are always trying to do work requiring careful, plodding, painstaking, methodical ways; while thoughtful, philosophic, and deliberate people oftentimes find themselves distressed, bewildered, and inefficient in the hurly-burly of some swift-moving vocation.

SOME OTHER MISFITS

Mild, easy-going, timid, self-conscious men we frequently find in vocations which require aggressiveness, courage, fighting ability, self-confidence, and a considerable amount of hard-headed brutality. On the other hand, we sometimes find the fighting man in a profession which is considered to be quiet and peaceable.

Similarly, we have often seen lawyers, whose profession requires of them a good deal of combativeness, shrewdness, a certain degree of skepticism, and a large amount of hard-headed determination to win, no matter what the cost, handicapped by extreme sensitiveness, sympathy, generosity, non-resistance, credulity, humility, and self-consciousness. Physically, they were wonderfully capable of success as lawyers. Intellectually, they, perhaps, were even better fitted for the profession than many of their brothers in the legal fraternity. But, emotionally, they were absolutely unfit for the competition, the contest, the necessity for combat and severity in the practice of law.

Contrawise, we have often seen hard-headed, shrewd, skeptical, grasping, unprincipled, aggressive, fighting men in professions where they did not belong; in professions requiring sympathy, credulity, kindness, tact, generosity, unselfishness, and other such qualities. We have not, in this chapter, outlined all of the different classes of misfits. That would be impossible. We have, however, referred to the most common of them. Probably nine-tenths of all the misfits which have come under our observation could be classified under one or more of the heads we have outlined in the foregoing chapter.

CHAPTER IV

THE PHYSICALLY FRAIL

Some years ago there came into our offices in Boston a young man twenty-six years of age. He was about medium height, with keen, intelligent face, fine skin, fine hair, delicately modeled features, refined looking hands, and small, well-shaped feet.

He was inexpensively, but neatly, dressed, and, while somewhat diffident, was courteous, affable, and respectful in demeanor. After a little conversation with him, we asked him if he would be willing to appear before one of our classes and permit the students to try to analyze him, decide what his aptitudes were, and for what profession he was best fitted. An evening or two later he appeared and we placed him before the class. After some little examination of his appearance, this is the judgment passed upon him by those present:

"Fairly observant; capable of learning well through his powers of observation; good intellect, of the thoughtful, meditative type; a fair degree of constructive ability; in disposition, optimistic, cheerful; inclined to take chances; sympathetic, generous, sensitive, kindly, well disposed, and agreeable; rather lacking in self-confidence and, therefore, somewhat diffident, but courteous and friendly in contact with others; responsive and, therefore, easily influenced by his associates, and affected by his environment. Lacking in sense of justice and property sense. A man of natural refinement and refined tastes; fond of beauty, elegance and luxury. Energetic and alert mentally, but rather disinclined to physical effort. Somewhat deficient in aggressiveness, but endowed with an excellent constructive imagination, and so great mental energy that he would be able to take the initiative in an intellectual way, especially in the formation of plans and in the devising of means and ways. Fond of change, variety; loves excitement; likes social life, and somewhat deficient in constancy, conservatism, prudence, and responsibility. Keen, alert, somewhat impatient and restless. Well fitted by nature for intellectual work of any kind; with training would have done well as teacher, writer, private secretary or high-class clerical worker, but expression indicates that, through lack of training, he has failed in physical work and has fallen into evil ways."

After this analysis had been carefully made, we excused the young man and explained that thirteen of his twenty-six years had been spent in jail. He had been left an orphan early in life and secured so little education that he was almost entirely illiterate.

THE EASY DESCENT TO CRIME

As soon as he was old enough, he was set to work at the only thing he could do, namely, manual labor. He was small and slight for his age, and the services he was able to render were not worth much. He, therefore, received very small pay. Because of his physical disabilities, he was behind the other boys in his gang and suffered frequently from the tongue-lashings of an unsympathetic foreman. His pay was not commensurate with his tastes. He constantly felt the desire for finer, better, cleaner things than he was able to earn. The work was hard for him; he suffered much from the punishment inflicted upon his tender hands, from muscular soreness and from weariness. As the days rolled on, he grew weaker, rather than stronger, and became weary earlier in the day. Finally, the time came when he felt that he could endure the taunts of his foreman no longer, and he was about to give up when the foreman, exasperated with his inefficiency, his clumsiness, and his weakness, discharged him.

Having been discharged, it was difficult for him to find another place to work. At this critical stage, being out of money, and having fallen in with idlers--and worse--he was influenced to use his keen intellect and ability in plans and schemes, to commit a small crime, which yielded him $10 or $15. Being a novice in crime, not naturally a criminal, he did not protect himself from discovery and punishment, and, as a result, was sent to a reformatory. After a short term in the reformatory, his behavior was so good that he was released. After his release, a kind-hearted person, who had observed him and liked his appearance, secured another position for him. This also was at manual labor. At first he entered upon his new work with a determination to succeed, to live down the stain upon his character caused by his previous speculation, and, therefore, to live an honorable and successful life.

STRUGGLING AGAINST ODDS

He worked hard and did his best, but the best he could do was not good enough. He possessed no manual skill, he had no strength, and little by little he again became physically tired out, mentally discouraged and sore, and, having once committed a crime, found it easy to seek his former associates and drop again into the old ways. An opportunity presented itself to rob a companion's pocket of a few dollars, and he did so. Again he was sent to the reformatory, this time for a longer term. Then, until he came to our office, his career was a repetition of what has already been related. A few months or a year or two in a reformatory, a jail, or a penitentiary, a month or two trying to rehabilitate himself in some form of manual labor, and, then, inefficiency, incompetency, lack of skill, lack of strength, and discharge, to be followed by another attempt to add to his resources by some petty crime.

For several years following this first interview with Mr. L. we followed him, and did our best to assist him to enter upon some vocation for which he was better fitted. Again and again we and other friends of his helped him to secure work, but always it was the old story. His mind was so active, so intelligent, so eager for expression, that the drudgery, the monotony, the routine, the small pay, and the consequent lack of the many elegances and luxuries he so strongly desired were too much for him. His crimes were never serious, and never those requiring great courage. He never stole any very large sums. For this reason much of his time was spent in the work house or in jail, rather than in the penitentiary. In addition to petty thieving, he had acquired some little ability as a confidence man, and was capable of ensnaring small sums from credulous or sympathetic people on various pretexts. The last time we heard of him he had called upon a friend of ours, professed his complete and permanent reform, wept over his former failures, and promised faithfully--and with the greatest possible fervency and apparent sincerity--to do better in the future. He said that he had an opportunity to make a trip on a whaling vessel and he thought this opportunity would be the best thing in the world for him, as it would take him away from his old, evil associates and give him an opportunity to save money and make good in a new life. He wished our friend to give him $4 to buy a ticket to New Bedford. Our friend gave him the money and also a postal card, on which he had written his own address. "Now, L.," he said, "I believe you, and I want you to show me that you are playing square with me. When you get your new position and are about to sail, I want you to write me about it on this postal card, and mail it to me so that I will know that you are carrying out your promises."

THE OLD, OLD STORY

L. promised faithfully, and said, "I want to write a letter to my mother, and tell her where I am going. I wish you would let me have an envelope and a stamp." Our friend obliged him with the necessaries, and L. left the office beaming with gratitude and profuse in his promises to return the loan as soon as he came back from his trip on the whaling vessel. A few days later my friend received a postal card, dated at New Bedford, Massachusetts. In one corner of the postal card was the notation, "Received at the post office at New Bedford in an envelope, with a letter, requesting that it be mailed here. (Signed) Postmaster."

Here was a man so well-intentioned by nature, of such a kindly, sympathetic, generous disposition, so intelligent, so naturally capable mentally that, with proper training and properly placed in a vocation in which he could have used his talents, he would doubtless have become an excellent asset to society.

This case is typical of many others. They have natural aptitudes which fit them to become useful, but their talents have never been trained, their aptitudes have never been given an opportunity to develop. They have no inherent tendencies toward crime. In fact, there is no "criminal" type. Most--but not all--criminals fall into their evil ways simply because they have never been taught how to direct their mental and physical energies in a way which will give them pleasure, as well as profit.

DESCRIPTION OF THIS TYPE

The physically frail individual of this type is frail because the brain and nervous system are so highly developed that they require a great deal of his vitality and endurance to nourish them and to sustain their activities. The result is that mental powers grow and thrive at the expense of physical.

Such people have large heads in proportion to their bodies. Their heads also are inclined to be very much larger above the ears and in the neighborhood of the forehead and temples than at the jaw and at the nape of the neck. This gives their heads a rather top-heavy effect--like a pear with the small end down--and their faces a triangular shape. Their jaws are usually fine and slender, and their chins not particularly broad and strong.

Such people have very fine hair and fine skin. Their nerves are sensitive and close to the surface. Their entire build of body is delicate and slender. Their hands and feet also are usually delicately and slenderly fashioned; their shoulders are narrow and oftentimes sloping. It is folly to talk of building up rugged, muscular and bony systems by means of strenuous exercise in people thus endowed. Much, of course, can be done to strengthen and harden the muscles, but they are frail physically, by nature, and can never be anything else.

VOCATIONS FOR THE PHYSICALLY FRAIL

People with this type of organization are not inclined to be skillful with their fingers. They do not care for physical work of any kind; they do not take an interest in it and, therefore, cannot do it well. Properly trained, men and women of this type take their place in the professions. They are teachers, preachers, lawyers, educators, reformers, inventors, authors, and artists. Among those of mediocre abilities we find clerks, secretaries, accountants, salesmen, window trimmers, decorators, advertisers, and others working along similar mental lines. When such people are not trained and educated, they are misfits always, because they do not have opportunities to use to their fullest extent the natural intellectual talents with which they have been endowed.

THE MENTALLY MECHANICAL

There is a type of boy who is oftentimes thrown into the wrong vocation in life, owing to a lack of appreciation of his true abilities on the part of parents or teachers. This boy has a large head and small body, and is intensely interested in machinery. He probably learns to handle tools, after a fashion, at a very early age; spends his spare time in machine shops; is intensely interested in locomotives and steamships, and otherwise manifests a passion for machinery and mechanics. Oftentimes, on account of this, he is very early apprenticed to a mechanic or is given a job in some place where he will have an opportunity to build, operate or repair machinery.

Some years ago we visited in a family in which there was a boy of this type. At that time his chief interest was in locomotives. He had a toy locomotive and took the greatest delight in operating it. Whenever he went near a railroad station he improved every opportunity to examine carefully the parts of a locomotive and, if possible, to induce the engineer to take him up into the cab and show him the levers, valves and other parts to be seen there. As soon as he was old enough, he begged his father to be permitted to go to work in a railroad shop. Fortunately, however, his father was too intelligent and too sensible to be misled by mere surface indications. The boy was encouraged to finish his education. Being a bright, capable youngster, he learned readily and rapidly. By means of proper educational methods, giving him plenty of opportunity for the exercise of his mechanical activities, he was induced to remain in school until he secured an excellent college education. As he grew older his interest in machinery did not wane. He found, however, that it was becoming almost wholly intellectual. He lost all desire to handle, build, operate or repair machinery. When, in later life, he became the owner of an automobile, he was more than willing to leave all of the details of its care to his chauffeur and mechanician.

As he cultivated his mental powers, he became more and more interested in the use of his constructive aptitudes in the formation of ideas. He liked to put ideas together; to work out the mechanics of expression in writing. Instead of building machinery, he loved to build plots. Instead of operating machinery, his abilities turned in the direction of working out the technique of literary expression. Instead of repairing machinery he loved rather to revise and rewrite his stories and plays. In other words, the constructive talent, which he had shown as a child in material mechanics, turned in the direction of mental and intellectual construction as he grew older.

COMMERCIAL CONSTRUCTIVENESS

There are many boys who exhibit in their early years a great love of machinery, and it is usually considered a kindness to them to prepare them for either mechanics or engineering. In mechanical lines, they are misfits, because they are frail and insufficient physically. In engineering lines they are more at home, because the engineer works principally with his brains. But very often they would still be more at home in the realms of literature or oratory.

In a similar way boys often manifest great interest in machinery in their youth, and afterward, if given the right opportunities, show their constructive ability in the organization of business enterprises and the successful devising of plans and schemes for pushing these enterprises to success.

Sometimes those of this type of organization devote themselves rather to invention and improvement than to the direct physical handling of machinery. The following brief story of the struggles of Elias Howe[7] should be an inspiration to every individual who fights physical frailty; also, a lesson to him as to the way in which he should express his mechanical ability:

[Footnote 7: From "Great Fortunes," by James D. McCabe. Published by George Maclean.]

INTELLECTUAL TRIUMPH OF A FRAIL MAN

"Elias Howe was born in the town of Spencer, Massachusetts, in 1819. He was one of eight children, and it was no small undertaking on the part of his father to provide a maintenance for such a household. Mr. Howe, Sr., was a farmer and miller, and, as was the custom at that time in the country towns of New England, carried on in his family some of those minor branches of industry suited to the capacity of children, with which New England abounds. When Elias was six years old, he was set, with his brothers and sisters, to sticking wire teeth through the leather straps used for making cotton cards. When he became old enough, he assisted his father in his saw-mill and grist-mill, and during the winter months picked up a meager education at the district school. He has said that it was the rude and imperfect mills of his father that first turned his attention to machinery. He was not fitted for hard work, however, as he was frail in constitution and incapable of bearing much fatigue. Moreover, he inherited a species of lameness which proved a

85

great obstacle to any undertaking on his part, and gave him no little trouble all through life. At the age of eleven he went to live out on the farm of a neighbor, but the labor proving too severe for him he returned home and resumed his place in his father's mills, where he remained until he was sixteen years old.

"At the age of twenty-one he married. This was a rash step for him, as his health was very delicate, and his earnings were but nine dollars per week. Three children were born to him in quick succession, and he found it no easy task to provide food, shelter and clothing for his little family. The light heartedness for which he had formerly been noted entirely deserted him, and he became sad and melancholy. His health did not improve, and it was with difficulty that he could perform his daily task. His strength was so slight that he would frequently return from his day's work too exhausted to eat. He could only go to bed, and in his agony he wished 'to lie in bed forever and ever,' Still he worked faithfully and conscientiously, for his wife and children were very dear to him; but he did so with a hopelessness which only those who have tasted the depths of poverty can understand.

"About this time he heard it said that the great necessity of the age was a machine for doing sewing. The immense amount of fatigue incurred and the delay in hand sewing were obvious, and it was conceded by all who thought of the matter at all that the man who could invent a machine which would remove these difficulties would make a fortune. Howe's poverty inclined him to listen to these remarks with great interest. No man needed money more than he, and he was confident that his mechanical skill was of an order which made him as competent as any one else to achieve the task proposed. He set to work to accomplish it, and, as he knew well the dangers which surround an inventor, kept his own counsel. At his daily labor, in all his waking hours, and even in his dreams, he brooded over this invention. He spent many a wakeful night in these meditations, and his health was far from being benefitted by this severe mental application. Success is not easily won in any great undertaking, and Elias Howe found that he had entered upon a task which required the greatest patience, perseverance, energy and hopefulness. He watched his wife as she sewed, and his first effort was to devise a machine which should do what she was doing. He made a needle pointed at both ends, with the eye in the middle, that should work up and down through the cloth, and carry the thread through at each thrust, but his elaboration of this conception would not work satisfactorily. It was not until 1844, fully a year after he began the attempt to invent the machine, that he came to the conclusion that the movement of a machine need not of necessity be an imitation of the performance by hand. It was plain to him that there must be another stitch by the aid of a shuttle and a curved needle with the eye near the point. This was the triumph of his skill. He had now invented a perfect sewing machine, and had discovered the essential principles of every subsequent modification of his conception. Satisfied that he had at length solved the problem, he constructed a rough model of his machine of wood and wire, in October, 1844, and operated it to his perfect satisfaction.

"It has been stated by Professor Renwick and other scientists that Elias Howe 'carried the invention of the sewing machine further on toward its complete and final utility than any other inventor has ever brought a first-rate invention at the first trial.' ...

"Having patented his machine, Howe endeavored to bring it into use. He was full of hope, and had no doubt that it would be adopted at once by those who were so much interested in the saving of labor. He first offered it to the tailors of Boston; but they, while admitting its usefulness, told him it would never be adopted by their trade, as it would ruin them. Considering the number of machines now used by the tailoring interests throughout the world, this assertion seems ridiculous. Other efforts were equally unsuccessful. Every one admitted and praised the ingenuity of the machine, but no one would invest a dollar in it. Fisher (Howe's partner) became disgusted and withdrew from his partnership, and Howe and his family moved back to his father's house. Thoroughly disheartened, he abandoned his machine. He then obtained a place as engineer on a railroad, and drove a locomotive until his health entirely broke down....

"In 1850 Howe removed to New York, and began in a small way to manufacture machines to order. He was in partnership with a Mr. Bliss, but for several years the business was so unimportant that upon the death of his partner, in 1855, he was enabled to buy out that gentleman's interest, and thus became the sole proprietor of his patent. Soon after this his business began to increase, and continued until his own proper profits, and the royalty which the courts compelled other manufacturers to pay him for the use of his invention, grew from $300 to $200,000 per annum. In 1867, when the extension of his patent expired, it is stated that he had earned a total of two millions of dollars by it."

STARVED BY HIS HANDS, ENRICHED BY HIS HEAD

Robert Burns was a failure as plowman and farmer. Rousseau was a failure at every kind of physical work. Henry George nearly starved himself and his family to death trying to make a living as a journeyman printer. The following extract from the autobiography of Jacob Riis[8]--another excellent example of this type of organization--shows how useless it was for him to attempt to make his living at physical labor:

[Footnote 8: From "The Making of an American," by Jacob A. Riis. Macmillan & Company, New York.]

A missionary in Castle Garden was getting up a gang of men for the Brady's Bend Iron Works on the Allegheny River, and I went along. We started a full score, with tickets paid, but only two of us reached the Bend. The rest calmly deserted in Pittsburgh and went their own way....

The iron works company mined its own coal. Such as it was, it cropped out of the hills right and left in narrow veins, sometimes too shallow to work, seldom affording more space to the digger than barely enough to permit him to stand upright. You did not go down through a shaft, but straight in through the side of a hill to the bowels of the mountain, following a track on which a little donkey drew the coal to the mouth of the mine and sent it down the incline to run up and down a hill a mile or more by its own gravity before it reached the place of unloading. Through one of these we marched in, Adler and I, one summer morning with new pickaxes on our shoulders and nasty little oil lamps fixed in our hats to light us through the darkness where every second we stumbled over chunks of slate rock, or into pools of water that oozed through from above. An old miner, whose way lay past the fork in the tunnel where our lead began, showed us how to use our picks and the timbers to brace the slate that roofed over the vein, and left us to ourselves in a chamber perhaps ten feet wide and the height of a man.

We were to be paid by the ton, I forget how much, but it was very little, and we lost no time in getting to work. We had to dig away the coal at the floor with our picks, lying on our knees to do it, and afterward drive wedges under the roof to loosen the mass. It was hard work, and, entirely inexperienced as we were, we made but little headway.

When toward evening we quit work, after narrowly escaping being killed by a large stone that fell from the roof in consequence of our neglect to brace it up properly, our united efforts had resulted in barely filling two of the little carts, and we had earned, if I recollect aright, something like sixty cents each. The fall of the roof robbed us of all desire to try mining again....

Up the railroad track I went, and at night hired out to a truck farmer, with the freedom of his hay-mow for my sleeping quarters. But when I had hoed cucumbers three days in a scorching sun, till my back ached as if it were going to break, and the farmer guessed he would call it square for three shillings, I went farther. A man is not necessarily a philanthropist, it seems, because he tills the soil. I did not hire out again. I did odd jobs to earn my meals, and slept in the fields at night....

The city was full of idle men. My last hope, a promise of employment in a human-hair factory, failed, and, homeless and penniless, I joined the great army of tramps, wandering about the streets in the daytime with the one aim of somehow stilling the hunger that gnawed at my vitals, and fighting at night with vagrant curs or outcasts as miserable as myself for the protection of some sheltering ash-bin or doorway. I was too proud in all my misery to beg. I do not believe I ever did.

There was until last winter a doorway in Chatham Square, that of the old Barnum clothing store, which I could never pass without recalling those nights of hopeless misery with the policeman's periodic 'Get up there! move on!' reinforced by a prod of his club or the toe of his boot. I slept there, or tried to when crowded out of the tenements in the Bend by their utter nastiness. Cold and wet weather had set in, and a linen duster was all that covered my back. There was a woolen blanket in my trunk which I had from home--the one, my mother had told me, in which I was wrapped when I was born; but the trunk was in the 'hotel' as security for money I owed for board, and I asked for it in vain. I was now too shabby to get work, even if there had been any to get. I had letters still to friends of my family in New York who might have helped me, but hunger and want had not conquered my pride. I would come to them, if at all, as their equal, and, lest I fall into temptation, I destroyed the letters. So, having burned my bridges behind me, I was finally and utterly alone in the city, with the winter approaching and every shivering night in the streets reminding me that a time was rapidly coming when such a life as I led could no longer be endured.

Not in a thousand years would I be likely to forget the night when it came. It had rained all day, a cold October storm, and night found me, with the chill downpour unabated, down by the North River, soaked through and through, with no chance for a supper, forlorn and discouraged. I sat on the bulwark, listening to the falling rain and the swish of the dark tide, and thinking of home. How far it seemed, and how impassable the gulf now between the 'castle,' with its refined ways, between her, in her dainty girlhood, and me sitting there, numbed with the cold that was slowly stealing away my senses with my courage. There was warmth and cheer where she was. Here an overpowering sense of desolation came upon me. I hitched a little nearer to the edge.

What if----? Would they miss me much or long at home if no word came from me? Perhaps they might never hear. What was the use of keeping it up any longer, with, God help us, everything against, and nothing to back, a lonely lad?...

It was not only breakfast we lacked. The day before we had had only a crust together. Two days without food is not good preparation for a day's canvassing. We did the best we could. Bob stood by and wagged his tail persuasively while I did the talking; but luck was dead against us, and 'Hard Times' stuck to us for all we tried. Evening came and found us down by the Cooper Institute, with never a cent. Faint with hunger, I sat down on the steps under the illuminated clock, while Bob stretched himself at my feet. He had beguiled the cook in one of the last houses we called at, and his stomach was filled. From the corner I had looked on enviously. For me there was no supper, as there had been no dinner and no breakfast. To-morrow there was another day of starvation. How long was this to last? Was it any use to keep up a struggle so hopeless? From this very spot I had gone, hungry and wrathful, three years before when the dining Frenchmen for whom I wanted to fight thrust me forth from their company. Three wasted years! Then I had one cent in my pocket, I remembered. To-day I had not even so much. I was bankrupt in hope and purpose. Nothing had gone right; and worse, I did not care. I drummed moodily upon my book. Wasted! Yes, that was right. My life was wasted, utterly wasted.

A voice hailed me by name, and Bob sat up, looking attentively at me for his cue as to the treatment of the owner of it. I recognized in him the principal of the telegraph school where I had gone until my money gave out. He seemed suddenly struck by something.

[Illustration: Photo by Marceau, N.Y. FIG. 9. Richard Mansfield, Actor-Manager. A fine, balanced combination of artistic talent, creative power, and capacity for great emotion, with good judgment, financial sense, great energy, great determination, uncompromising devotion to ideals, fine powers of expression, and executive ability of the driving, compelling, rigid type. Note high head, domed above temples and wide across center of forehead; large nose; long, straight upper lip; firm mouth; prominent chin; long line from point of chin to crown of head; intense expression.]

[Illustration: FIG. 10. Hon. A.I. Cutting (same as FIG. 11). Intellectual, idealistic, yet practical; mild, but very shrewd and persistent; good-natured, friendly, social, sympathetic, kindly, yet with good commercial and financial judgment. Observe height of head, with dome above temples; moderate width of head; pleasant, but firm-set, mouth; fine texture and fine chiseling of features; strong, prominent chin, and genial, kindly, friendly expression.]

[Illustration: FIG. 11. Hon. A.L. Cutting. Ambitious, aspiring, hopeful, cheerful, friendly, social. A good public speaker. Excellent planner, prudent, far-sighted, and deliberate in speech and action. Note high head, both at crown and above temples, long behind ears; high forehead; well-formed eyes and nose, and prominent chin.]

[Illustration: FIG. 12. The late Melville Fuller, Chief Justice of the Supreme Court of the United States. Unusually keen analytical powers, unaffected by sentiment or irrelevant considerations. Great ability to get down to essentials. Note fullness of brows and of upper corners of forehead; keen, penetrating eyes, and long nose with depressed tip.]

[Illustration: FIG. 13. Frank A. Vanderlip, President of National City Bank, of New York. A man of both financial and political acumen--also humanitarian. Note high, domed head; width across center and lower part of forehead; inclination to stoutness; large, well-formed features; long lines of face.]

[Illustration: *Copyright American Press Association.* FIG. 14. Hon. Joseph W. Folk, of Missouri. A keen politician, shrewd lawyer, and hard fighter. Note height and width of head; large, prominent nose; square, firm jaw; long upper lip; dogged set of mouth; unflinching eyes, and inclination to stoutness.]

[Illustration: FIG. 15. The late Senator Nelson W. Aldrich, of Rhode Island. Keen, practical observation, financial judgment, diplomacy, shrewdness, energy, intellect, industry, courage, determination, and command. Note well-developed brows; height and width of forehead, especially across center; long, well-developed nose; straight, firm mouth; broad, square, prominent chin; long ears; long line from point of chin to crown of head, and keen, shrewd, alert, penetrating expression of eye.]

[Illustration: FIG. 16. Showing large, well-developed base of brain, usually an indication of a tendency to stoutness. Note fullness of back of head at nape of neck.]

"'Why, what are you doing here?' he asked. I told him Bob and I were just resting after a day of canvassing.

"'Books!' he snorted. 'I guess that won't make you rich. Now, how would like to be a reporter, if you have got nothing better to do? The manager of a news agency downtown asked me to-day to find him a bright young fellow whom he could break in. It isn't much--$10 a week to start with. But it is better than peddling books, I know,'

"He poked over the book in my hand and read the title. 'Hard Times,' he said, with a little laugh. 'I guess so. What do you say? I think you will do. Better come along and let me give you a note to him now.'

"As in a dream. I walked across the street with him to his office and got the letter which was to make me, half starved and homeless, rich as Croesus, it seemed to me.

"When the sun rose I washed my face and hands in a dog's drinking trough, pulled my clothes into such shape as I could, and went with Bob to his new home. The parting over, I walked down to 23 Park Row and delivered my letter to the desk editor in the New York News Association up on the top floor.

"He looked me over a little doubtfully, but evidently impressed with the early hours I kept told me that I might try. He waved me to a desk, bidding me wait until he had made out his morning book of assignments; and with such scant ceremony was I finally introduced to Newspaper Row, that had been to me like an enchanted land. After twenty-seven years of hard work in it, during which I have been behind the scenes of most of the plays that go to make up the sum of the life of the metropolis, it exercises the old spell over me yet. If my sympathies need quickening, my point of view adjusting, I have only to go down to Park Row at eventide, when the crowds are hurrying homeward and the City Hall clock is lighted, particularly when the snow lies on the grass in the park, and stand watching them awhile, to find all things coming right. It is Bob who stands by and watches with me then, as on that night."

TALENT IN THE BUD AND BLOSSOM

The big important lesson underlying all of these concrete examples is that the individual of this type never ought to attempt to do any kind of work in which success depends upon physical effort. Whatever talents he may have will express themselves always best in an intellectual way. It may be art, it may be music, it may be machinery, it may be business, it may be mining or agriculture, it may be any one of many other active pursuits which have also a purely intellectual side. In his early youth his mind naturally turns to the more material manifestation of his talent. But, with proper training and given the proper opportunities, he will always gravitate surely to the mental and intellectual phases of his bent.

92

The boy who is interested in machinery may become an inventor or he may become a playwright or an author. The boy who is interested in plants and flowers may become a botanist or a naturalist, or, perhaps, even a poet. The boy who is deeply interested in battles and fighting may be far better adapted to the profession of historian than to the trade of soldier. The boy who likes to build houses and factories in his play, and seems to be deeply interested in the construction of edifices, may not be fitted to become a contractor or a draughtsman. If he is of this intellectual type, he is far more likely to become an architect, or, perhaps, to idealize his talents even further and devote himself to literature on the subject of architecture, home planning, and home decoration. The boy of this type, who in his youth seems to take a particular interest in horses, cattle, dogs, and other animals, may not necessarily be best qualified for a stock breeder or a dairyman. Possibly he should become a veterinarian or even a physician and surgeon. Or his bent may be in the direction of science, so that he makes a name as a naturalist.

The first and most important thing for people of this type, and for parents having children of this type, is to get it firmly fixed in their minds, once for all, that they are not fitted for hard physical work. The next important thing, of course, is to secure a broad and complete education along general lines. If there is any striking and particular talent along any one line, such an education is more than likely to bring it out and to cause it to seek further development. In case there is no such distinct predilection manifested, further and more minute study of the individual will have to be made in order to determine just what kind of intellectual work will give him the best opportunities for success and happiness. Even in the want of such a careful analysis, it is, nevertheless, true that an individual of this type, who has no marked inclination toward any one form of mental activity, is always far better placed, far happier, and far more successful if trained to do any kind of intellectual work than if left untrained and compelled to try to earn his own living by the use of his bones and muscles.

CHAPTER V

THE FAT MAN

When we were children and went to the circus, our favorite performer in the sawdust ring was always the clown, and our favorite clown was the fat one. In fact, we do not remember ever having seen a clown who was not a fat man.

Alas! how many were the tribulations of our rotund friend! How he was buffeted, and paddled, and slapped! How often he tumbled and fell! How maliciously inanimate objects flew up and hit him in the face! How constantly his best efforts went for naught, how invariably he was misunderstood! How great was the glee with which everybody persecuted him and knocked him about the ring! And yet, notwithstanding all his troubles, did he win from us a sympathetic sigh or even the fraction of a tear, except tears of laughter? All his troubles seemed funny to us.

Millions are still laughing at the comic tribulations of dear old John Bunny, although he has gone beyond the power of things to trouble him. We have laughed and are still laughing at Thomas Wise. From the days of Falstaff down to those of the "movies," we have enjoyed laughing at the plights of a fat man on the stage.

FAT MEN RULE THE WORLD

In real life it is much the same. Every fat man knows that only by unusual patience, good nature, and friendly tolerance can he live with his fellows. He is the butt of all jokes; he must smile at a constant patter of pleasantries about his unusual size. He hears the same old stupid japes over and over and over again. If he weren't the prince of good fellows and the best-natured man in the world, it would fare ill for those who torment him.

As a matter of fact, it may be better for the rest of us than for the fat man that he is good natured, easy going, genial, fond of a good laugh; because fat men rule the world. Perhaps that is why it is so funny to us to see them in trouble. It is one of the foibles of humanity always to find pleasure in the mishaps of its rulers and superiors. The pranks of the schoolboy are intended to cause perplexity and distress to his teacher. This is true of the college youth in his playfulness. The same human trait manifests itself in a thousand other ways.

The fat man was born to rule. He enjoys the good things of life. He is fond of luxuries. He has a keenly developed sense of taste, and a nice

94

discrimination of flavor. He likes to wear good clothing. He likes soft, upholstered chairs, comfortable beds, a goodly shelter. Like old King Cole (always pictured in our nursery books with a Garguntian girth), he enjoys "his pipe and his bowl and his fiddlers three." He is fond of a good joke, and laughs more heartily than any one else at it. In fact, enjoyment and pleasure may be said to be the keynote of the typical fat man's personality. But he is too heavy for physical activity. His feet are too small for the weight of his body. He does not care for strenuous physical exercise. It is not his idea of a good time to follow a golf ball all over a twenty-acre field. He does it only because he thus hopes to reduce his flesh and enable himself to become once more the romantic figure he was in his youth. For, while the fat man may be a master of comedy, and while he may be a ruler of the people, he is not romantic. The big fellows do not well sustain romantic rôles, except in grand opera, where nearly everything but the music is illusion and elusive. Our novelists all tell us that as soon as a man's girth begins to increase, he looks ridiculous in a fine frenzy. J.M. Barrie makes a very keen point of this in his story of Tommy and Grizel. It was the increasing size of his waist band that drove poor Tommy to such extreme measures as to cause his final downfall and death. His one great aim in life was to be romantic, and when the lady of his desires giggled about his increasing size it was too much.

Scientific research, philosophy, and the more strenuous and concentrated forms of mental activity seem to require a certain degree of asceticism in order to be wholly efficient. We are told that the person who feeds too well causes his mind to grow rather ponderous in its movements. He is inclined to fall asleep if he remains quiet and practices severe mental concentration for too long a time.

HE PLANS WORK FOR OTHERS

If, therefore, the fat man cannot work at physical labor, if he is not fitted for romance, if he is incapacitated by his love of the good things of life for severe mental labor, what can he do to fill his purse, supply his table, clothe his portly person, and surround himself with the elegancies and luxuries which are so dear to his heart?

Evidently the fat man found out long ago that the eager, active, restless, energetic, muscular, raw-boned soldier and workman was far more interested in the exercise of his muscles and in outdoor activity than he was in securing niceties and luxuries. He also learned that the thinker, the philosopher, the scientific experimenter, and all who took delight in mental effort were more deeply interested in their studies, in their research, in their philosophies, and in their religions than they were in money, food, clothing, and shelter. So he set about it, with his jovial personality, his persuasiveness, and keen sense of values, to organize the thinkers and philosophers under his direction, so that he could take and use for himself the product of their mental labors. He was perfectly willing to agree to feed and take care of them, to clothe and shelter them, in return for what they could give him. They didn't eat much. They didn't care much for fine clothing. They were perfectly satisfied in very plain and rather ascetic surroundings. They were, therefore, a rather inexpensive lot of people for him to keep.

Taking the plans, schemes, inventions, and discoveries from those who thought them out, the fat man carried them to the muscular fellows, who were just spoiling for a fight or for some opportunity to exercise their physical powers. These he organized into armies--to fight, to till the soil, and to build and manufacture. These armies carried out the ideas the fat man got for them from the lean and hungry thinkers. They gloried in hardship. They rather enjoyed roughing it, and took delight in privation. Therefore, they also were a comparatively easy burden on the hands of the fat man; who was thus enabled to sit upon a golden throne, in a comfortable palace, surrounded by all the beauties and luxuries gathered from the four winds, and enjoy himself while directing the work of both the intellectual giant and the physical giant.

THE SLENDER SCHOLAR AND THE RUGGED SOLDIER

Kant, Schopenhauer, Hegel, Spencer, Emerson, and Bergson were philosophers, and were all lean and slender men. Lord Kelvin, Lister, Darwin, Curie, Francis Bacon, Michelson, Loeb, Burbank, and most of our other scientists are also of the thin, lean type. Shakespeare, Longfellow, Holmes, Ruskin, Tindall, Huxley, and a long list of other intellectual and spiritual writers were men who never put on much flesh. James Watt, Robert Fulton, Elias Howe, Eli Whitney, S.F.B. Morse, Marconi, Alexander Graham Bell, the Wright Brothers, and nearly all of our other great inventors have also been men whose habit was slender. Alexander, Napoleon, Washington, Grant, Kitchener, and most of our other great soldiers, while robust, are of the raw-boned, muscular type. They do not belong in the list of the fat men. The same is true of our great railroad builders, of Stanley, Peary, Livingston, and other explorers, of De Palma, Oldfield, Anderson, Cooper, Resta, and our other automobile racing kings. You look in vain among the aviators for a huge, rotund figure. Spend a week in New York City looking over subway workers, structural iron workers, guards, brakemen, motormen, carpenters, bricklayers, truckmen, stevedores, and boatmen. Go out into the country, look over the farm hands, the gardeners, the woodsmen, and all who work with their hands in the midst of nature, and in all the list you will find very few, if any, fat men. Fat men are, therefore, doing neither the actual intellectual nor the actual physical work of the world.

THE FAT MAN'S MODERN THRONE

Study butchers, bakers, chefs, provision merchants, and others who deal in food products. Among them you will find a good many corpulent figures. They are interested in good things to eat. They know how to handle them. They know how to purchase them, and they know how to sell them. They are able to tickle the palate of the lean and hungry scholar, of the robust and active soldier or worker, and, especially, of men as epicurean as themselves. They are, therefore, successful in the handling of food products. Go a little further--study foremen, superintendents, managers, and presidents of corporations. In many a large upholstered chair, which represents, in our modern life, the golden throne of the olden days, you will find a fat man. Here, as of old, they are taking the ideas of the thinkers and the muscular powers of the workers, and combining the two to make profit for themselves. At the same time, they are finding for the thinker a market for his ideas that he himself could never find. Unless the fat man fed him, the lean man would become so lean that he would finally die of starvation. The big fellow is also finding a market for the muscular power, energy, and skill of the worker; a market which the worker, by himself, could never find.

THE FAT MAN'S VALUABLE SERVICE

Recently we made a study of a large corporation. Amongst other things, we found it required ten thousand dollars capital to provide the building, machinery, help, tools, advertising, selling, and other necessities of that business for every employee on the payroll. It also required unusual organizing ability and unusual selling ability to gather together the means for manufacturing the product and getting it into the hands of the consumer. It also required considerable genius to collect the money for the product and apply it to the needs of the workers in the form of payroll. These services of the fat man are often forgotten by those who work under his direction.

In order that huge industries may be built up and employment secured for hundreds of thousands of men, large bodies of capital must be gathered together. This is a work for financiers. Go down into Wall Street, in New York; La Salle Street, in Chicago; State Street, in

Boston, and look over the financiers there. A considerable number of them are fat men. Because thinkers and workers cannot appreciate financial value, many of them complain loudly because the fat man sits in an easy chair and reaps the profits from their efforts. They restlessly agitate for an economic system which will yield them all the profits from their ideas and labor. They want to eliminate the capitalist--to condemn the fat man to a choice between scholarship or working as they work and starvation. They know human aptitudes so vaguely that they want to turn the corpulent into farm hands or philosophers and the great mass of lean and bony into financial rulers.

There is a prevalent notion among the unthinking that capital takes about four-fifths of the products of labor's hands and keeps it. A committee of the American Civic Federation, after three years of careful investigation in industries employing an aggregate of ten million workers, found that this idea is based upon the assumption that capital gets and keeps all the gross income from production except what is paid to labor. It leaves out of account the cost of raw materials, the upkeep of buildings and machinery, and miscellaneous expenses. When these are subtracted from gross income, the committee found, labor receives two-thirds of the remainder in wages and salaries, capital one-third for interest, upkeep of capital, and profit.

FINANCIER AND JUDGE

With some exceptions, neither the deep thinker nor the hard physical worker is capable of handling finances. They are lacking in financial acumen, due, no doubt, to the fact that the thinker is interested chiefly in the object of his thought, the worker chiefly in the exercise of his powerful muscles. Neither of them is sufficiently eager for the good things of life to have a true and unerring sense of financial values. The lean man is nervous. He is inclined to be irritable; he probably lacks patience. Therefore, he is not well qualified to judge impartially. The active, energetic, restless man is not contented to sit quietly for hours at a time and listen to the troubles of other people. He must get away, be out of doors, have something to do to exercise those splendid muscles of his. Therefore, it is left to the fat man to sit upon the bench, to listen to tiresome details of the woe of those who have had trouble with one another. Because he is neither nervous nor irritable; because his mind is at rest; because he is well fed and well clothed and has no need to be anxious, he can take time to be impartial and to judge righteous judgment between his fellowmen. And so you will find fat men on the bench, in politics, in the halls of legislature, on the police force, and in other places where they have an opportunity to use their judicial ability.

HOW MISFITS HAPPEN

So unerring is the fat man's judgment of values, as a general rule, that it is not at all likely that he would ever find himself a misfit were it not for the fact that many men are lean and slender or muscular and robust up to the age of 30 or 40, and after that put on flesh rapidly. These men, therefore, are often deceived in regard to themselves. In the slenderness of youth, they feel active and are active. In short, they have the qualities, in these early periods of their life, which we should expect in men of similar build. They are, therefore, too likely to enter upon vocations for which they will find themselves unfitted as the years go by and they put on more flesh. It often happens that men of this class graduate from the ranks of thinkers or workers into the ranks of managers, financiers, bankers, and judges, as they put on flesh and become better and better adapted for that particular kind of work. The only trouble is that sometimes they are not well enough trained--they do not have sufficient education for the higher positions. In these cases they remain misfits. Oftentimes they succeed in getting into positions of comparatively mediocre executive nature, when they could assume and make a success of very much higher positions if they had a true knowledge of their vocations.

A FAT MAN'S SUCCESS

The story of Hon. Alfred L. Cutting, of Weston, Massachusetts, perhaps illustrates as well as any other in our records the aptitudes and vocational possibilities of this type. Mr. Cutting comes of good old New England stock, his ancestors on both sides having settled in Massachusetts comparatively early in the seventeenth century. His father and his grandfather before him were merchants, and young Alfred began working in the parental general store as soon as he had finished school.

As a youth, Mr. Cutting was quite distinctly of the bony and muscular type, being very active, fond of rowing and fishing, a great lover of nature and of long tramps through the beautiful hills of eastern Massachusetts. As he entered manhood, however, he began to put on more flesh and to take less interest in strenuous outdoor sports. At the same time, he began to take a hand, in a quiet, modest way, in the town politics of Weston. While still a comparatively young man, he was elected a member of the board of selectmen of this town and has held this position with singular acceptability to his fellow-citizens almost continuously ever since.

For a number of years, Mr. Cutting was associated with his father and brother in the general store, but, as time went on, he became ambitious to enlarge his activities. He, therefore, assisted in the organization of the New England branch of the Sheldon School, of Chicago, and was its manager for a number of years. When he first undertook this work, Mr. Cutting had never made a public speech in his life, and, while he was interested in politics and ambitious for success along this line, he felt greatly handicapped by what he considered to be his inability to face an audience acceptably. It was at about this time that we first formed the acquaintance of Mr. Cutting and, upon consultation, informed him of his natural aptitudes and talents. He immediately began a careful study of public speaking, supplementing this study with actual practice both in politics and in his capacity as manager of the Sheldon School. In 1908 and 1909 he was a member of the House of Representatives for the State of Massachusetts, gaining credit for himself as a member of important committees and rendering to his own constituency unusually faithful and efficient service.

SUCCESS IN EXECUTIVE CAPACITY

As manager for the Sheldon School, Mr. Cutting selected and trained a number of salesmen and assistants in the leadership of whom he did excellent work, he himself delivering lectures before boards of trade, chambers of commerce, trade conventions, and other such bodies in all parts of New England. He has since, however, given up this particular line of work to devote himself to politics, to his civic duties, and to the management of his growing mercantile business. He is, at present, chairman of the board of selectmen for the town of Weston, an office which he has held with distinction for five years. He is also a member of the executive committee of the Republican Club of Massachusetts. In 1913 he was the Republican candidate for representative in Congress for the thirteenth district, at the special election held during that year to fill the vacancy caused by the promotion of the Hon. John W. Weeks to the United States Senate. This was the year when the Progressive vote was very large and the Republican candidate for governor in Massachusetts was thousands of votes behind the Progressive. Notwithstanding this unusual political situation, Mr. Cutting, though not elected, led his Progressive opponent by more than 3,000 votes, and, by his splendid leadership, helped lay the foundation for the Republican victory in the same district the following year. At this writing, Mr. Cutting has just won a notable victory at the polls, having been elected a member of the board of county commissioners for Middlesex County by a very large plurality. He carried every district in the county except two, and in nearly every district he ran far ahead of his ticket.

POLITICAL PRINCIPLES AND PRACTICES

Mr. Cutting's ability, however, is by no means fully indicated by the offices which he has held. He has never been an office seeker, but has preferred rather to work as a political leader. His great interest in politics arises, first, from his ardent desire for excellence and efficiency in the public service. Under his leadership, the town of Weston has built and maintains more miles of excellent roads, at less cost to the tax payer, than any other town of its area in the State. Its schools and other public institutions are similarly efficient and conducted with a similar degree of economy. Second, Mr. Cutting enjoys politics because he loves the game. Like all true sportsmen, he plays to win, but is neither chagrined or cast down if he loses. He is always able to rejoice with the victor if beaten in a fair fight.

FINANCIAL ACUMEN

Mr. Cutting is one of the organizers of the Metropolitan Bank of Boston, and a prominent member of its board of directors, thus indicating his growing interest in financial matters.

The portraits of Mr. Cutting, shown on pages 126 and 127, are well worthy of study. In them are evident his cheerfulness, his geniality, his shrewdness, his friendliness, and his honesty of purpose. These are shown largely in the expression, but also in the full, found development of his head just above the temples, in his long back head, and in the general squareness of the head. This squareness, especially in the back, indicates also his prudence, his tendency to take precautions and, through foresight, to forestall disaster. The narrowness of the head, just above the ears, indicates mildness of disposition and an ability to secure his ends by tact, diplomacy, and intellectual mastery rather than by open combat and belligerency. The fulness of the eyes indicates Mr. Cutting's command of language, and the broad, square chin his determination and deliberation; the long line from the point of the chin to the crown of the head, his love of authority and his ability to lead and to rule.

INDICATIONS OF APPROACHING STOUTNESS

The man of slender build who has indications clearly marked and easily recognizable of approaching stoutness should prepare himself for executive, financial, judicial, or merchandising work. He should study law, economics, finance, banking, politics, political economy, public speaking and other such branches. If he has the ability to write, he should prepare himself to write on financial or political subjects. Many of our most noted political writers are fat men. Such writers as Alfred G. Lewis, Samuel G. Blythe, and others are good examples of this type.

Indications of approaching stoutness are not difficult to detect. Heredity has a powerful influence. The young man who resembles his father in facial appearance and coloring, will probably grow stout if his father is a fat man. When the face inclines to be round, the cheeks rather full, and the lips full, there is a fair probability that the individual will take on flesh. A concave form of face is also another good indication. The concave face is shown in Figure 31. It will be seen that it is prominent at the point of the chin, and not so prominent at the mouth, and prominent at the top of the forehead, near the hair line, and not so prominent at the brows. The nose, also, is inclined to be sway backed. Another indication which should have a bearing in the choice of a vocation is the thickness of the neck, especially, at the back, and a fulness of the back head, at the base of the brain. Such fulness is shown in Figure 16.

Wideness of the head, in comparison with length and height, is also another indication that the individual may put on flesh as he grows older. The man or woman who has a majority of these indications will do well to prepare himself or herself for a position of command.

The world is a richer, pleasanter, better fed, better clothed, and happier place because of its fat men. It is true, they enjoy the good things of life themselves, but, as a general rule, they also like to see others enjoy them, and well deserve the rich rewards they reap. We are glad that so few of them are ever poor and hungry.

[Illustration: FIG. 17. Beaumont, Aviator. His square jaw, strong chin, large nose, large ear, convex profile, and alert, keen expression all indicate activity, energy, love of motion, desire for speed, and physical courage.]

[Illustration: Photo by Paul Thompson. N. FIG. 18. The late Lincoln Beachy, Aviator. A man of consummate physical courage and coolness. Note long lines of face and unusually long, prominent chin.]

[Illustration: _Copyright by Harris & Ewing_. FIG. 19. Col. George W. Goethals, Builder of the Panama Canal and Governor of Canal Zone. Of the intellectual but bony and muscular type. Short, stocky, enduring, and resistant. Finer and kindlier than FIG. 20 or FIG. 21, as shown by texture and expression, but firm, dogged, and just. A natural-born executive for construction or mechanical work. Note firm mouth and chin, with slight droop at corners, showing determination and self-control.]

[Illustration: *Copyright American Press Association.* FIG. 20. Field Marshal von Hindenberg, of the German Army. A splendid example of the bony, muscular type. Unusually determined, persistent, enduring, and resistant. Prudent, far-sighted, dogged, unsentimental, capable of enduring great hardship. Note short, stocky build; big, square chin and jaw; long, square head; relentless expression of mouth and eyes; coarse texture, and big, heavy-tipped nose. A great executive, especially as a relentless driver and rigid disciplinarian.]

[Illustration: *Copyright American Press Association.* FIG. 21. Rear Admiral Frank E. Beatty, of the American Navy. A fine example of the bony and muscular type. Rugged and enduring, keen, alert, and resourceful. Finer and kindlier than von Hindenberg, but not quite so fine, intellectual and kindly as Goethals. Just and determined as an executive, of which he is an excellent type. Note finer texture and more genial expression.]

[Illustration: FIG. 22. William Lloyd Garrison, the Great Abolitionist. A man of the bony and muscular type, with the passion of his type for freedom. A man of high ideals, great courage, determination, and perseverance. Note large, well-formed features; forehead prominent at brows; long upper lip, and high, spirited expression. Such a man cannot be overlooked.]

[Illustration: _Photo by Pach, N.Y._ FIG. 23. Samuel Rea, Railroad Builder and Executive. Very alert, keen, practical, matter-of-fact, hard-headed; a good observer, a quick thinker. Very decisive, determined, and persistent. Understands construction, mechanics, and operation. Note well-developed brows; moderately low, square forehead; height of crown; width of head; large, well-formed nose, mouth, chin, jaw, and ears, and keen, but calm, self-possessed expression.]

[Illustration: FIG. 24. Lon Wescott Beck, the Sign Poster of Death Valley. An out-of-doors man. Loves grandeur of scenery, wide spaces. Note long, square, prominent chin; long lines of face; width between eyes, and width at top of head.]

CHAPTER VI

THE MAN OF BONE AND MUSCLE

Consider the record of the man of action.

He built the pyramids and temples of Egypt, raised up the monuments and artistic triumphs of Greece, fared forth across the plains of Arabia and the deserts of Africa on horses and camels before the dawn of history. He wore the coat of mail of the Roman legion; he penetrated through the northernmost forest of Europe; he pioneered in barbarous England. Thousands of years ago he built ships and sailed them, and, finally, drove them across the sea. Thus he found two new continents. In America, he cut down forests, built roads, established industry, fought battles for freedom, invented and built steamships, telephones, telegraphs, cotton gins, aeroplanes, railroads, submarines thousands of electric light and power stations, and millions of shops and factories. He explored darkest Africa; found both the North and the South Poles. This man drives his steamships at thirty knots an hour, his locomotives at 70 miles an hour, his automobiles at 100, and his aeroplanes at 120. He is setting higher and yet higher records for running, leaping, swimming, rowing, throwing weights, and driving horses. He has organized great athletic contests, baseball leagues, tennis associations, golf clubs, and other organizations for the promotion of physical activity. The man of bone and muscle has climbed to the peaks of all the mountains of the world; has dug down into the depths of the earth after her treasures of gold and silver and the baser metals, precious stones, and other products of the mines. This man tills the fields, manufactures all fabricated products, and carries goods to the ends of the earth. This active type mans navies, fills the ranks of armies, erects great buildings, and cut through the backbone of a continent.

ACTIVITY AND SPEED

This man loves motion. He is not satisfied with slow, languid motion, but demands speed, greater and ever greater speed. And so his horses, his locomotives, the machines in his factory, his automobiles, his aeroplanes, his motor-cycles, his farm implements, his ocean liners, his motor boats, are being constantly studied, constantly improved, and constantly raised to higher and higher performances in speed of production, speed of transportation, speed of accomplishment.

This man not only demands speed, but he demands space. The man who can travel at a hundred miles an hour needs many hundred miles in which to travel. This is why nearly all of his activities are in the big out-of-doors; this is why he is constantly exploring and pioneering in order to extend his boundaries. He has a craving for more space in which to breathe, more scope of action.

This ardent and irrepressible desire for physical freedom, for physical liberty of action, also leads to the desire for political and economical freedom. All of our great liberators, from Moses down to Lincoln, have been men of this active, muscular, bony, type. Because they desire freedom for themselves, they want freedom for everyone else. They often go to extremes and strive to secure freedom for those who have no use for it, who do not care for it after it is won for them, and who only abuse it when they should enjoy its blessings.

THE MAN OF MUSCLE GROWS A BRAIN

In the early days of the race, the man of this type had little intelligence. He was supposed to be, principally, bone and muscle with no brain. He did the physical work which was assigned to him and other men did the thinking, the planning, and the directing. But, as the race has increased in intelligence, the man of bone and muscle has developed a brain. Manual skill, educators tell us, is one of the best of all means for gaining knowledge and increasing intelligence. So now the muscular man can think, now he can plan, now, especially, does he manifest his thinking, planning and constructive ability along lines for increasing speed, getting more out of machinery, buildings, inventions, manufacture, agriculture, horticulture, transportation. In all these lines the man of action is also a man of thought. This is well; this is an improvement, and our active, hustling, pioneer type of man is happier, more efficient, more prosperous in his intelligent state than he was in his purely physical state. But here, also, he gets into trouble. So long as his mental activity is accompanied by considerable physical activity, his health is good, he is satisfied, he enjoys his work and he is successful in it. But the time comes when the work to be done by brain becomes so important that many men of this type give up physical activity entirely and devote all of their time to mental work.

THE ACTIVE MAN'S DILEMMA

Strange that we have not learned that any faculty possessed must be exercised or the possessor surely falls into evil ways. Strange that we have not seen that the man who explores the unknown world in mighty pioneering work, who frees it from oppression, who carries on its tremendous physical and industrial development, could never be satisfied if imprisoned within the four walls of an office. Thus hampered and confined, unless he finds expression for his speed mania, he grows irritable, ill, nervous, depressed. He troops, by the thousand, into the consulting rooms of the physician and surgeon. And always and always is the same prescription given: "You must get away from your work; you must get out into the open; you must get plenty of outdoor exercise."

Exercise, exercise, exercise, has become the slogan. Magazines are devoted to it. Whole libraries of books are published showing the relationship between exercise and health. Sanitariums multiply whose principal means of cure are located in the gymnasium, in the garden, in the woods, at the wood pile, and on the farm. Fortunes have been made in the manufacture of the equipment for exercise: Indian clubs, dumb bells, and whole shiploads of so-called sporting goods, the object of all of which is to enable the active man to get some relief from the ache of his muscles or nerves due to lack of exercise.

EXERCISE FOR EXERCISE'S SAKE DULL

But the man of muscle is, as we have said, frequently a man of brains. He has common sense; he has a desire for accomplishment and achievement. To such a man, the mere pulling of cords, or the swinging about of his arms and legs, the bending of his back, just for the sake of exercise, seems a trifle stupid.

Very few men of this type ever keep up exercise for exercise's sake for any very long period of time. They read in some magazine about the benefits of exercise. Perhaps, on account of some trouble, they go to their physicians, and exercise is prescribed. So, with a great show of resolution and not a little feeling of martyrdom, they buy a pair of Indian clubs, or wall exercisers, or a weight machine, or, perhaps, merely buy a book of "exercises without apparatus," and make up their minds to take their exercises regularly every morning. At first they attack the task with great enthusiasm--but it is still a task. Perhaps marked improvement is shown. They feel much better. They push out their chests and tell their friends how they get up, take a cold bath every morning, and then take ten or fifteen or twenty minutes of rapid calisthenics. In a righteous glow, they relate how it shakes them up and makes their blood course through their veins; how they breathe deeply; how the process clears out their heads; and how much better they feel

They wind up: "You ought to do it, too, old man; it would make you young again."

By and by, however, to stand gazing blankly at the wall of a bathroom, or out of the window of a bed-chamber, and put your arms up five times and then straight forward five times, then repeat five times, etc., etc., grows dull. You lose interest You hate the task--you revolt. Even if, by power of will, you keep it up, you do so under protest. It is a physical truth that that which is disagreeable is also physically harmful. In order to be wholesomely nourishing, food must taste good. The same is true in regard to exercise. There is no very great benefit in exercise which is drudgery.

WHEN GAMES PALL

To take the "task" element out of exercise, many kinds of games have been invented--some indoor, some outdoor, some for men of little activity, some of great strenuousness and even danger. But it requires a particular type of man or woman to take interest in a game, to play it well and profitably, as a form of exercise. To enter into a game whole-heartedly, one must have a keen zest for combat. The man who plays purely for the sport, and not to win, doesn't win. And the man who doesn't win, loses interest. Not all men, not even all active men, have this desire to win. To them a game soon becomes dull--nearly as dull as any other form of exercise. They do not see that they are any further ahead in anything worth while simply because they have knocked a golf ball about more skilfully--or luckily--than some other fellow, or pulled a little stronger oar than their opponents. There are plenty of men to whom it is humiliating to be beaten, who are not good losers, and because they are not good losers they are not very often winners. Such men do not really enjoy games at all, and, as a general rule, do not play them with enthusiasm and persistence.

For those, then, who do not enjoy calisthenics of any kind, who take very little interest in games and contests, there remain, for exercise, gardening, farming, carpentry, forestry, hunting, fishing, mountain climbing, and other such forms of physical activity. All of these, however, require considerable leisure, and some financial investment. They are out of the reach of many of those in lower clerkships and other such employment. These men, by the thousands, work in offices which are, perhaps, not as well ventilated as they should be, under artificial light. They travel to and from their work in crowded street cars and subways, and live in little dark, narrow flats and apartments, with one window opening out on sunlight and fresh air, and all other windows opening on courts and so-called light and air-shafts. Golf, tennis, baseball, rowing, etc., are good forms of exercise for these men--but few of them care for games. Gardening, forestry, carpenter work, mountain climbing, hunting, or fishing are out of the question in a city flat. So the majority jump up in the morning, hurry on their clothes, snatch a bite of breakfast, run for a car, get to work, burrow in the warrens of industry until lunch time, rush out, snatch a sandwich and a cup of coffee at some lunch counter, and back to work again until dinner time. Another dive into the bowels of the earth in the subway, home to the little flat, dinner at seven o'clock or even later, and then the short evening. This little time from eight o'clock until ten at night is practically the only time the worker has for himself, except for holidays and his annual two weeks' vacation. How shall he get sufficient physical exercise during that time to satisfy all his needs? If he is so constituted that he enjoys such things, he may go to a gymnasium or to a bowling alley, but he is just as likely to go to a pool room or to a dance hall. Of course, it is far better for him to play pool or to dance than to sit quietly at home, as many do.

SOLUTION OF THE PROBLEM

This whole question is a serious one. Even those who have the time, the means, the opportunity, and the inclination find themselves confronted with problems. Even with all of their opportunities, most of them do not get enough outdoor physical activity. And so they fret, they fume, they beat their wings against the bars, they are unhappy, dissatisfied, and therefore, oftentimes inefficient and unsuccessful. Even when they are successful, they have fallen far below what they might have accomplished had they been engaged in some vocation which would have given them not only physical activity out of doors, but *some intense vital interest* in the *result* of that activity. In other words, their vocation should supply them with the necessary physical exercise as part of the day's work. They should see themselves advancing, making money, achieving something worth while, creating something beautiful or useful, making a career for themselves, instead of merely playing or exercising for the sake of exercise. Then they would be happier. Then they would be better satisfied with their lot. They would be more efficient and far more successful.

Current literature abounds in true stories of those who have gone forward to the land and have found help, happiness, and success in the cultivation of the soil. This one has redeemed an abandoned farm in New England. That one has taken a small ten-acre farm in southern California. Another has carved out health, happiness, and a fair degree of fortune for himself on the plains of Washington or Idaho, or among the hills of Oregon. Old southern plantations have been rehabilitated at the same time with their new owners or tenants.

ONE MAN'S "WAY OUT"

Near Gardiner, Maine, is a little forty-five acre poultry and fruit farm which pays its happy owner $3,800 a year clear of all expense. Seven years ago this farm was abandoned by its former owners, who could not make it pay. Five years ago it was purchased by its present owner for a song--and only a half-line of the song was sung at the time. He was a clerk who had lived the little-flat-dark-office-and-subway life until tuberculosis had removed him from his job and threatened his life. Farm work--on his own farm--proved to be a game at which he could play with zest and success. The stakes were a life and a living--and he has won. We--and you, too, no doubt--could multiply narratives from observation and experience, to say nothing of reading.

A WORLD OF OPPORTUNITY

All these experiences and the reports of them are both a part of and a stimulus to the "back to the land movement." This movement has its mainspring in two plain economic facts, namely: first, clerical and other indoor vocations have become overcrowded; second, while crops grow bigger year by year, the number of mouths to feed multiplies even faster, and unless more land is tilled and all land cultivated more intensively, we shall eat less and less, as a race, and pay more and more for what we eat. Here is opportunity for the men of bone and muscle-- opportunity for health, prosperity, usefulness to humanity, enjoyment and happiness. Other opportunities lie in the conservation of our forests and the planting and development of new timber lands; in the building up of new industries for manufacturing our raw materials; in restoring the American flag to the seas of the world; in extending our foreign trade; in opening and operating inland waterways; in irrigating or draining our millions of square miles of land now lying idle; in the development of Alaska, and the harnessing of our great mines of "white coal"--water-power.

Our foreign trade requires men of this type to travel in all parts of the world as commercial ambassadors, diligently collecting, compiling, and sending back to the United States information necessary . in manufacturing goods for foreign consumption; also information regarding credits, prices, shipping, packing--in short, complete and detailed knowledge about commerce with foreign lands, how to secure it and how to hold it.

The world's greatest opportunities to-day, perhaps, lie within the grasp of the men of this active type. Instead of pioneering in exploration, as in former years, they are needed to pioneer in production. From the earliest history of the race, these restless men have been faring westward and ever westward, adding to the wealth and resources of humanity by opening up new lands. But the crest of the westward moving tide has now circumnavigated the globe, and the Far West meets the Far East on the Pacific Ocean. Here and there are comparatively small, neglected tracts of land still to be developed, but there are no longer great new empires, as in former days. The great welling sources of human life have not ceased to flow, even though the final boundaries of its spread have been reached. Population will continue to grow and its demands upon the resources of the earth to increase. The man who discovers a way to make a hundred bushels of wheat grow on an acre of land where only twenty-five bushels grew before is as great a benefactor of the race as the discoverer of a continent. The invention of the electric light, the telephone, the automobile, the trolley car, and the aeroplane have added as much to the products and power of the race as the pioneering of thousands of square miles of fertile hills and plains. The man who can find a cheap and easy way to capture and hold nitrogen from the air will add more to the wealth of the race than all the discoverers of all the gold mines.

America needs to find efficient and profitable methods for manufacturing her own raw materials. Up to the present time, our exports have been coal, petroleum, steel rails, wheat, corn, oats, lumber, and other products which carry out of the country the riches of our soil. We have been exporting raw materials to foreign lands, where they have been refined and fabricated by brain and hand and returned to us at some five hundred to a thousand times the price we received for them. With the increase of population, we need to capitalize more and more the intelligence and skill of our people, and less and less the virgin resources of our lands. Ore beds, coal measures, copper, lead, gold and silver mines, forests, oil wells, and the fertility of our soils can all become exhausted. But the skill of our hands and the power of our intellects grow and increase and yield larger and larger returns the more they are called upon to produce.

The man of bone and muscle--the restless, active, pioneering, constructing man--would do well to consider these things before

110

determining upon his vocation, and especially before entering upon any kind of non-productive work. The world has need of his particular talents and he should find his greatest happiness and greatest success in the exercise of them in response to that need.

We have seen so many men of this active type so badly placed that individual examples seem almost too commonplace for citation. Yet, a few may be instructive and encouraging.

William Carleton's remarkable story, entitled "Rediscovering America," is, in fact, the story of a man who was a middle-aged failure in a clerical position, and who afterward made a remarkable success of his life by taking up contracting and building. James Cook, a misfit as a grocer, afterward became famous as a naval officer and explorer. Henry M. Stanley, office boy to a cotton broker and merchant, afterward won immortal fame as a newspaper correspondent and explorer. What would have become of Theodore Roosevelt had he followed the usual line of occupation of a man in his position and entered a law office instead of becoming a rancher? We might add other experiences of similar importance from the biographies of other great men.

DESCRIPTION OF ACTIVE TYPE

The active type of man is, of course, easily recognized. He has broad, square shoulders, and is well muscled. He is either of the wiry, elastic, exceedingly energetic type, with muscles like steel springs and sinews like steel wire--very agile, very skillful, very quick, and somewhat jerky in his movements--or he is tall, raw-boned, strong, enduring, graceful, easy in his movements rather than quick, and yet with considerable manual skill. Or he may be of the short, stocky type, with broad shoulders, short neck, short arms, short legs, with big, round muscles and an immense capacity for endurance. The railroads of the early days, in this country, were built by Irishmen. They were either the large, raw-boned type or the quick, agile, wiry type. The railroads, subways, and other construction work of to-day are built mostly by Italians, Hungarians, Greeks, and others from the south of Europe. These men are of short, stocky, sturdy, and enduring build. As a general rule, they are far better fitted for this class of work than the tall or medium-sized, large-boned or wiry type. As an evidence of this, take notice of the fact that the Irishmen who built the railroads in the sixties own and manage them to-day.

These active men usually have square faces. That is to say, there is a good development of the outer corners of the lower jaw, which gives to the face a square appearance. Oftentimes their cheek bones are both high and wide. As a general rule, they have large aquiline or Roman noses. When they are of the enduring type and capable of long-sustained muscular activity, they have prominent chins. Their hands are square. Their feet are large. If they have mechanical and constructive ability, as most of them have, their foreheads are comparatively high and wide just above the temple. Professional baseball players, professional dancers, middle-weight and light-weight prize-fighters, most aviators, automobile racers, and athletes belong to the wiry, springy, medium-sized type of this particular class of men. U.S. Grant, Robert E. Peary, Henry M. Stanley, Ty Cobb and Ralph DePalma belong to this type. Abraham Lincoln, W.E. Gladstone, Joseph G. Cannon, William G. McAdoo, Woodrow Wilson, and other men of this build belong to the raw-boned type. Napoleon Bonaparte, with his tremendous activities on only four hours' sleep a day, is a good example of the short, stocky type. While men of these types may make brilliant successes in purely mental vocations, as the result of the development of their intellects, and may keep themselves in a fair degree of health and strength by games, exercise, mountain climbing, farming, or some such avocation, they are, nevertheless, never quite so well satisfied as when they have something to do which not only gives them opportunity for the use of their intellects, but also involves a certain degree of physical activity as a part of their regular work.

CHAPTER VII

SLAVES OF MACHINERY

To multitudes of men and women the lure of levers, cranks, wheels and pinions is as seductive, as insidious, as heavenly in its promises, and as hellish in its performances, as the opium habit. The craving for opium, however, is an acquired taste, while the passion for machinery is born in thousands. We have seen children, while yet in their baby-cabs, fascinated by automobiles, sewing machines, and even little mechanical toys. We knew a boy on a farm who built a fairly workable miniature threshing machine with his own hands before he was old enough to speak the name of it in anything but baby-talk. We have seen boys work in the broiling sun day after day hoeing potatoes, pulling weeds, gathering crops, and doing other hard jobs for small pay, carefully saving every penny to buy a toy steam engine.

Parents usually look upon these evidences of mechanical ability with pleasure. They regard them as sure indications of the vocation of the child and oftentimes do everything in their power to encourage him in these lines. They little realize, however, the supreme danger which attaches to this very manifestation. Nor have they looked far enough ahead to see what is, in so many cases, the lamentable result.

THE RESTLESS "MACHINE CRAZY" BOY

The boy of this type hates to sit quietly on a hard bench in a school and study books. Some of the boys who went to school with us had imitation levers and valve-handles fastened about their desks in an ingenious way, and instead of studying, pretended that they were locomotive engineers. With a careful eye upon the teacher, who was his semaphore, such a boy would work the reverse lever, open and close the throttle, apply and disengage the brakes, test the lubrication, and otherwise go through the motions of running a locomotive with great seriousness and huge enjoyment.

These boys usually have considerable trouble with their teachers. They do not like grammar, frequently do not care for geography and history. They flounder dolefully in these studies and are in a state of more or less continual rebellion and disgrace. Because of their intense activity and restlessness, they irritate the teacher. She wants quiet in the school-room. Their surreptitious playing, rapping and tapping on desks, and other evidences of dammed-up energy and desire for more freedom and more scope of action, interferes with the desired sanctity of silence.

Outside of school hours and during the long vacation, the fatal fascination of machinery draws these young people to factories, railroad yards, machine shops, and other places where they may indulge their fancy and craving for mechanical motion. The boy who hangs around a machine shop or railroad yard is always pressed into voluntary and delighted service by those who work there. In a small town in Wisconsin we once knew a boy who worked willingly and at the hardest kind of labor in a railroad yard for years, voluntarily and without a cent of pay. In time he was entrusted with a small responsibility and given a small salary. Even if the boy does not begin in this way, the result is substantially the same. He may take the bit in his teeth, leave school and go to work at some trade which will give at least temporary satisfaction for his mechanical craving, or he may, through economic necessity, be forced out of school and naturally gravitate into a machine shop or factory. Oftentimes a few dollars a week is a very welcome addition to the family income. To the boy himself, three, four, five or six dollars a week seems like a fortune. Neither the parents nor the boy look ahead. Neither of them sees that when the little salary has increased to fifteen, sixteen, eighteen or twenty-five dollars a week, the boy will have reached the zenith of his possibilities. There will then be no further advancement, unless, during his apprenticeship and journeymanship, or previously to them, he has secured mental training which will enable him to go higher, hold more responsible positions and earn larger pay.

"MAN OR MACHINE--WHICH?"

In former days, the boy who left school and took up employment in a factory learned a trade. He became a shoe-maker, or a harness-maker, or a wheelwright, or a gun-maker. To-day, however, the work on all of these articles has been so subdivided that the boy perhaps becomes stranded in front of a machine which does nothing but punch out the covers for tin cans, or cut pieces of leather for the heels of shoes, or some other finer operation in manufacture. Once he has mastered the comparatively simple method of operating his particular machine, the boy is likely to remain there for all time. His employer--perhaps short-sighted--has no desire to advance him, because this would mean breaking in another boy to handle his machine. Also, it would mean paying more money.

Al Priddy, in his illuminating book, "Man or Machine--Which?"[9] thus describes the case of the slave to the machine:

[Footnote 9: The Pilgrim Press, Boston.]

"The workingman has been taught that his chief asset is skill. It has been his stocks, his bonds, the pride of his life. Poor as to purse and impoverished in his household; his cupboard bare, his last penny spent on a bread crust, he is not humbled; no, he merely stretches out his ten fingers and two callous palms, exactly as a proud king extends his diamond-tipped sceptre, to show you that which upholds him in his birthright. 'My skill is my portion given to the world,' he says. 'I shall not want. See, I am without a penny. I touch this bar of steel, and it becomes a scissors blade. My skill did it. I take this stick of oak and it becomes a chair rung. My skill is the grandest magic on earth, the common magic of every day. By it I live and because of it I hold my head royal high.'

"But the machine now attacks and displaces this skill. The cunning of trained fingers is transferred to cranks, cogs and belts. The trade secrets are objectified in mechanical form; able to mix the product, compound the chemicals, or make the notch at the right place.

"Besides this loss of skill, the workman loses, in the grind of the machine, his sense of the value of his work. Next to his pride of skill

114

the workman has always been proud to be the connoisseur: stand back near the light with his product on his upraised hand, showing to all passers-by what he has done. Perhaps it was a red morocco slipper for a dancer, or a pearl button to go on the cloak of a little child, or maybe it was a horseshoe to go on the mayor's carriage horse. On a day a party of visitors would come to the little shop and the owner would pick up a hand-forged hammer and say, 'See what John made!' But, in our modern industry, no one man ever completes a task. Each task is subdivided into twenty, forty, a hundred or more portions, and a workingman is given just one to work on, day by day, year after year, for a working generation.

"After the time has come when the workman can find no distinct esthetic pleasure in his work, his loyalty to his employers suffers a shock.

"Then, when this indifference or disloyalty is full grown, the employer has full on him acute and formidable labor diseases. The man who should stand at his shoulder faces him, instead, with a hostile poise. The mill full of people over whom he holds power, upon whom he depends for his success, and who, in turn, depend upon his initiative and capital for their bread and butter, is turned into an armed camp of plotting enemies, who, while they work, grumble, and who, while they receive their wages, scheme for the overthrow of the entire concern! His mills, instead of being shelters for his brothers and sisters, are nests of scratching eagles--ready to rend and claw!

"It is further given out that the machine robs man of his industrial initiative; that the complicated and specialized machine decreases his mental alertness. In addition to his skill and his appreciation of his product, the workman has ever prized the appeal his labor has made to his individual intelligence. His work has brought thinking power with it. His day's task has included the excitement of invention and adventure. In the heat and burden of the week has come that thrilling moment when his mind has discovered the fact that a variation in method means a simplification of his task. Or, in the monotonous on-going of his labor, he has suddenly realized that by sheer brain power he has accomplished a third more work than his neighbor. He has counted such results compliments to his initiative, to his thinking power. They have brought a reward three times more satisfying than a mere increase in wage, for, in his eyes, they have been substantial testimonies to the freedom of his mind, something which every reasonable person puts higher than any king's ransom. But the coming of the machine deadens the workman's inclination toward inventive

115

adventure.

"So the multitude of men and women stand before the cunning machinery of industry, in the pose of helplessness before a mechanical finality. They cannot help feeling that in so far as their special task is involved, the machine has said the last word. The challenge dies out of their work. The brain that has ever been on the quiver of adventurous expectancy relaxes its tension, and the workman moodily or indifferently lets his machine do its perfect work, while his undisciplined, unchallenged thoughts wander freely over external, social, or domestic concerns. It may give an indolent, unambitious, selfish type of employee a certain amount of satisfaction to know that the machine frees his mind of initiative, but to the considerate workman it is a day of tragedy when his brain power receives no challenge from his work, and that day has dawned in the minds of millions of men who throng our industries.

"So, then, when this machine-robber, without heart or conscience, makes of little repute the workman's most shining glory--skill; steals rudely from him the esthetic pleasure in his product, and leaves him mentally crippled before his work, how little force has that honored appeal, 'The dignity of labor'! Talk as we will, in this machine-ridden time, the 'dignity of labor' is but a skeleton of its former robust self. Take away the king's throne, the courtier's carpet, the royal prerogative, and then speak about 'The Divine Right'! All that 'dignity of labor' can mean in these days is simply that it is more dignified for a man to earn a wage than it is to be a doorway loafer. The workingman's throne--skill--has gone. His prerogative--skill--has been taken away. The items that have formerly given dignity to labor have been largely displaced, so far as we have adventured, by the machine, and the future holds out no other hope than this, that machines shall more and more increase. There is little 'dignity' in a task that a man does which may be equally well done by his fourteen-year-old boy or girl. There is little 'dignity' in a task which less and less depends upon independent knowledge."

But must these workers remain always slaves of machine? Is there no escape for them? Is there no "underground railroad" by which they may win their way to freedom?

Here is what Al Priddy has to say about it:

"The most convincing way in which man may master the machine is when he invents a new and better one, or improves an old one. This is the real triumph of mind over matter, of skill over machinery.

"With all its arrogance among us, machinery is always final in itself; incapable of change; incapable of progression or retrogression. Till the clouds fade from the sky, or the earth cracks, a machine will remain the same from the day of its creation until the day of its last whirl--unless man says the word to change it. Once started on its mission, there is nothing in the world can change the motion and purpose of a machine save man's mind. So, then, whatever relation man might have toward a machine, this stands sure: he will ever be able to stand before it and say: 'I am thy master. I can change thee, make thee better or worse. I made thee. I can unmake thee. If thou dost accomplish such mighty works, more honor to the mind which conceived thee!'"

"But it is suddenly discovered by an industrial diagnosis that the machine has never been properly operated, even by the most skilled operators. It has been proved that 'there is more science in the most "unskilled" task than the man who performs it is capable of understanding.' This dictum of Mr. Taylor, a practical experimenter, has been dramatically proved in many directions. In the task of the sand shoveler, or the iron lifter, for instance, it was proved that by scientifically undertaking such work, fifty selected men, properly drilled, scientifically rested, intelligently manoeuvred, could accomplish a third more than one hundred ill selected and improperly managed men, in less time and under a larger salary. It is suddenly found that, contrary to theory, a machine, to be economically operated, leaves open man's chance for skill and does not rob him of it."

Perhaps a few cases taken from our records will indicate how men of this kind are able to come up from slavery and take successful places in their true vocations.

FROM BOILER-ROOM TO CHIEF ENGINEER'S OFFICE

G---- manifested very early indications of the lure of machinery for him. While yet in his cradle, he would play contentedly for hours with a little pulley or other mechanical trifle. Before he was able to walk, he could drive nails with a hammer sturdily and with more precision than many adults. This also was one of his favorite amusements, and it was necessary to keep him provided with lumber, lest he fill the furniture with nails. As he grew older he became more and more interested in machinery and mechanical things. He took to pieces the family clock and put it together again. He nearly always had the sewing machine partly dismantled, but could always put it together again, and it usually ran better after he had finished his work. He built water-wheels, wind-mills, and other mechanical toys. When he was about fourteen years old he built a steam engine. He used a bicycle pump for the cylinder and pieces of an old sewing machine, a discarded wringer, some brass wires, and other odds and ends for the rest of the parts. So perfect mechanically was this product that when steam was turned on it ran smoothly, and with very little noise, at the rate of three thousand revolutions a minute. In this engine he employed a form of valve motion which he had never seen, and which had never been used before. While not particularly efficient, and therefore not a valuable invention, it at least showed his ability to adapt means to ends mechanically.

After G---- began earning money for himself by mechanical and electrical work, he would go without luxuries, food and clothing, tramping to the shop almost barefoot one entire winter, for the sake of buying tools and equipment to carry on his mechanical experiments. It is not surprising, therefore, that he left school at an early age to engage in actual work in railroad shops. He afterward secured a position as a locomotive fireman. Circumstances arose which made it necessary for him to give up railroading. He secured a position as fireman on a stationary engine.

A HARD FIGHT FOR AN EDUCATION

It was while he was engaged in this kind of work that the suggestion was made to him that he ought not to try to go through life with only the rudiments of an education. It was pointed out that, while he had undoubted mechanical and inventive ability, he would have small opportunity to use it unless he also had the necessary technical and scientific knowledge to go with it. At first his interest in mechanics was so intense and his interest in school in general so comparatively slight, that he did not look with very much favor upon the suggestion. However, as time went on and he saw more and more of the results of such action as he was contemplating, he became more and more interested in completing his education. He therefore entered a good preparatory school and, with some little assistance from relatives, worked his way through by doing electrical and mechanical work about the little college town. In this kind of work he soon became well known and was in constant requisition. Occasionally his ingenuity and resourcefulness enabled him to do successfully work which had puzzled and baffled even those who were called experts. Having finished his preparatory course, he began a course in mechanical and electrical engineering in one of the best known of our universities. About this time practically all assistance from relatives had been withdrawn, owing to changed circumstances, and he was left almost

118

entirely dependent upon his own efforts. The story of his struggles would fill a volume. Oftentimes he was almost entirely without food. There was one month during which he was unable to collect money due him for work done. Because he was a poor university student he had no credit. So he lived the entire month on $1.25. He thus explains how it was done:

LIVING A MONTH ON $1.25

"After visiting all of my clients trying to collect money, I came to the conclusion that it would be useless to expect anything to come in to me for at least thirty days. At this time I had $1.25 in my pocket. My room I had paid for in advance by doing a piece of work for my landlord. I also had about a cord of good oak wood which I had sawed and split and piled in the hallway under the stairs. I had a little sheet-iron stove which I used for both heating and cooking. I sat down and carefully figured out how I could make my $1.25 feed me until I could collect the money due. Twenty-five cents purchased three quarts of strained honey from a bee-keeper friend of mine. The dollar I invested in hominy. Every morning, when I first got up and built the fire, I put on a double boiler with as much hominy as would cook in it. While it was cooking I sat down and studied hard on my calculus. By the time I had got a pretty good hold of the pot-hooks and the bird-tracks in the calculus lesson, the hominy would be ready to eat. Hominy and honey is not a bad breakfast. While perhaps you would like some variety, it is also fairly edible for lunch. If you are very, very hungry, as a growing boy ought to be, and have been hard at work putting up bell wires and arranging batteries, doubtless you would rather eat hominy and honey for dinner than go without. The next morning the combination doesn't taste quite so good, and by lunch time you are beginning to wonder whether hominy and honey will satisfy all your cravings. In the evening, however, you are quite sure that, in the absence of anything else, you will have to have some hominy and honey in order to keep yourself alive. By the end of the first week you feel that you can never even hear the word hominy again without nausea and that you wish never to look a bee in the face. By the end of the second week you have become indifferent to the whole matter and simply take your hominy and honey as a matter of course, trying to think nothing about it and interesting yourself as much as possible in calculus, generator design, strength of materials, and other things that an engineering student has to study.

"The month finally passed. I felt as if I had eaten my way out of a mountain of hominy and waded through a sea of honey. Collections began coming in a little and I went and bought a beefsteak. You may have eaten some palatable viands. I have myself partaken of meals that cost as much as I made in a whole week's work in my school days. But let me assure you that no one ever had a meal that tasted better than the beefsteak and fried potatoes which finally broke the hominy and honey regime."

After this our young friend hired a little larger room, laid in a few cheap dishes and cooking utensils and took two or three of his fellow students to board. He did the marketing and the cooking and made them help him wash the dishes. Two were engineering students and the third was a student in the college of agriculture, all working their way through college. A few cents saved was a memorable event in their lives. Our young engineer furnished table board at $1.25 a week, and out of the $3.75 a week paid him by his boarders was able to buy all of his own food as well as theirs, and pay his room rent.

THE HARD FIGHT JUSTIFIED

After many troubles of this kind, G---- finished his engineering course and secured a position in one of the largest corporations in the United States at a salary of fifty dollars a month. At the time when he went to work for the big corporation there were probably three or four hundred other graduate engineers added to the staff. So keen was his mind along mechanical and engineering lines, and so great were his natural aptitudes, that within a few months his wages had been increased to $60 a month and he had been given far more responsible work. Almost as soon as he took up work with the corporation, he began making improvements in methods, inventing machinery and other devices, and thinking out ways and means for saving labor and making short cuts. Within a few weeks after his joining the force he had invented a bit of apparatus which could be carried in the coat pocket, and which took the place of a clumsy contrivance which required a horse and wagon to carry it. In this way he saved the company the price of horses, wagons, drivers, etc., on a great many operations. From the very first the young man rose very much more rapidly than any of the others who had entered the employ of the company at the time he did. Soon he was occupying an executive position and directing the activities of scores of men. To-day, only nine years after his leaving school, he occupies one of the most important positions in the engineering department of this great corporation, and while he does not have the title, performs nearly all the duties of chief engineer.

The point of all this story is that this young man, while he had plenty of mechanical ability and enjoyed machinery, was not fit to be a locomotive fireman or stationary engine fireman. He had, in addition to his mechanical sense and great skill in the use of his hands, a very keen, wide-awake, energetic, ambitious, accurate intellectual equipment, which did not find any adequate use in his work as a mechanic or fireman. Nor could he ever have found expression for it unless he had taken the initiative as a result of wise counsel and secured for himself the necessary education and training. With all his ingenuity, he would always have been more or less a slave to the machine to be operated unless he had trained his mind to make him the master of thousands of machines and of men.

FROM TURRET LATHE TO TREASURY

About eight years ago, while we were in St. Paul, Minnesota, a young mechanic, J.F., came to us for consultation. He was about twenty years old, and expressed himself as being dissatisfied with his work.

"I don't know just what is the matter with me," he said. "I have loved to play with mechanical things. I was always building machinery and, when I had an opportunity, hanging around machine shops and watching the men work. On account of these things my father was very sure that I had mechanical ability, and when I was fifteen years old took me out of school and apprenticed me in a machine shop. This shop was partly devoted to the manufacture of heavy machinery and partly to repairs of all kinds of machinery and tools. I have now been at work in this shop for five years. I am a journeyman mechanic and making good wages, and yet, somehow or other, I feel that I am in the wrong place. I wish you could tell me what is the matter with me."

After examining the young man and the data submitted, we made the following report:

ANALYSIS OF AN EMBRYO FINANCIER

"While you have undoubted mechanical ability, this is a minor part of your intellectual equipment. You are also qualified for commercial pursuits. You have a good sense of values. You understand the value of a dollar even now and you have natural aptitudes which, with proper training and experience, will make you an excellent financier. You also have executive ability. You like people and you like to deal with them. You like to handle them, and because you enjoy handling people and negotiating with them, you are successful in doing so. While you are fairly active physically, you are very much more active mentally. Your work, therefore, should be mental work, with a fair amount of light physical activity mingled with it, instead of purely physical work. You ought to hold an executive position and ought to have charge of thee finances of some concern which is engaged in the building and selling of machinery. You have worked, up to the present time, with heavy, coarse, crude machinery. But you are of fine texture, refined type, and naturally have a desire to work with that which is fine, delicate and beautiful--something into which you can put some of your natural refinement and artistic ability. You are still young. You have learned a trade at which you can earn fairly good wages. You ought, therefore, to prepare yourself in some way for business. Work during the summer, and then during the winter resume your studies, preparing yourself for an executive position in connection with manufacturing and selling fine machinery. Study accounting, banking, finance, salesmanship, advertising, mechanical engineering and designing. At the earliest possible moment give up your work in a machine shop where heavy machinery is manufactured and begin to get some actual experience in the manufacture of something finer and more artistic; for example, the automobile."

A few years later, in Boston, a young man came to us, well dressed, happy, and prosperous. He said he wished to consult us. After a few minutes' talk with him, we said: "We have given you advice somewhere before. This is not the first time you have consulted us." He smiled, and said: "Yes. I consulted you in St. Paul, some years ago. At that time you advised me to secure an executive position in the automobile business. This advice struck me at the time as being wise, and satisfied my own desires and ambitions. I lost no time in following your directions and was soon engaged as a mechanic in an automobile factory. I attended night-school at first, but finally made arrangements to spend half my time in school and the other half in the factory, learning every part of the business. At the present time I am the vice-president and treasurer of the ---- Motor Company, and one of the designers of the ---- Motor Car. We are doing an excellent business and making money. Whereas I was certainly misfit in my old job, I am well and happily placed since I have learned my true vocation."

EVOLUTION OF AN ELECTRICAL ENGINEER

D.B., of Chicago, was a young man admirably endowed with mechanical ability. From his earliest years he was especially interested in matters electrical. His father told us that he always had dry-cell and other batteries around the house. He used to try to make magnetos out of horseshoe magnets, and at one time attempted to build a dynamo. When he was sixteen years of age, having finished grammar school and having had one or two years of high school training, young B. became so ambitious to get into electrical work that his father, thinking that he was intended for exactly this vocation, consented to his leaving high school and taking a position as assistant to the linemen of a telephone company. He worked at this a year or two, and finally became a full-fledged lineman. He did well as a lineman and after a year or so attracted the attention of an electric light and power company, who enticed him away from the telephone company and gave him charge of poles and wires in a residential district. Here his unusual ingenuity and quickness soon became so manifest that he was taken off the outside and placed in charge of a gang of men wiring houses and installing electric fixtures. This was a pretty good job for a young fellow and paid good wages; at least, the wages seemed quite large to young B. at the time. By this time, however, he was twenty-one and decided to marry. He needed more money.

GETTING HIS BEARINGS

He had a long talk with a very kind and wise advisor, who finally said to him: "See here, B., you have abilities that ought to be put to use at something better than stringing wires and hanging bells."

"Why, I am a foreman now," said B.

"Yes, I know you are a foreman, but who plans all the work you do?"

"Why, the Super."

"Yes, the Super hands the plans down to you, but who plans the work for him?"

"Why, the Chief."

"Now, look here; the Chief comes to his office at ten o'clock in the morning. He uses his head until noon. He leaves at noon, and perhaps he doesn't come back until two or three o'clock. He uses his head then until five or, sometimes, until four; then he goes off to play golf. But as the result of those few hours' use of the Chief's head, the Superintendent, and you six or eight foremen, and all the two hundred men under your direction work a whole day or a week, or even a month, as you know. You are merely carrying out in a mechanical, routine kind of a way the thoughts and ideas that another man thinks. Now, you have the ability to think for yourself."

"I could think for myself," said he, "but I can't do all the figuring that is necessary in order to decide just what size wire should go here, and what kind of equipment should go there, and all the different things.

That's beyond me."

"Yes, it is beyond you now, but it doesn't need to be beyond you. You have the mental ability to learn to use those formulae just as well as the Chief does. The thing necessary is for you to learn how to do it, to get needful education. Now, you are young, and you're strong, and you've got lots of time before you. If you want to make more money, the way to do it is to learn to use your head and save weeks, months of time, as well as the labor of your hands."

"If I went off to college or university for two or three years, I don't think Bessie would wait for me," said he. "She wants to get married. I want to, too, and I think we ought to do it."

AN EDUCATION BY CORRESPONDENCE

"Well," said his counselor, "you don't need to go off to school. You can take electrical engineering in a correspondence course, even after you are married. You're making good wages now as a foreman. Your hours of work are only eight a day, and you have plenty of time in the evenings and on holidays and other times to study this subject. Besides, you will probably make better progress studying it while you work at the trade than you would in school and withdrawn from the practical applications of the principles that you are learning."

The result of all this was that D.B. did take a correspondence course in electrical engineering. It was pretty tough work. He had not studied for years. One of the first things he had to learn was how to study; how to concentrate; how to learn the things he had to know without tremendous waste of energy. After a little while he learned how to study. Then he progressed, a little at a time, with the intricate and complicated mathematics of the profession he had determined to make his own. Again and again he was puzzled, perplexed, and almost defeated. But his young wife encouraged him, and when things got so bad that he thought he would have to give it all up, he would go and talk with his counselor, who would inspire him with new ambition, so that he would go to work again. So, month after month, year after year, he struggled away with his correspondence course in electrical engineering. Little by little, he got hold of the technical knowledge necessary for professional engineering work.

A VICTORY FOR THE CORRESPONDENCE SCHOOL GRADUATE

At first he was greatly handicapped by the prejudice of some of his superiors against correspondence school courses, which were very much newer at that time than they are now and regarded as much more of an experiment. His superiors were graduates of universities and looked down with contempt upon any merely "practical" man who tried to qualify as an engineer by studying at home at night and without the personal oversight of authorities in a university. But D.B. was dogged in his persistence. Missing no opportunities to improve and advance himself, he was, nevertheless, respectful and diplomatic. And he repeatedly demonstrated his grasp of the subject. Eventually he was promoted to the position of superintendent of the electric light and power company. There was only one man then between him and the desired goal, namely, the chief engineer.

At the time B. became superintendent the chief engineer was a young university graduate, and was perhaps a little too egotistical and dogmatic on account of his degree and honors. Soon after B. took charge as superintendent, the company decided to build a new central power station. The design was left to the young chief engineer, and the practical work of carrying it out to our friend. When, finally, the design was complete and passed on to D.B. for execution, he felt that it was defective in several ways. He spent several nights of hard study on it and became convinced that he was right. He therefore took the whole matter to his superior and tried to explain to him how the design was defective.

"I made that plan, and it is right," said the chief engineer. "Your business isn't to criticize the plan, but to go ahead and carry it out. Now, I don't care to hear any more about it."

"But," said B., "if we carry out this plan the way it stands, it will mean the investment on the part of the company of something like $35,000 which will be practically dead loss. I can't conscientiously go to work and carry out this plan as it stands. I am sure if you will go over it again carefully, pay attention to my suggestions, and consult the proper authorities, you will find that I am right."

"That's what comes of studying a correspondence course," said the chief. "You get a little smattering of knowledge into your head. Part of it is worth while, and part of it is purely theoretical and useless, and because you have had some practical experience, you imagine you know it all. Now, you have lots yet to learn, B., and I am willing to help you, but I want to tell you that that plan and those specifications are technically correct, and all you need to do is to go ahead and carry them out. I'll take the responsibility."

"Very well," said B., "if you want those plans and specifications carried

125

out as they are, you can get someone else to do it. I would rather resign than to superintend this job which I know to be technically wrong."

His resignation had to be passed upon by the general manager, who, before accepting it, sent for him.

"What's the trouble, B.?" said he. "I thought you were getting along fine. We like your work, and we thought you liked the company. Why do you want to leave?"

"I don't like to say anything about it, Mr. Jones," said B., "but the plans passed on to me to carry out in the construction of that new power-house down in Elm Street are technically wrong. They mean an expenditure of $35,000 along certain lines which will be pretty nearly a dead loss. When you come to try to use your equipment there, you will find that it all has to be taken out and replaced by the proper materials.

"Suppose you get the plans, B., and show them to me, and explain just what you mean," said the general manager, who was also a professional engineer of many years' successful experience.

So B. produced the plans and explained his proposition.

"Why, of course you are right," said the general manager. "I'm surprised that Mr. F. should have thought for a moment that he could use that type."

The result was that B. was reinstated and the chief engineer reprimanded. Stung by his reprimand and angered because the correspondence school graduate had bested him, the chief engineer resigned. His resignation was accepted and B. became chief engineer of the company. Later, he was promoted to the position of chief engineer of an even larger corporation, and, finally, occupied an executive position as managing engineer for a municipal light and power plant in one of the large cities of the country.

THE GENESIS OF AN INVENTOR

Some years ago we spent a few months in a very comfortable and homelike hotel in one of the largest cities in the Middle West. Down in a nook of the basement of this hotel was a private electric light plant. In charge of the plant was an old Scotch engineer delightful for his wise sayings and quaint philosophy. The fireman, a young man named T., was rather a puzzle to us. He had all the marks of unusual mechanical ability, and yet he seemed to take only the slightest interest in his work, and was constantly being reproved by his chief for laziness, irresponsibility, and neglect of duty. "What's the use?" he asked us, after we gained his confidence, and had asked him why he did not take greater interest in his work. "What's the use? After years of experience shoveling coal into a firebox and monkeying around these old grease pots, I suppose I might get an engineer's certificate. Then what would I be? Why, just like old Mack there--$75 to $100 a month, sitting around a hot, close basement twelve hours a day or, perhaps, twelve hours at night, nothing to look forward to, no further advancement, no more pay, and, finally, T.B. would carry me off because of the lack of fresh air, sunshine and outdoor exercise. No, thank you!"

"Well, then, why don't you do something else?"

"I don't know what to do. I like mechanics, and some job of this kind is the only thing I know how to do or would care to do. Yet, I don't care for this. I must confess that I am puzzled as to what in the world I was made for, anyhow."

"What you need is to give your time and attention to the intellectual side of engineering rather than the purely mechanical and physical. You are of the intellectual type, and you are as badly placed trying to do mere mechanical work as if you were an eagle trying to cross the country on foot."

"I believe you are right in that. I am going to get an education."

AMBITION, INDUSTRY, AND PERSISTENCE

He began at once with correspondence courses in mechanical and electrical engineering. Twelve hours a day he shoveled coal in his basement boiler-room. Some four to eight hours a day he studied in his little room up under the roof. It takes an immense amount of courage, persistence, and perseverance to complete a correspondence course in engineering, as anyone who has tried it well knows. There is lacking any inspiration from the personality and skill of a teacher. There is no spur to endeavor from association with other students doing the same kind of work and striving for the same degree. There are no glee clubs, athletic games, fraternities, prizes, scholarships, and other aids to the imagination and ambition, such as are found in a university. It is all hard, lonely work. But what the student learns, he knows. And, somehow, he gains a great knack for the practical use of his knowledge. Night after night T. toiled away, until he had finished his course and secured his certificate of graduation.

By this time T.'s ambition began to assume a definite form. He was determined that he should have the honor and the emoluments which would come to him as a result of solving one of the toughest problems in engineering--one which had puzzled both technical and practical men for many years. He therefore saved up a few dollars and, packing his little belongings, departed to complete his education in one of the most famous technical engineering schools of the country. Tuition was high. Board cost a good deal of money. Books were distressingly expensive. Tools, machine shop fees, and other incidentals ate into the little store he had brought with him, and inside of two months it was gone. He hunted around and finally secured a job running an engine. This meant twelve hours in the engine room every night. In addition, he did what other students considered a full day's work attending lectures and carrying on his studies in the laboratories and classroom. He went almost without necessary food and clothing in order to buy books, tools, and other equipment. But he was young, he was strong, and, above all, he was happy in his mental picture of the great object of his ambition. In due time he had taken his degree, having specialized on all subjects bearing upon the solution of his great problem.

PATIENT TOIL HIS GENIUS

Coming back from the university after having finished his course, T. found a position as engineer in an electric light and power plant. Then he began saving up money to purchase the necessary equipment for a laboratory of his own. Finally, he had a little building and was one of the proudest young men we ever saw. Little by little, he added to his apparatus the things he needed. Several nights a week, after his hard day's work in the engine room, he toiled, trying to solve the problem upon which he had fixed his mind. About this time he married, and he and his wife moved into a narrow little flat. Years passed, children came into the little flat, and still he worked at his problem. Again and again, and still again, he failed. Yet, each time he failed, he told us he was coming closer to the solution. At last came the day, after many heart-breaking experiences, when the problem, while not fully solved, had at least revealed a solution which was commercially valuable.

His years of self-denial and toil seemed to be about to end in success. But he found that he had only begun another long period of discouraging and almost desperate work. It was a struggle to scrape together the necessary funds for securing a patent. If he was to complete and perfect his invention, he must have more capital. So, with his model, he made the rounds of manufacturers of engines, manufacturers who used engines, railroads, steamboat companies, electric light and power companies; in fact, everywhere he thought he might get some encouragement and financial assistance. His little family was living on short rations. He himself had not eaten as he ought for years. One after another, the men in authority said: "Yes, your proposition looks good, but I don't think it can ever be made practical. Some of the brightest men in the engineering profession have spent years trying to solve that problem, and have not found the answer to it. I do not believe that it will ever be found. You seem to have come near it, but yet you have not found it, and we cannot see our way clear to put any money into it."

REAPING HIS REWARD

T. argued, pleaded, and demanded an opportunity for a demonstration, but all in vain. Then, one day, a lawyer, who had been consulted by T., said: "I have no money to invest in anything myself, but I'll tell you frankly and honestly, it looks good to me. Now, I happen to be on very good terms with Mr. J. over at the T. & B. Company. He has been interested in this problem for years and has worked along toward its solution. He understands every phase of it, and I believe he will do something with your device. Unless I am mistaken, he will be interested in it, and will give you an opportunity to demonstrate it. If your demonstration works out as well as you think it will, he has the authority to put you in a position where you can go ahead and perfect it if it is perfectible. I will give you a letter of introduction to him." And thus began T.'s prosperity. He now lives in a beautiful home on a wide boulevard. His invention, still short of perfection, but highly valuable, is coming slowly into use, and would probably be in very widespread use were it not for the fact that he is constantly working on it, perfecting it, improving it, and hoping finally to have a complete solution to the problem.

CHAPTER VIII

THE IMPRACTICAL MAN

"My life is a failure," wrote Sydney Williams to us, "and I do not know why."

In middle life my grandfather Williams moved his family across the Potomac River from Virginia in order to study to enter the ministry. He is said to have freed some slaves at that time, so he must have been a 'planter,' He became a Congregational minister. My grandfather Jacobs was a carpenter; but, as I knew him, and for some years before my birth, he was a helpless invalid from paralysis on one side.

My father graduated from college and then became a minister. He preached for many years, then he took up work with a religious publishing house, finally having charge of the work at St. Paul. He was there, I believe, when he was elected president of a small school for girls. He assumed his new duties in June and I was born the following November. (I am the youngest of eleven children, of whom there are now three boys and five girls still living, three boys having died while still babies before my birth.)

Until I was nearly twelve years old we lived at the girls' school, which father succeeded in greatly enlarging. Mother taught me to read a little and write a little. She and others read to me a great deal. I had no playmates except my nephews and nieces, to whom I was continually being pointed out as a 'model.' Out of the sight of the grown-ups, I was not always such a model as they could have wished; yet I did feel a certain amount of responsibility that was oppressive and repressive. When nearly eleven, I was sent to the public school, where I was soon promoted with two others. The next year father and mother moved into a larger town, so that I had a few months of real home life before my father's death in April, 1893.

Then my mother, her mother, and I went to Wisconsin to live with a married sister of mine whose husband was the Presbyterian minister there. I entered the fourth grade of the public school that fall; but, by the end of the school year, I had completed the fifth grade.

My mother died in May, 1896. I continued to live with my sister. Finished the seventh grade that June, but entered preparatory school that fall. In November, 1897, my brother-in-law moved to Iowa, and I made the mistake of deciding to go with him. While living in Wisconsin, I had become acquainted with a fine lot of boys. One of them organized a small military company; I was elected quarter-master and, later, lieutenant. I now know that that was because we were considered 'rich,' Also in Wisconsin I overcame some of my extreme bashfulness in regard to girls, derived from babyhood experiences. In fact, one reason I decided to leave Wisconsin was the fear that the friendship with one girl might become too serious; I was beginning to shun responsibility.

ATTAINMENTS IN SCHOLARSHIP

In Iowa I entered the high school and completed the tenth grade the next June (1898). My elder brother was my official guardian and he wanted me to make a change. As a result, in September, 1898, I had my first experience of being away alone by entering a famous academy. There I earned the reputation of being a 'grind,' and graduated second in my class in June, 1901. While there I went out for football, and made the third team and even played once on the second. My poor eyesight hindered me somewhat, but still more the fact that I was not eager to fall down on the ball on the hard ground when it did not seem to me necessary. I was quite ready to get hurt, if there was any reason for it. That, too, was a mistake on my part.

That September I entered Harvard University. My father had left some insurance, and mother left some of it to me for a college education. She expected, as did my sisters and brothers, that I would become a minister. By the end of my Freshman year I had decided that I could not do so, but from that time I was unable to decide what I did want to do or could do. Consequently I did not get the good out of a college education that I might have. Moreover, though I stood fairly well in most of my classes, I did not always understand the subjects as well as the professors thought I did. As soon as it became possible to elect subjects, I dropped Latin, Greek, and German, and specialized in history, economics, etc. I graduated 'Cum Laude,' But that was really a failure, considering what I might have done.

But I did well enough to receive recommendation for a $500 fellowship that enabled me to return for another year. I did work which caused me to be recommended for an A.M. degree. But I felt that I had so little in comparison with others, that I was actually ashamed to receive it. Socially, however, that extra year was a very delightful one for me.

During two summers as an undergraduate, I worked at Nantasket Beach selling tickets in the bathing pavilion for $50 a month, besides room and board. I made good, much to the surprise of the superintendent.

HUNTING A JOB

So then I was finally through college in June, 1906. It is almost incredible how very childlike I still was, so far as my attitude toward the world was concerned. I had high ideals, and I wanted to get into business, but where or how I did not know. Moreover, my money was gone. A student gave me a note with which I intended to get his previous summer's job as a starter on an electric car line owned by a railway company. The position was abolished, however, so I became a conductor on a suburban line. Unfortunately, my motorman was a high-strung, nervous Irishman, who made me so nervous that I often could not give the signals properly, and who made life generally unpleasant for me. He professed a liking for me and did prevent one or two serious accidents. At the same time, he said I was the first 'square' conductor he had ever worked with, and, no doubt, he missed his 'extra,' After three weeks of him, and of the general public's idea that I must, of course, be knocking down fares, I resigned. However, the superintendent offered me a job as 'inspector' of registers on the main line, a job that he was just creating. When the rush was over after Labor Day, I was again out of a job. I might have secured a clerkship with the railway company, but I was foolish enough not to try.

A few weeks later found me established in the district office of a correspondence school not very far from New York City as a representative. At first I gave good promise of success, but I lost my enthusiasm and belief in the school and became ashamed to be numbered as one of its workers because of the character of most of the local field force at that time and before my time. The reputation of the school in that place was not very good. Also I was not successful in collecting the monthly payments from those who had hard luck stories or had been lied to by the man who had enrolled them. By the end of two months I was ready to quit, but my immediate superior begged me to stay, in order to keep him from having to break in a new man just then. At the end of about four months I did resign to save being kicked out. Mind you, I was to blame, all right; for I had given up a real continuous effort beyond the merest routine and the attempt to collect the monthly payments. While I was there I did write a few contracts, among them a cash one amounting to $80. But, toward the end, my lack of success was due to my utter disgust with myself for being so blamed poor and for shirking.

AN ATTEMPT IN ORANGE CULTURE

Going back to a brother in New York, I tried to land a job, but, of course, in such a state of mind, I could not. Then I went to my older brother in Cincinnati, where he was, and is, the pastor of a large church. Unfortunately, he did not take me by the back of the neck and kick me into some kind of work, any kind. At last, in March, 1908, he helped me to come out West. I landed in Los Angeles, and indirectly through a friend of his I secured a job on an orange ranch in the San Gabriel Valley, which I held until the end of the season. Once more I was happy and contented. It was certainly a pleasure to work.

That fall, or rather winter (1908), I secured a place near San Diego, where I had shelter and food during the winters and small wages during the active seasons in return for doing the chores and other work.

I had become possessed with a desire for an orange grove, and refused to consider how much it would take to develop one. I was finally able to secure a small tract of unimproved land. But I found that the task of

132

clearing it would be too great for me because of the great trees, so for this and other reasons I snatched at a chance to file on a homestead in the Imperial Valley. This was in May, 1910. Later that summer I was able to sell my piece of land near San Diego at a profit, so that in September I went over to get settled on my homestead. I employed a fellow to help me make a wagon trail for a mile or more and to build my cabin for me. I moved in the first of November. Early in 1912 I decided it would be impossible to irrigate enough land there to make a living at that time. Also the difficulties of living alone so far out in the desert were greater than I had anticipated. With the help of a friend, I was able to make final proof in July and pay the government for the 160 acres, instead of having to continue to live on it. I did stay, however, until the general election in 1912.

AT WORK IN A SURVEYING CREW

Then I went to Los Angeles to get something to do. The town was full of people seeking work, as usual, most of whom could present better records than I could. To be sure, my friends and even my old correspondence school boss gave me splendid recommendations, but I felt my lack of business training and feared that 999 out of any 1,000 employers would not take a chance with me on such a record as I had. Consequently I did not try very hard. For a while I was with a real estate firm trying to secure applications for a mortgage. The commission was $25, but, naturally, that did not go far toward expenses. It was not long before I was in a bad mental condition again through worrying, self-condemnation, and uncertainty. It would not have been difficult to prove that I was 'insane.'

Finally an acquaintance of mine, a prominent lawyer, took up my case. He has a good personal and business friend who is the general manager of a large oil company with headquarters here in Bakersfield. When first appealed to, this gentleman refused point blank, because he had a bad opinion of college graduates in general (I really don't blame him or other business men); but the lawyer used his influence to the utmost with the result that I came up here in March, 1913, and was sent up into the oil fields. I was put under the civil engineer, and for two months I was sort of 'inspector' and 'force account' man in connection with the building of a supply railroad, but I gradually worked into the regular surveying crew, first as substitute rear chainman, and then as the regular one. Before long I was head chainman. I could have remained a chainman with the same crew to this time, but I left a little over a year ago, as there once more seemed a chance to earn a place in the country.

ANOTHER ATTEMPT AT ORANGE CULTURE

A young fellow, now located near Bakersfield, whom I had known in San Diego, told me great tales that I was too anxious to believe, and finally made some fine promises to help me get a piece of what he said was his land and to bring it to a productive state. But when I reached his place, in February, he was not ready, willing or able to carry out his promises. He kept me hanging on, however, and as I had used up my savings in a month's attendance at the short course of the State agricultural college and in bringing my goods from Bakersfield, I was compelled to get work from him as one of his orchard gang. I helped to set out several hundred trees and berry plants, and later knew what it meant to hoe for ten hours a day. I left him the latter part of July in order to work out a scheme I had thought of.

[Illustration: FIG. 25. "Sydney Williams." For analysis see pages 206 to 210. Here is a fine, capable intellect, good sense of humor, optimism, cheerfulness, great refinement, and excellent critical powers in art and literature. But there is a deficiency of practicability. Note smallness and flatness of brows, narrowness of head just above the ears, fineness of features and height of head in center, above temples.]

[Illustration: FIG. 26. "Sydney Williams." Note flatness of brows; smallness and fineness of features; fineness of texture; height of forehead and crown.]

[Illustration: FIG. 27. Prof. Adolf von Menzel, Sociologist. A man of great intellect, especially interested in theoretical and statistical studies of people, in the mass, but not greatly interested in practical, material affairs. Note immense dome of forehead and head, with flatness at brows.]

[Illustration: FIG. 28. Edgar Allan Poe, Poet. Impractical, deficient in financial sense, but keenly alive to a world of fancy, ideals, dreams, imagery, beauty, mysticism and tragedy. Note high forehead, wide above, flat at brows and concave at sides; small nose and mouth, deep-set, gloomy eyes; dark complexion; and lack of symmetry and balance in head and features.]

[Illustration: FIG. 29. Samuel Taylor Coleridge, Author. Highly intellectual, sentimental, impractical, sensitive, emotional. A man of high ideals and beautiful thoughts, and creative power. Note high, dome-shaped head; flat, high brows, fine, delicate features; weak mouth, and general softness of contour and expression.]

[Illustration: _Copyright by Harper & Brothers, N. Y_. FIG. 30.

134

Thomas De Quincy, Author. A man of fine, discriminating, logical intellect along purely mental lines, but impractical in material affairs. Note high, prominent forehead, with flat, poorly-developed brows, weak nose and mouth and narrow head.]

[Illustration: FIG. 31. O. Henry, at the age of thirty. Impractical, lacking in desire for money and financial judgment. Creative, humorous, a lover of human nature, mild, rather easy-going, idealistic, constant. Note high forehead, flat at brows, full at sides along top, concave nose, full lips, prominent chin.]

[Illustration: FIG. 32. Edwin Reynolds, of Wisconsin. Of the practical, matter-of-fact, literal type of intellect. Interested in facts, keenly observant, quick in thought, alert and positive in his mental activities. Note high, sloping forehead, very prominent at the brows, large nose, high in the bridge and well-developed.]

"The first part of September I moved back to Bakersfield. I tried out my scheme by mail on two of the most prominent men in the country (one of the times when I had plenty of nerve). It did not work and the time did not seem auspicious for trying it on a greater number, especially as I did not have money enough to do it properly.

"While still working for the orchard man, I began to do some work in getting subscriptions for the Curtis publications. I did get a few. Later, about the middle of October, I went to Los Angeles, where I had a booth at an exhibition for three weeks in the interest of a publishing house. But it did not pay expenses, and I was deeper in debt than ever. I landed in Bakersfield nearly 'broke.' Thanks to the kindness of the people where I roomed and boarded, I was able to pull through until I obtained a loan last week, secured by a mortgage on my homestead.

"I was entirely unable to force myself to do any real canvassing while I was absolutely in need of each commission, but, now that I once more have a bank account, I hope to make myself keep at it until I can feel moderately successful. That is the one job I have fallen down on over and over (I have not even mentioned many of the attempts), and I believe I could be a real salesman if I could only get over my fear of approaching people on any proposition of immediate profit to me."

Here we have in detail the old, old story. How often have you heard of the man who graduated with high honors at the head of his class and was unable to make a living afterward? How many men of highest scholarship have you met who could not make a living for themselves and their families? Not long ago we were offered the services of a man who had degrees from several universities in America and Europe, who was master of several languages, and who was glad to offer to do a little translating at twenty-five cents an hour.

AN ANALYSIS OF SYDNEY WILLIAMS

What handicaps these men? They have good intellects, or they would be unable to win high honors in colleges and universities. It is fitting that they should educate themselves highly, since they are so capable of attainment in scholarship. Surely, they ought to do some intellectual work of some kind, because they are not fitted for manual labor. Where do they belong? What is their particular type? What opportunities are there for their unquestioned talents?

Here is what we wrote to Sydney Williams:

"From photographs and data submitted, I should judge your type of organization, character and aptitudes to be as follows:

"You have inherited only a fairly good physical constitution. You will always need to take care of yourself, but there is absolutely no reason why you should worry in regard to your health.

"Under stress and strain your nervous system may give you trouble, and there may be some tendency to digestive disturbances, but if you will practice moderation, live on a well-balanced and sensibly selected diet, and keep yourself from extremes of every kind you will probably maintain very fair health and strength for many years.

"Intellectually you have a good, active mind of the theoretical type. Your mind is quick to grasp theories, ideals, abstractions, and such intangible and purely mental concepts. Your imagination is active, and is inclined to run away with plans, schemes, and inventions, with speculations and with visions of future prospects. However, your plans and inventions are liable to be purely along mental and intellectual lines, rather than practical.

"You do not observe well. You are a little too careless in regard to your facts. You therefore have a tendency to go ahead with your theories and your plans upon insufficient data or upon data which are not accurate because they have not been properly verified.

"This deficiency in observation also handicaps you, because you do not see things in their right relation, and your judgment is, therefore, liable to be erratic and unsound.

"You should compel yourself to get the facts. You should suspend judgment until you have made sure that all of the premises from which you argue to your conclusions are sound and accurate. Take nothing for granted. Compel yourself to stick to the facts. Not only ask yourself the question, 'Will it work?' but make sure that the affirmative answer is absolutely accurate before you go ahead.

"Many of your characteristics are those of immaturity, notwithstanding your years, your education, and your experience. You still retain many youthful tendencies. You are inclined to be impulsive. You are very responsive emotionally, and when your emotions are aroused you are prone to decide important matters without reference to facts, reason, and logic. Another very youthful characteristic in you is your tendency to be headstrong, wilful, stubborn, and opinionated. When you have arrived at one of your swift conclusions you find it very difficult to take advice. Even when you do listen to what others say, you do not listen well. Your mind jumps ahead to conclusions that are erroneous and which were never in the mind of the person giving you the advice.

"As you can readily see, it is this inability to get competent counsel from others, coupled with your own lack of observation and lack of deliberation, that leads you into so many situations that turn out to be undesirable. Here, again, you need to go more slowly, to act more according to your knowledge and less according to impulse, to make sure that you understand what other people say, especially when seeking for advice. As a result of your rather emotional character, you are liable to go to extremes and do erratic things, to be over-zealous for a short period; also, at times, to be high tempered, although your temper quickly evaporates. In all of these things you will see the need for cultivation of more self-control, more poise, more calmness, more maturity of thought, speech, and action.

"You are very idealistic. Your standards are high. You naturally expect much. It is your hope always, when making a change, that you will get into something which will more nearly approach perfection than the thing you are leaving.

"But you are also critical. Indeed, you are inclined to be hypercritical, to find too much fault, to see too many flaws and failures. For this reason, nothing ever measures up to your ideals--you are always being disappointed.

"You need to cultivate far more courage. By this I mean the courage which hangs on, which meets obstacles, which overcomes difficulties, which persists through disagreeable situations. Your impulsiveness leads you into plenty of things, but you are so hypercritical, and you become so easily discouraged when eventualities do not measure up to your ideals, that you fail to finish that which you start.

"Naturally, of course, if you were to be more deliberate and more careful in forming your judgments, you would find things more nearly ideal after you got into them. Then, if you would stick to them, you could make a much greater success of them.

"Your intention to be honest, is, no doubt, above reproach. However, your conduct or the results may at times be equivalent to dishonesty, being so regarded by others. This, of course, is the result of your immaturity, your impulsiveness, and your tendency not to see things through.

"You are very keenly sensitive. With your great love of beauty and refinement, anything which is coarse, crude, and ugly in your environment is very depressing to you. You also find it difficult to associate happily with those who are coarse and crude by nature. Unquestionably, such people frequently hurt you cruelly when they have no intention of doing so. It would be well if you would learn to accept other people for what they are worth, rather than being so critical of them and so easily hurt. Praise and blame are usually meant impersonally and should be so received. In other words, people praise or blame the deed and not the doer.

"Your appreciation of financial and commercial values and methods is deficient. This is due to many different things, but principally to your lack of observation, your inability to see things in their right relations, and your limited sense of values. For these reasons you are not and cannot become vitally interested in financial and commercial affairs. If your wants were supplied, and you had something interesting to do, money would receive practically no consideration from you. For your own sake, you ought to attach more importance to monetary considerations, cultivate a greater sense of values, develop more practical commercial sense. On the other hand, however, you should not attempt any vocation in which a high development of these qualities is necessary.

"In practical affairs, you show a tendency not to learn by experience. This is because of deficiency in your observation of facts. You do not really understand the essential facts of the experiences through which you pass, and, therefore, they do not impress or teach you.

"In your choice of a vocation you should make up your mind once for all that, on account of the qualities I have described, you are not

138

commercial or financial, and, therefore, you do not belong in the industrial or commercial world. Your talents are educational, dramatic, professional, literary. You are decidedly of the mental type. Your world is a mental world, an intellectual world. Ideas, ideals, and theories are the things with which you can deal most successfully.

"Owing to your distaste for detail, and the difficulty you have in applying yourself to a task until it is finished, and also on account of your very keen and sensitive critical faculties, you are probably better fitted for success as a critic than as a producer.

"A position in a house publishing books and magazines, where your duty would be to read, analyze, and criticise manuscripts, would offer you far better opportunities than anything you have yet attempted.

"You could probably do well in a mail-order house as correspondent.

"You also have some dramatic ability which, if developed and trained, might make you a success, either on the stage or in the pulpit. In this connection, I merely call your attention, in passing, to the opportunities in the motion picture drama. Here is where dramatic ability is everything and the heavier demands upon the actor in the ordinary drama, especially in the way of physical development, voice, etc., do not enter.

"Another line which might possibly interest you would be that of a salesman in an art or music store, where customers come to you, or in a book store. You probably would do better selling to women than to men.

"Whatever you do, you should work under direction, under the direction of some one whose judgment, wisdom, honesty, and high principles you respect. Under wise leadership you have your very best opportunities for success. In attempting to be your own manager and to go your own way, you suffer from the serious handicaps to which I have already referred.

"In selecting from among the vocations I have enumerated the one that is best for you, you will, of course, be guided very largely by opportunities. At this distance I do not know just which is your best opportunity, and, therefore, cannot counsel you definitely to undertake any one of these vocations in preference to the others. If the opportunity is at hand, perhaps the position of literary or dramatic critic with a publishing house would be most congenial for you and offer you the best future. If not, then one of the others. You might even undertake a position as salesman in a book store or an art store while preparing or waiting for an opening in one of the other lines suggested.

"Whatever you undertake, however, compel yourself, in spite of obstacles, in spite of your very natural criticisms of the situation, to stick to it until you make a success of it.

"As you grow older, if you will patiently and conscientiously cultivate more deliberation, more practical sense, more self-control, and more poise, you will become more mature in judgment and gradually overcome to a greater and greater degree the handicaps which have so far interfered with your progress and the best and highest expression of your personality."

HANDICAPS OF THIS TYPE

To make a long story short, Sydney Williams and men of his type have unusual intellectual powers of analysis, criticism, memory, abstraction, and philosophy. They can master hypotheses, higher mathematics, and Hebrew irregular verbs, but they are babes in all practical affairs. They have some such conception of the plain facts of human nature, ordinary financial values, and efficient methods of commerce as a man with color blindness has of the art of Corot. Like the children they are, these people seldom suspect their deficiencies. Oftentimes they are ambitious to make a success in a commercial way. They try salesmanship, or, if they have a little capital, they may embark in some ambitious business project on their own account. They even go into farming or agriculture or poultry raising, or some kind of fancy fruit producing, with all of the optimism and cheerfulness and confidence in their ability that Sydney Williams felt for his orange growing. When they fail, it is more often through their own incompetence than because some one comes along who is mean enough to take candy from a baby. They usually dissipate their assets by impracticable schemes before the unscrupulous can take them. The only hope for such men is to learn their limitations; to learn that, even though they may be ambitious for commercial success, they are utterly unqualified for it; that, although they may wish to do something in the way of production or selling, they have neither talent, courage, secretiveness, persistence, nor other qualities necessary for a success in these lines. They are too credulous. They are too impractical. They are too lacking in fighting qualities, and, therefore, too easily imposed upon. They are usually lazy physically and find disagreeable situations hard, so that they are out of place in the rough-and-tumble, strenuous, hurly-burly of business, manufacturing, or ordinary professional life.

Perhaps a few stories would indicate what these men can do, do well, and what they can be happy and satisfied in doing. There is a real need for them in the world.

A CAREER IN MUSIC

George R. came to us late one evening in a little town in Illinois. He was nervous, weak, and diffident.

"I am now," he said, "a salesman in a dry goods store. But I have only held the job three months and do not expect that I will be permitted to remain more than a week or so longer. I have been warned several times by the floor-walker that my errors will cost me my position. God knows, I do my best to succeed in the work, but it is like all the other positions I've held. Somehow or other I don't seem to be able to give satisfaction. While I am on my guard and as alert as I know how to be against one of the things I've been told not to do, I am just as sure as sunshine to go and do some other thing which is against the rules. If I don't do something against the rules, then I forget to do something I was told to do. If I don't forget to do something I've been told to do, then I am quite likely to make some outlandish mistake that no one ever thought of framing a rule to fit. The result of it all is that in about another week or, at the most, two, I'll be out of employment again. I have tried driving a delivery wagon. I've tried grocery stores. I've tried doing collections. I began once as clerk in a bank. Immediately after leaving college, I started in as newspaper reporter. I've been a newsboy on railroad trains. I sold candies and peanuts in a fair ground. I have been night clerk in a hotel. I've been steward on a steamboat. I've been a shipping clerk in a publishing house, and I have been fired from every job I have ever had. True enough, I've hated them all, but, nevertheless; I have tried to do my best in them. Why I cannot succeed with any of them, I don't know, and yet I have a feeling that somehow, somewhere, sometime, I will find something to do that I will love, and that I can do well."

"Music," we said, "unquestionably music."

"Do you think I could?" he said wistfully. "Music has been my passion all my life long. It has been my one joy, my one solace in all my wanderings and all my failures. But I have always been afraid I would fail also in that, and, if I should, it would break my heart sure. But if you think I have the talent, then I shall give my whole time, my whole thought, my whole energy to music hereafter."

141

It was rather late in life for this young man to begin a musical career. While he had always been fond of music, he had been sent to college for a classical course by parents to whom a classical course meant everything that was desirable in an education. He had learned to play the piano, the violin, the guitar, the mandolin, and some other instruments, without education, because of his natural musical talent. He played them all as he had opportunity, for his own amusement, but, because of his ambition for commercial success, had never thought of music as a career. We wish we might tell you that this young man was now one of the foremost composers or conductors of his time. It would make an excellent story. Such, however, is not the case.

He devoted himself to securing a thorough musical education, supporting himself and paying his expenses in the mean-while by playing in churches, musicales, motion picture shows, and other places. He also received a few dollars nearly every week for playing the violin for dances and other functions in a semi-professional orchestra. Truly this was not "art for art's sake." Any critical musician could probably tell you that such use of his musical talent forever shut off any hopes of his becoming a true artist. On the other hand, it did fill his stomach and clothe him while he was securing a sufficient musical education to enable him to make a very fair living as teacher on various musical instruments and as a performer at popular concerts, recitals, etc. Best of all, he was happy in his work, felt himself growing in success and, while there were probably heights which he never could scale and to which he may have turned his longing eyes, he doubtless got a considerable amount of satisfaction out of the fact that he was no longer being kicked around from pillar to post in the commercial world.

VOCATIONS FOR THE IMPRACTICAL

Herbert Spencer felt that he was a complete and utter failure as a civil engineer, but he made a magnificent success as a scientist, essayist, and philosopher.

The number of great authors, scientists, philosophers, poets, actors, preachers, teachers, lecturers, and musicians who were ludicrously impractical is legion. Literature abounds in stories of their idiosyncrasies. These people deal with abstractions, ideas, with theories, and with emotions. They may be very successful in the spinning of theories, in the working out of clever ideas, and in their appeal to the emotions of their fellow-men. They may write poetry which is the product of genius; they may devise profound philosophy.

This is their realm. Here is where they are supreme, and it is in this kind of work they find an expression for all of their talent.

Right here there is need for careful distinction. There is a great difference between the impractical man who has energy, courage, and persistence, and the impractical man who is lazy and cowardly. No matter what a man's natural talent may be, it takes hard work to be successful in such callings as art, music, the pulpit, the stage, the platform, and the pen. Inspiration may seem to have a great deal to do with success. But even in the writing of a poem inspiration is probably only about five per cent.; hard work constitutes the other ninety-five per cent. It is one thing to have vague, beautiful dreams, to be an admirer of beauty, to enjoy thrills in contemplation of beautiful thoughts or beautiful pictures. It is quite another thing to have the energy, the courage, and the dogged persistence necessary to create that which is beautiful.

NO EASY ROAD TO SUCCESS

We offer no golden key which unlocks the doors to success. Much as we regret to disappoint many aspiring young men and women, we must be truthful and admit that there is no magic way in which some wonderful, unguessed talent can be discovered within them and made to blossom forth in a night, as it were. Many people of this type come to us for consultation, evidently with the delectable delusion that we can point out to them some quick and easy way to fame and fortune. Again we must make emphatic by repetition the hard, uncompromising truth that laziness, cowardice, weakness, and vacilation are incompatible with true success. No matter what a man's other aptitudes may be, no matter how great his talent or his opportunities, we can suggest absolutely no vocation in which he can be successful unless he has the will to overcome these deficiencies in his character.

Many a man is deluded into the fond supposition that he is not successful because he does not fit into the vocation where he finds himself. The truth is that he probably is in as desirable a vocation as could possibly be found for him. The reason he is not successful is because he has failed to develop the fundamental qualities of industry, courage, and persistence.

HOW TO BECOME MORE PRACTICAL

143

When the impractical man learns his limitations he is all too likely to go to extremes in depreciating his own business ability. Many such people are seemingly proud of their deficiencies in business sense. "I am no business man. You attend to it, I'll trust you," they say. While a lack of natural business ability may not be a man's fault, it is nothing to be proud of. You may not be born with keen, financial sense, but that is no reason why you may not develop more and more of it and make yourself a better business man. As a matter of fact, every man is in business--he has something to sell which he wishes the rest of the world to buy from him. He has himself, at least, to support, and more than likely he has others dependent upon him. He has no right, therefore, to neglect business affairs and to permit others to impose upon him and to steal from him and from those dependent upon him the proper reward for his labor.

Even the youth who is poor in mathematics can learn something about geometry, algebra, and trigonometry; even he who "has no head for language" can learn to speak a foreign tongue and even to read Latin or Greek. It is not easy for either one of them and perhaps the one can never become a great mathematician nor the other a great linguist, but both can learn something, both can improve their grasp of the difficult subject. There are probably few readers of these pages who have not in their school days overcome just such handicaps in some particular subject of study.

In a similar way those who are impractical and have little business sense can improve in this respect and they ought to. Such people ought to study practical affairs, ought to give their attention to financial matters. In fact, one of the best ways to increase financial judgment is to form the intimate acquaintance of some one who has a keen sense of financial values. If such a person can be persuaded to talk about what he knows, the impractical man will do well to take a keen interest in what he says, to qualify himself to understand it, and, if possible, to get the point of view from which a good business man approaches his problems and studies his affairs. Actual practice is, of course, necessary for development, and the impractical man ought to take an interest in his affairs and ought to do his best to handle them. Naturally, he needs to seek competent counsel in regard to them, but he should pay some attention to the counsel given, try to learn something from it, watch results of every course of action and in every possible way study to make himself more practical and less theoretical and abstract in his attitude toward life in general and toward business affairs in particular.

Not long ago we attended a meeting of two and three hundred of the

144

most prominent authors, poets, and playwrights in America. We were not at all surprised to note that nearly every one of those who had made a financial success of his art was a man of the practical, commercial type who had developed his business sense along with his artistic or literary talent.

A PAUPER, HE DREAMED OF MILLIONS

Some years ago we formed the acquaintance of a delightful man who is so typical of a certain class of the impractical that his story is instructive. When we first formed the acquaintance of this gentleman he was about thirty years of age, rather handsome in appearance, with great blue eyes, very fine silky blonde hair, and a clear, pink, and white complexion. His head, somewhat narrow just above the ears, indicated a mild, easy-going, gentle disposition. The large, rounded dome just above temples was typical of the irrepressible optimist. His forehead, very full and bulging just below the hair line, showed him to be of the thoughtful, meditative, drearily type, while flatness and narrowness at the brows told as plainly as print of the utter impracticability of his roseate dreams.

True to his exquisite blonde coloring, this man was eager, buoyant, irrepressible, impatient of monotony, routine, and detail--social and friendly. True to his fine texture, he shrank from hardship, was sensitive, refined, beauty loving and luxury loving. Because of his mild disposition and optimism and also because of his love of approval, he was suave, affable, courteous, agreeable. He made acquaintances easily and had many of the elements of popularity.

Because he was ambitious to occupy a position of prominence and distinction, because he wished to gratify his luxurious and elegant tastes, and because in his irrepressible optimism it seemed so absurdly easy to do, he was eager to make a large fortune. Lacking the aggressiveness, energy, willingness to undergo hardship and to work hard and long, patiently enduring the hours and days of drudgery over details that could not be neglected, he dreamed of making millions by successful speculation.

LOOKING FOR A SHORT CUT TO WEALTH

It is easy to see why a man of this type, with his futile dreams of easy conquests in the field of finance, should have scorned the slow and painful process of acquiring an education. Yet the tragedy of his life was that his only hope of usefulness in the world was through the careful cultivation and development of his really fine intellect. It is also easy to see why such a man would lack the patience to learn a trade even if he had had the manual skill to carry on any trade successfully-- which he had not. For the same reasons he would not take pains to qualify himself for any occupation, although he might have made a fair success in retail salesmanship perhaps, notwithstanding his far greater fitness for educational, ministerial, or platform work. On the contrary, he roamed about the country occupying himself at odd times with such bits of light mental or physical work as came his way. Being without training and taking no real interest in his work, he never retained any job long. Sometimes, lured by the will-o'-the-wisp of some fancied opportunity to make a million, he gave up his work. Sometimes he merely got tired of working and quit. But most often he was discharged for his incompetence. It is difficult indeed for any man to attend properly to the cent-a-piece details of an ordinary job when he is dreaming of the easy thousands he is going to make next week.

This charming gentleman was always out of funds. Although he carefully tonsured the ends of his trouser legs, inked the cuffs of his coat, blackened and polished his hose and even his own, fine, fair skin where it showed through the holes of his shoes, and turned his collars and ties again and again, he was nearly always shabby. On rare and ever rarer occasions he would do some relative or friend the inestimable favor and honor of accepting a small loan, "to be repaid in a few days, as soon as a big deal I now have under way is consummated." These loans were his only successes in the realm of practical finance. Inasmuch as the repayment of them was contingent upon the closing of an ever-imminent, but never consummated, "big deal," they cost him nothing for either principal or interest. For a few weeks after the successful negotiation of one of these loans, he would be resplendent, opulent, fastidious, even generous. All too soon the last dollar would slip through his unheeding fingers. If during a period of affluence he had succeeded in establishing a little semblance of credit, he would maintain his regal style of living as long as it lasted. Then he would come down to the hall bedroom or even the ten-cent lodging house, the lunch wagon, and the pawn shop. But even at the lowest ebb of his fortunes, he never seemed to lose his cheerfulness, his good nature, his grand manners, and his easy, confident hope and conviction about the huge sums that were to come into his possession "within a few days."

A DILETTANTE IN REAL ESTATE

Do not imagine that this man's dreams of great and easy fortunes were mere idle fancies--far from it. He was nearly always engaged in negotiations for some big deal. One of his favorite pastimes was to hunt up large holdings of real estate offered for sale, go to the owners, represent himself as a real estate broker, and secure permission to put these properties on his "list." This permission obtained, he would go about trying to find buyers. But his ideas of real estate values, of the adaptation of properties to purchasers, of the details of a real estate transaction and of salesmanship were so vague and so impractical that if he ever succeeded in selling a piece of real estate, we have not yet heard of it. He lacked the practical sense necessary to inform himself upon such important matters as taxes, assessments, insurance rates, trend of population, direction and character of commercial expansion, bank clearings, freight shipments, volume of retail and wholesale business, projected municipal and public service improvements, crop reports, output of manufacturers, and many other items which form the basis for intelligent negotiation, in a real estate deal. He could talk only in glittering generalities, and his suggestions were usually so impracticable that he failed to secure the confidence of those who were in a position to purchase properties so valuable as those he invariably hit upon for his ambitious projects.

AN UNDESERVED BAD REPUTATION

Here, then, was a man of unusual intelligence and capacity along theoretical, abstract, philosophical, and spiritual lines. His intentions were good. He was kindly, sympathetic, generous to a fault, refined, ambitious, high principled at heart and a thorough gentleman by birth, training, and instinct. Yet, because of a lack of clear knowledge, his life has been one of hardship, privation, disappointment, disillusionment, galling poverty, and utter failure. He has been subjected to ridicule and the even more blighting cruelty of good-natured, patronizing, contemptuous tolerance. His reputation is that of a lazy, good-for-nothing, disreputable dead beat and loafer. And yet, in a sense, nothing is further from the truth. Notwithstanding his many disappointments, no one could have been more sincere than he in believing that just around the corner fortune awaited him.

DIAGNOSIS OF THE IMPRACTICAL MAN'S CASE

The fundamental difficulty with the impractical man is two fold. First, his powers of observation are so deficient that it is difficult for him to obtain facts. It is an axiom of conscious life that there is pleasure and satisfaction in the use of well-developed powers and a disinclination to use powers which are deficient in development. Because it is difficult for the impractical man to obtain facts, he has little desire to obtain

147

them. He takes little interest in them, does not appreciate their value. He, therefore, assumes his facts, takes them for granted or proceeds almost wholly without them. Even when he does take the trouble to ascertain the facts, he is inclined to be hasty and slipshod in his methods. He, therefore does not obtain all of the necessary information bearing upon his problem. He does not painstakingly verify his knowledge through repeated observations, under all kinds of conditions. So he is frequently mistaken and reasons to his conclusions upon supposed facts which are not facts at all.

Second, the impractical man, as a general rule, has well-developed powers of reason, logic, and imagination. His mind easily and unerringly leaps from premises to conclusion and weaves long and beautiful chains of reasoning, each link perfectly formed. The only trouble is that none of the chains are attached to anything solid and substantial at either end. With highly developed powers of imagination, it follows that the impractical man loves to dream, to build castles in the air. When he attempts to form a judgment or reach a conclusion, he may possibly begin by attempting to ascertain the facts. But observation for him is a slow and painful process. He does not enjoy it. He has no patience with it. Mere facts restrict him. Practical reasoning is like walking painfully, step by step, along a narrow, steep pathway, leading to a fixed destination at which the traveler arrives whether he wills it or not. The impractical man's form of reasoning, starting at the same place, soars into the air, dips and sweeps in magnificent and inspiring curves and finally sets him down at whatever destination seems most desirable to him. His well-developed powers of imagination are usually more than willing to supply the deficiencies in his powers of observation. In his own realm he is a valuable member of society--often becomes rich and famous. But he is a misfit in any vocation which deals wholly with concrete things.

DESCRIPTION OF THE IMPRACTICAL MAN

The impractical man is easily recognized. He may be blonde or brunette, large or small, fine textured or coarse textured, energetic or lazy, aggressive or mild, friendly or unfriendly, ambitious or unambitious, honest or dishonest--but his mark is upon his forehead. If his brows are flat or if his forehead immediately above and at the sides of his eyes is undeveloped or only a little developed, his powers of observation are deficient. He is not interested in facts and his judgment is based upon hasty and mistaken premises. As a general rule, in such cases, the upper part of the forehead is well developed. This is always the case if the man is intelligent. If the forehead is both low and retreating and flat at the brows, then the individual lacks both power of observation and reasoning power, and is very deficient in intellect.

Figures 27 and 28 and 29 and 30 show some very common types of the impractical man. Note the flatness of the brows in every case. Figures 32, 50, and 54 show the foreheads of practical men.

CHAPTER IX

HUNGRY FOR FAME

The born artist has a passion for creation. This is true whether his art expresses itself through paints and brushes, through chisel and stone, on the stage, through musical tones, through bricks and mortar, or through the printed page. The born artist may or may not have, as companion to his passion for creation, a hunger for fame, an ear which adores applause. Few artists, however, have ever become famous who were not spurred on by an eager desire for the plaudits of their fellows.

It is possible to have the passion for creation without the hunger for fame. It is also possible to have a hunger for fame without the passion for creation. In the "Light That Failed," Kipling tells of little Maisie, who toiled and struggled, not to create beauty, but for success. Yet, poor Dick, who loved her, was forced to admit that there was no special reason why her work should be done at all.

Horace Annesley Vachell, in "Brothers," tells the story of Mark Samphire's tragedy. "When, after three years of most gruelling, hard work as an art student, he turned to his great master and asked: 'When you were here last you said to a friend of mine that it was fortunate for me that I had independent means. You are my master; you have seen everything I have done. Pynsent knows my work, too, every line of it. I ask you both: Am I wasting my time?'

"Neither answered.

"'No mediocre success will content me,' continued Mark. 'I ask you again: Am I wasting my time?'

"'Yes,' said the master gruffly. He put on his hat and went out.

"'He's not infallible,' Pynsent muttered angrily.

"'Then you advise me to go on? No, you are too honest to do that. I shall not go on, Pynsent; but I do not regret the last three years. They would have been wasted, indeed, if they had blinded me to the truth

149

concerning my powers.'"

WHEN THE DIVINE FIRE IS NOT AFLAME

The art schools of Paris! History, fiction, reminiscence, your own knowledge, perhaps your own experience, join in piling mountain-high the tale of wasted years, blasted ambitions, broken hopes and shattered ideals. Worse than this, perhaps, they tell of homes, galleries and shops disfigured with mediocre work and criminally hideous daubs.

The music studios of Paris, Berlin, New York, and other large cities, the schools of dramatic art, the theological seminaries, and the departments of literature in our universities could add their sad testimony. Theatrical managers, editors of magazines, publishers, art dealers, and lyceum bureaus are besieged by armies of aspiring misfits.

Probably there is no more difficult and hazardous undertaking in all the experience of the vocational counsellor than that presented by people of this type. The mere fact that a young man has painted scores of pictures which have been rejected has no bearing on the case. Artistic and literary history is studded with the glorious names of those who struggled through years of failure and rejection to final success. This is, in fact, true of nearly all of the great artists and writers. True, the mere dictum of any authority, however high, would have very little effect in turning the true creative artist from his life work, but what a pity it would have been if Richard Mansfield, Booth Tarkington, Mark Twain, and a host of others had paid any attention to the advice of those who told them they never could succeed! And yet, unless the vocational counsellor can encourage and urge on those who have the divine spark, and turn back from their quest those who have it not, he has failed in one of his most important tasks.

ELEMENTS OF SUCCESS IN ART

Let us, therefore, examine some of the elements of success in art. We have seen that the born artist has a passion for creation. He *must* draw, or paint, or act, or sing, or write. That which is within him demands expression and will not be denied. His love is for the work and not for the reward or the applause. These are but incidental. His visions and dreams are of ever greater achievements and not of an ever increasing income or wider popularity. Work well done and the conscious approval of his own mind are the sweetest nectar to his soul.

But this passion of creation is, perhaps, not enough in itself. "Art is a jealous mistress." Even the passion for creation must wait upon slowly and painfully acquired technique, and, in the case of painting,

150

sculpture, instrumental music, and some other forms of art, upon inherent capacity and manual skill. Many an artist's soul is imprisoned in a clumsy body which will not do its bidding.

"Art is long," and he who is unwilling or unable to keep alive the divine spark through years of poverty had better turn back before he sets forth upon the great adventure. Searching the portraits of the world's great artists, living and dead, you will not find a lazy man amongst them.

AN ATTEMPT TO MIX INDOLENCE AND POETRY

During our school days we made the acquaintance of Larime Hutchinson, then a lad of twenty, shy, self-conscious, pathetically credulous, and hobbled by a prodigious ineptitude which made him a favorite butt for schoolboy jokes and pranks. Larime was in great disfavor with the teachers because he almost never had his lessons. He was also in disfavor with the college treasurer because he did not pay his bills. Larime's father was a country minister and could send him only a few dollars a month. The rest of his financial necessities he was supposed to meet by sawing wood, mowing lawns, attending furnaces, and other such odd jobs. But Larime never could hold these jobs because he was too lazy to do them well. He was also in high disfavor with his schoolmates, first, because of his timidity and self-consciousness; second, because of the strange air of superiority which, paradoxically enough, he managed to affect even in spite of these handicaps. A little confidential consorting with this peculiar young man soon revealed the fact that he yearned to be heralded with great acclaim as "The Poet of the New World." Not only did he yearn; he confidently expected it. Nay, more; he already was "The Poet of the New World," and awaited only the day of his acknowledgment by those who, despite their prejudices and envy, would eventually be compelled to accord him his true position. To prove his claims, Larime read us some of his "poetry." It was bad, very bad, and yet it was not quite bad enough to be good.

Such visions of glory as obscured Larime Hutchinson's sensible view of the practical world are, perhaps, common enough in adolescence, and, as a general rule, work no serious harm. There were, however, two fatal defects of character in this case. The first was that Larime continued to dream and to write what he thought was verse, when he ought to have been at work plowing corn, for he had qualities which, with industry, would have made him a successful farmer. Second, he was mentally too lazy for the drudgery even the greatest poet must perform if he is to perfect his technique.

151

A MIND FOCUSSED ON DETAILS

The case of Marshall Mears, a young man who consulted us a few years ago with reference to his ambition to become a journalist and author, well illustrates a different phase of this same problem. This young man was of the tall, raw-boned, vigorous, active, energetic, industrious type. There was not a lazy bone in his body. In addition to his energy, he had unusual powers of endurance, so that he could work fifteen, eighteen, or twenty hours a day for weeks at a time without seeming to show any signs of fatigue. He was ambitious for success as a writer. He was willing to work, to work hard, to work long, to wait for recognition through years of constant effort. He had secured a fairly good education and, in many ways, seemed well fitted for the vocation he had chosen to pursue.

A careful examination, however, showed two fundamental deficiencies in Marshall Mears which training could only partially overcome. First, his was one of those narrow-gauge, single-track minds. He was incapable of any breadth of vision. His mind was completely obsessed with details. He would go to a lecture, or to a play, and invariably, instead of grasping the main argument of the lecture, or the lesson of the play, he saw only a few inconsequential details of action in the play, and remembered only stray and somewhat irrelevant statements made by the lecturer. A novel or an essay appealed to him in the same way. Present to him a business proposition and his whole attention would be absorbed by some chance remark. He was a devoted admirer of the late Elbert Hubbard and he had longed for years to hear the great man lecture. Finally his opportunity came and he was greatly elated, and not a little excited, as he looked forward to what he believed to be one of the treats of a lifetime. When he returned from the lecture, as we had feared, instead of being uplifted and delighted, he was manifestly disappointed.

"Didn't you like the lecture?" we asked.

"I cannot understand," he complained, "why as intelligent a man as Hubbard should split his infinitives."

Naturally, a man with a mind like this could not construct a plot or outline an article. His writings, like his conversations, were long drawn out, meandering and painfully tiresome recitations of trifling and, for the most part, irrelevant detail.

We counselled him to lay aside his pen and take hold of plow handles instead. He has since become a successful farmer, perfectly happy, working out all the infinitude of minutiae in connection with the intensive cultivation of small fruits.

LACK OF DISCRIMINATION A HANDICAP

Still another phase of this problem is presented by the case of N.J.F. This man also wanted to be an editor and writer. He was a big, fine-looking fellow, fairly well educated, had some ability in written expression, and frequent good ideas. With his aptitudes, training, and talents, it seemed, at first sight, that he certainly ought to be able to succeed in an editorial capacity. Further examination showed, however, a lamentable lack of discrimination, a deficient sense of the fitness of things, and consequently, unreliable judgment. These deficiencies are worse than handicaps to an editor. They are absolute disqualifications. An editor's first duty is to discriminate, to sift, to winnow the few grains of wheat out of the bushels of chaff that come to his mill. Editors must have a very keen sense of the fitness of things. It is true that the discriminating reader of newspapers and magazines may be tempted to feel at times that this sense of the fitness of things is very rare in editors. Unquestionably, it could be improved in many cases, and yet, on the whole, it must be admitted that newspaper and magazine editors perform at least one important function with a very fair degree of acceptability, namely, they purvey material which is at least interesting to the particular class of readers to whom they wish to appeal. If readers could be induced to wade through for a week the masses of uninteresting material which is submitted, they would doubtless have far greater respect for the intelligence, criticism, peculiarities, and sense of fitness of things of the editors.

But we digress. N.J.F. was incapable of sound judgment, not because he did not know the facts, but because, instead of reasoning logically to his conclusion, in accordance with the facts, he was entirely governed by his rather erratic feelings. In other words, he could not reason well from cause to effect; he did not understand people, and so could not sense what would interest them, and his powers of criticism, such as he possessed, were destructive rather than constructive.

Contrary to our advice, N.J.F. persisted in his editorial ambitions and in time managed to persuade the owner of a certain publication to entrust him with its editorial management. Almost immediately the periodical began to lose subscribers. Down, down, down went its circulation until it almost reached the vanishing point. Finally, it expired. The trouble was not that its pages contained anything bad, harmful or illiterate, but simply that there was page after page of dry, discursive, uninteresting, valueless material. It was a pity, because, under a competent editor, the periodical in question had occupied an important and useful place in the current literature of the period, and also because, as a dealer in coal, lumber, lime, and building materials, N.J. F. would have been a useful and successful member of the community.

[Illustration: FIG. 33. John Masefield, Poet. Idealistic, sentimental, dreamy, impractical, but intensely responsive to beauty, rhythm and imagery. Has creative power. Note high, straight forehead, very high head, fine texture, finely chiseled features, and dreamy, mystic expression.]

[Illustration: FIG. 34. Edward DeReszke, Opera Singer. Great artistic and musical talent, with capacity for sentiment and emotion. Note width of brows; dome of head over temples; fulness of eyes, curves of nose, cheeks and lips, Also large physical frame, especially chest and abdomen.]

[Illustration: _Copyright by A. Dupont, N.Y._ FIG. 35. Puccini. Composer. Has artistic talent and creative ability together with, energy, ambition, persistence, courage, determination. Rather mild in disposition. Not a particularly good business man. More interested in music than in money. Note width of forehead at eyes and at upper corners and its narrowness between; high nose; brunette color; square, strong jaw and chin; straight, firm mouth, and calm, determined expression.]

[Illustration: FIG. 36. John S. Sargent, R.A., Portrait Painter. Keen powers of observation, high ambition, great energy, fine discrimination, excellent powers of expression, and social qualities. Note unusual development of brows, height of head; fulness of forehead at center; fulness of eyes, large, high nose, and fulness of backhead.]

[Illustration: _Photo by American Press Association._ FIG. 37. Pietro Mascagni. Composer. Musical, emotional sensuous, impulsive, spasmodically energetic. Note width of forehead at brows, full lips, dimpled chin, heavy cheeks, thick-lidded eyes, large nose, and intense, ardent expression.]

[Illustration: FIG. 38. Richard Burton. Author. Has fine, sentimental, idealistic, artistic and literary talents, intellectual, creative and inventive ability, together with energy, determination, and ambition. Note height and width of forehead; fulness back of upper corners; large, but finely chiseled features, and thoughtfully intense, but calm, serious, poised expression.]

154

[Illustration: FIG. 39. Mendelssohn, Composer. Very refined, sensitive, responsive, emotional and delighted with appreciation and applause. Creative, musical, capable of great industry and perseverance. Note width of forehead at brows; large, glowing eyes; finely chiseled, regular features; short upper lip; beautifully curved lips; high head, rounded above temples. Compare this with Figure 20.]

[Illustration: FIG. 40. Massenet, Composer. Artistic ability, backed up by ambition, energy, determination, courage, and persistence. Note width of lower portion of forehead; large, well-formed nose; firm mouth, jaw and chin; height and width of head; square hands and finger-tips. Also very emotional and intense nature. Note round, dome-shaped head, smooth fingers, and dreamy expression.]

THE INSANITY OF GENIUS

The greatest artists, musicians, writers, and thinkers are men of genius and are, therefore, in a sense, abnormal. Lombroso, in his work, "The Man of Genius," produces a great deal of interesting evidence showing the similarity between the manifestations of genius and those of insanity. Lombroso's conclusions have been more or less discredited, but later investigations and practically all students agree that the true genius is more or less an abnormality. In his case, some one or two faculties are developed out of all reasonable proportion to the others. Naturally enough, in such cases there is no need for a vocational counsellor. The genius devotes himself to his music, or his painting, or his writing, because there is nothing else he can do, nothing else in which he takes any interest, and because the inner urge is so powerful as to be irresistible.

But grossly deceived are those who imagine that the fire of genius burns away any necessity for drudgery. On the other hand, genius seems to consist very largely of a capacity for almost infinite drudgery. A prominent engineer once said to us that all great inventions which become commercially practicable are the joint product of a genius and a drudge, or rather, of a genius and a corps of drudges. The genius, in a flash of inspiration, conceives a new idea. Having conceived it, he can only sit down and wait for a new inspiration, while the drudges take his idea, work out its details, modify and conform it to conditions, and, finally, harness it to the commercial wagon. This sounded well and has a great deal of truth in it. Yet the most slavish drudge in the Edison laboratories and factories is Edison himself. The hardest worker in all the Westinghouse plant was Westinghouse. And who but the Wright brothers themselves made a commercial success of the aeroplane?

155

Sometimes, it is true, one man conceives an idea which he is unable to work out and which must be made practical by others, but more often than not he stumbles on the idea more by accident than because he is looking for it. So the young man or the young woman who has hopes of winning fame in the world of art, music, or literature should assay himself or herself first of all for a willingness to work, to work hard, and to work endlessly.

INDICATIONS OF ENERGY

Such energy is indicated by the large nose, high in the bridge, which admits large quantities of oxygen into the lungs; by high cheek bones, oftentimes by a head wide just above the ears, by square hands and square-tipped fingers, by hard or elastic consistency of fibre. Persistence and patience are indicated by brunette coloring and plodding by a well-developed and rather prominent jaw and chin. Havelock Ellis and other anthropologists have noted the fact that dark coloring is more frequently found in artists and actors than light hair, eyes, and skin.

Artistic, musical, and literary ability are as various in their indications as they are in their manifestations. One man is a painter, another a sculptor, another an architect. One man paints flowers, another landscapes, another portraits, another allegorical scenes, and still another the rough, virile, vigorous, or even horrible and gruesome aspects of life. One musician sings, another plays the violin, still another the piano, and another the pipe organ. One conducts a grand opera, another conducts a choir. One musician composes lyrics, another oratorios, another ragtime, and still another symphonies. One man writes poetry, another stories, another essays, another history, another philosophy, and still another the hard, dry, mathematical facts of science. Obviously, it would only confuse the reader were we to attempt to describe the physical appearance of all these different classes.

INDICATIONS OF ARTISTIC TEMPERAMENT

In general, we may say that an appreciation of form, color, proportion, size, and distance is indicated by well-developed brows, broad and full at the outer angles, and by eyes set rather widely apart. But size, form, color, and proportion are but the mediums through which the artist's soul conveys its message. Whether or not one has the soul which can conceive a worthy message is indicated by the expression of the eyes, an expression which cannot be described but which, once seen and recognized, can never afterward be mistaken.

Inherent capacity for music is indicated by a forehead wide at the brows. Going over the portraits of all the famous composers and performers, you will find that while they differ in most other particulars, they are all alike in the proportionate width of the forehead at the brows. The kind and quality of music one may create depends partially upon training and partially upon the kind and quality of his soul, which, again, expresses itself in the eyes.

Capacity for literature and expression is indicated by fulness of the eye, by heighth and width of the forehead, and, perhaps, especially by the development of the head and forehead at the sides just above the temples and back of the hair line. Any portrait gallery of great authors will show this development in nine out of ten (see figures).

The artistic, musical, or literary man with fine, silken hair, fine, delicate skin, small and finely chiselled features, and a general daintiness of build will express refinement, beauty, tender sentiments, and sensitiveness in his work, while the man with coarse, bushy or wavy hair, coarse, thick skin, large, rugged features, and a general ruggedness and clumsiness of build, even when his size is small, will express vigor, virility, ruggedness, and even gruesomeness and horror, in his work. There may be in his productions a wild, virile type of beauty, as in the music of Wagner and the sculpture of Rodin, but the keynote of his work is elemental force.

The dilettante has conical hands, with small, tapering fingers; this is the hand which is popularly supposed to accompany artistic temperament. He loves art. He appreciates art. He may even win fame and fortune as a competent critic of art, but he cannot create it. Your true artist has square, competent hands, with blunt, square-tipped fingers. The hands shown in figure 57 page 317 are those of a music lover who can neither play nor sing. Those in figure 58 are the hands of a true artist on the piano and pipe organ. The true producing artist nearly always has square hands, with large thumbs set near the wrist, thus giving a wide reach between tip of thumb and tip of forefinger, as shown in figure 58. Actors and operatic singers sometimes have conical hands, with tapering fingers. They express emotion and beauty with voice, gesture, and facial expression rather than with their hands.

In the world of art and literature many are called but few are chosen. The pathway to the heights is steep and rugged and there are many pitfalls. There are many by-paths. Furthermore, it is cold and lonesome on the mountain-top. Before anyone sets out on the perilous journey he should read Jack London's "Martin Eden," Louis M. Alcott's autobiography, the story of Holman Hunt, the Autobiography of Benjamin Franklin, and the biographies of others who have attained fame in these fields.

CHAPTER X

WASTE OF TALENT IN THE PROFESSIONS

In the old days the physician was often a priest. There was mystery, magic, authority, and power in the profession. There were almost royal privileges, prerogatives, robes, insignia, and emoluments.

Humanity sheds its superstitions slowly. Science and common sense have smitten and shattered them for centuries, yet many fragments remain. And so there is still a good deal of mysticism, magic, and awe connected with both the art of healing and the priesthood. Hence, the lure of these professions. Romantic and ambitious youth longs to enter into the holy of holies, looks forward with trembling eagerness to the day when authority shall clothe him like a garment, when his simple-hearted people, gathered about him, will look up to him with adoration in eyes which say, "When you speak, God speaks."

There are other appeals to aspiration in the professions. When the layman seeks for social preferment, he must bring with him either the certificate of gentle birth or the indorsement of his banker. The professional man has a standing, however, far in excess of what he might command as the result of his financial standing.

The profession of law, in like manner, has, in the minds of the common people, always set a man apart from his fellows. About his profession, too, there is the charm of mystery, the thought of thrilling flights of oratory and high adventure in the courts of law, of opportunities for great financial success, and for political preferment.

Of late years the profession of engineering has called to the youth of the land with an almost irresistible voice. The development of steam and gasoline engines, of the electric current, and of a welter of machinery called for engineers. The specialization of engineering practice into production, chemical, industrial, municipal, efficiency, mining, construction, concrete, drainage, irrigation, landscape, and other phases, has still further increased the demand. Some few

158

engineers, by means of keen financial ability in addition to extraordinary powers in the engineering field, have made themselves names of international fame, as well as great fortunes. All these things have fired the ambitions of our youth, and the engineering schools are full.

OVER-CROWDING OF THE MEDICAL PROFESSION

Our colleges and universities, in their academic courses, do not fit their students for business, neither do they fit them for any of the professions. They are graduated "neither fish, nor fowl, nor good red herring," so far as vocation goes. Being an educated man, in his own estimation, the bearer of a college degree cannot go into business, he cannot "go back" into manual labor. So he must go forward. There is no way for him to go forward, so far as he knows, except to enter some technical school and prepare himself for one of the "learned professions."

Go into the graduating class in any college or university, and ask the young men what their plans for the future are. How many of them will reply that they are going into business? How many of them that they are going into agriculture? How many that they are going into manufacturing? Our experience is a very small percentage. Many of them have not yet made up their minds what they will do. The great majority of those who have made up their minds are headed toward the law, medicine, the ministry, or engineering. This is a great pity. Why should the teachers and counselors of these young men encourage them in preparing themselves for professions which are already over-crowded and which bid fair, within the next ten years, to become still more seriously congested? Perhaps the professors do not know these things. If so, a little common sense would suggest that it is their business to find out. Nor would the truth be difficult to learn.

In "Increasing Home Efficiency," by Martha Brensley Bruere and Robert W. Bruere, we read:

"We have pretty definitely grasped the idea that the labor market must be organized, because it is for the social advantage that the trades should be neither over-nor under-supplied with workers; but it seems to shock people inexpressibly to think that the demand for ministers and teachers and doctors should be put in the class with that for bricklayers and plumbers. And yet the problem is quite as acute in the middle class as among the wage-workers. Take the profession of medicine, for instance, a calling of the social value of which there can be no question, and which is largely recruited from the middle class. The introduction

159

of the Carnegie Foundation's Report on Medical Education says:

"'In a society constituted as are our Middle States, the interests of the social order will he served best when the number of men entering a given profession reaches and does not exceed a certain ratio.... For twenty-five years past there has been an enormous over-production of medical practitioners. This has been in absolute disregard of the public welfare. Taking the United States as a whole, physicians are four or five times as numerous in proportion to population as in older countries, like Germany.... In a town of 2,000 people one will find in most of our States from five to eight physicians, where two well-trained men could do the work efficiently and make a competent livelihood. When, however, six or eight physicians undertake to gain a living in a town which will support only two, the whole plane of professional conduct is lowered in the struggle which ensues, each man becomes intent upon his own practice, public health and sanitation are neglected, and the ideals and standards of the profession tend to demoralization.... It seems clear that as nations advance in civilization they will be driven to ... limit the number of those who enter (the professions) to some reasonable estimate of the number who are actually needed,'

"And in the face of this there were, in 1910, 23,927 students in preparation to further congest the profession of medicine! It's an inexcusable waste, for, though there's much the statistician hasn't done, there's little he can't do when he sets his mind to it. If he can estimate the market for the output of a shoe factory, why not the market for the output of a professional school? It ought to be possible to tell how many crown fillings the people of Omaha will need in their teeth in 1920 and just how many dentists must be graduated from the dental schools in time to do it."

PROBLEMS FOR LAWYERS AND PREACHERS

So much for the physician. While we have not at hand any exact statistics in regard to lawyers, there is a pretty general feeling amongst all who have studied the subject that the legal profession is even more over-crowded than the medical. God alone knows all the wickednesses that are perpetrated in this old world because there are too many lawyers for proper and necessary legal work and so, many of them live just as close to the dead line of professional ethics as is possible without actual disbarment. And yet, with all their devices and vices, the average lawyer is compelled to get along upon an income of less than $1,000 a year.

The ministry is, perhaps, even more over-crowded than either medicine or law. There are several reasons for this. In the first place, there are from four to a dozen churches in most places where one would render far better service. These churches are, many of them, poorly supported, and, therefore, inefficient. Yet each must have a pastor. Second, the fact that a theological or pre-theological student can secure aid in pursuing his education tempts many young men into the ministry. Recently a university student called upon us. He told us he was working his way through the university by supplying pulpits on Sunday. "But it's hard work," he confessed, "particularly when one must enthusiastically proclaim things he does not believe." This young man was, doubtless, an exception, but we have seen many poorly equipped for the ministry, "studying theology because they could not afford to take some other post-graduate work."

How greatly over-crowded this ancient and honorable profession has become may be guessed by the fact that a fine, intelligent man may spend four years in preparatory school, four years in college, and three years in a theological seminary, may acquire twenty-five years of successful experience, and still receive for his services only $500 a year. Moreover, he is expected to contribute to the cause not only all his own time and talent, but also the services of his wife and children. This, of course, is pretty close to the minimum salary, but the great majority of ecclesiastical salaries range very low--nor have they responded to the increase in the cost of living.

After all, the question is not one of the over-crowding of a profession, but of fitness for success in it. No matter how many may be seeking careers in any profession, the great majority are mediocre or worse, and the man with unusual aptitude and ability to work and work hard easily outstrips his fellows and finds both fame and fortune. The trouble is that the lure of the professions takes thousands of men into them who are better fitted for business, for mechanics, for agriculture, and for other vocations.

SUCCESSFUL, BUT NOT SATISFIED

Because they have the capacity to work hard, because they are conscientious and because they have some ordinary intellect and common sense, many men make a fair success in medicine, in the law, in the ministry, as college professors, as engineers, or in some other profession. All through their lives, however, they have the feeling that they are not doing their best work, that they would be better off, better satisfied, and happier if engaged in some other vocation. How well every true man knows that it is not enough to have kept the wolf from the door, it is not enough even to have piled up a little ahead. Every man of red blood and backbone wants to do his best work, wants to do work that he loves, work into which he can throw himself with heart and soul and with all his mind and strength. Merely to muddle through with some half-detested work, not making an utter failure of it, is no satisfaction when the day's work is done. Not only the man himself, but all of us, lose when he who might have been a great manufacturer and organizer of industry fritters away his life and his talents as a "pretty good doctor" or a "fair sort of lawyer."

Judge Elbert H. Gary was far from being a failure as a lawyer. Yet his life might have been a failure in the law in comparison to what he has accomplished and is accomplishing as the great head and organizer of the largest steel business in the United States. Oliver Wendell Holmes was successful as a physician and yet what would the world have lost if he had devoted his entire time and attention to the practice of medicine! Glen Buck once studied for the ministry. Imagine big, liberty-loving, outspoken Glen Buck trying to speak the truth as God gave him to see the truth and at the same time keep his artistic, literary, financial, and dramatic talents confined within the limits of a pastor's activities. So it is that some men are too meek and too small for the professions--others too aggressive, too versatile, and too independent for the routine of professional life. Still others have decided talents which qualify them for unusual success in other vocations. If a man has unusual intellectual attainment, he either does or does not acquire extensive education. If he does not, the probabilities are that he will enter business; he will become a merchant, a manufacturer, a promoter, a banker, or a railroad man. In some one of the departments of industry, commerce, transportation, or finance, he makes a place for himself by hard work, beginning at the bottom. If, on the other hand, circumstances are such that he can secure an education, then he passes by business, manufacturing, transportation, finance; he must forsooth become a doctor, a lawyer, a preacher, an editor, or an engineer. The question of vocation is thus, all too often, decided by the incident of education and not according to natural aptitudes.

INDICATIONS OF SUCCESS IN MEDICINE

The young man who is ambitious to enter upon a profession ought to study himself carefully before beginning his preparation. He ought to know, not guess, whether he is qualified for the highest form of success in his chosen vocation. And there is no reason why he should not know. In the appendix to this work we have outlined the leading characteristics required for success in medicine. Some of these are absolutely essential--others contributory. Among the essentials are health, a scientific mind, pleasure in dealing with people in an intimate way, ability to inspire confidence, and courage. Many a young man has taken highest honors in medical school only to fail in practice because he could not handle people successfully, or because he lacked the courage to face the constant reiteration of complaints and suffering by his patients. Sick people are selfish, peevish, whimsical, and babyish. It takes tact, patience, understanding, and good nature to handle them successfully.

INDICATIONS FOR SUCCESS IN LAW

It takes a combination of fox and lion to make a successful lawyer. And yet we are besieged with sheep and rabbits who are eager to enter law school or who have passed through law school and are wondering why they do not succeed in their profession.

There are at least two general types of lawyers, the court or trial lawyer and the counselor. The first must be a true catechist, a convincing public speaker, keen, alert, resourceful, self-confident, courageous, with a considerable degree of poise and self-control. He may be either aggressive, belligerent, and combative, or mild, persuasive, and non-resistant, but shrewd, intelligent, resourceful. A timid, dreamy, credulous man has no business in the law. A lawyer may love peace, but he should be willing to fight for it.

Because legal ethics forbid a lawyer to advertise or solicit business openly, it is necessary for him to secure a standing and clientele by indirect methods. Best of these is making and keeping friends, by mingling with all classes and conditions of people, by political activity, and in other ways making one's self agreeable and useful in the community. Thus a lawyer draws to himself the attention of the most desirable class of people. In order to be successful in this, the lawyer must possess qualities of sociability and friendship. A man who is not naturally social or friendly is not well qualified for any profession. Unless he intends to work with a partner who has these qualifications, and who will be the business getter of the firm, he would better leave the law alone.

INDICATIONS OF JUDICIAL QUALITIES

The second class of lawyer, the counsellor, is more of the judicial type. He is quite likely to be stout or to have the indications of approaching stoutness. He should be calm, deliberate, cautious, prudent, capable of handling details, a man with a splendid memory and with the capacity

163

for acquiring a great fund of knowledge about all kinds of things. He should be able to take an interest in almost any kind of business or profession and quickly master its fundamentals.

A MISFIT IN THE LAW

Men of the high-strung, nervous, timid, self-conscious, sentimental class are sadly out of place in the law. While they may be abundantly well equipped for success from an intellectual standpoint, physically and emotionally they are utterly unfit for it. A young man once sought us for counsel who had spent many years in colleges and universities acquiring one of the finest legal educations possible in this country. Because of his intellectual equipment, the study of the law was fascinating to him, and both his parents and his professors in law school expected him to make a brilliant success in practice. What was his intense disappointment, as well as theirs, when he opened an office, to find that almost everything connected with the practice of law was distasteful to him, so that he found himself incapable of doing it successfully. For several years he had made a desperate attempt to succeed and to learn to like his profession, but every day only made him hate it more ardently. As a natural result he did poorer and poorer work at it.

It was no wonder to us that this young man did not like the practice of law. In the first place, he was fond of change and variety. His was not a nature which could address itself to one task and concentrate upon that hour after hour and day after day, such as carefully scrutinizing every detail of a case and perfecting his preparation of it for presentation in court. In the second place, his was an unusually sensitive, refined, responsive, and sentimental disposition. So fine were his emotional sensibilities that it was almost more than he could endure to hear--as he was compelled to day after day--the seamy, inharmonious, sordid, and criminal side of life. The recital and consideration of these things depressed him, made him morbid and sapped his vitality and courage. For the swift repartee, keen combat, and mutual incriminations of the court room he was utterly unfitted. Any criticism was taken personally. He found it impossible to let the jibes, criticisms, and heated words of his opponents trickle off from him as easily as water does from a duck's back, which is the proper legal mental attitude in regard to such things. He told us that sharp, harsh, or bitter words entered his soul like barbed iron and he was upset and unstrung for hours afterward. A man with such an emotional nature as his and such an intellect is especially qualified for literature, and we are glad to say that he is now making a very flattering success in this particular field.

164

INDICATIONS FOR SUCCESS IN THE MINISTRY

Aside from spiritual qualifications, success in the ministry depends chiefly upon two talents: First, ability to speak well in public; second, social adaptability. The second is perhaps the more important. We have heard many ministers who were only indifferent public speakers, but who made a great success of their callings because of their social aptitudes, their ability to meet and mingle with all kinds of people, their cheerfulness, their optimism, their helpfulness, their tact and diplomacy. A traveling evangelist may depend principally upon his power as a public speaker, but the pastor of a church must depend far more upon his ability to make and keep friends among the members of his congregation and in the community.

The minister, of all the professional men, is most in need of ambition, a desire to please others and to help others, spiritual quality, humanitarianism, benevolence, faith, hope, veneration for the Deity, and for the supernatural elements of religion. The day has gone by when the solemn, joyless preacher can command a large congregation. People to-day want a religion which is bright and cheerful, which offers a surcease from the cares and sorrows of ordinary life. They want to be cheered, encouraged, inspired, and uplifted, rather than depressed and made sad and melancholy. Therefore, the successful preacher will not permit his intense conviction of the seriousness, earnestness, and solemnity of his calling interfere with his exhibiting always a bright, cheerful, and attractive personality.

To be successful the pastor must take an interest in all the members of his congregation; he must sympathize with them, mourn with them when they mourn, rejoice with them when they rejoice, cheer them when they are discouraged, counsel them when they are perplexed. Indeed, he must enter into their lives fully and wholly, also tactfully and diplomatically.

Perhaps the most successful preachers of the day are medium or blond in color. While those of dark complexion, dark eyes and dark hair, are more inclined to be religious, more inclined to take life seriously, more inclined to look forward and upward to the spiritual and the supernatural, and are also more studious, more capable of deep research and profound meditation, they do not, as a rule, have the social qualities, the aggressiveness, the cheerfulness, and the adaptability of the lighter complexioned people.

INDICATIONS FOR SUCCESS IN ENGINEERING

When engineering first became a profession there were only two classes of engineers, the civil and the military. Engineers in those days were chiefly concerned with the making of surveys and the construction of roads and bridges. The steam engine had not yet been made a commercial possibility, therefore there was almost no machinery in existence, and such little as there was did not require a professional engineer for its designing or operation. Nothing was known of electricity. Very little was known of chemistry and almost nothing was known of industry as it has been organized to-day. Since that time there has been an almost incredible development along all of these lines. As the result we now have almost as many kinds of engineers as there are classes of industry. There is the civil engineer, the mining engineer, the construction, the irrigation, the drainage, the sewage disposal, the gas production, the hydraulic, the chemical, the electrical, the mechanical, the industrial, the efficiency, the production, the illuminating, the automobile, the aeroplane, the marine, the submarine, and who knows how many other kinds. Indeed, there are also social engineers, merchandising engineers, advertising engineers, and even religious engineers. Naturally, it requires a slightly different kind of man to succeed in each one of the different branches of engineering, and it would be too great a task for the reader to try to wade through all of the qualifications here. It would also, no doubt, only result in confusion and a lack of understanding of the real fundamentals.

Fundamentally the engineer should be medium in coloring. The extreme blond is too changeable and usually not fond enough of detail to succeed in a profession which requires so much concentration and accuracy. Practically all successful engineers have the practical, scientific type of forehead. By this we mean the forehead which is prominent at the brows and, while high, slopes backward from the brows. Usually those succeed best in engineering who are medium in texture. The fine-textured individual, however, if he is qualified for engineering, will take up some of the finer, higher grades of it and make fine and delicate material or machinery, or will engage in some form of engineering which requires only intellectual work. Practically all successful engineers are of the bony and muscular type or some modification of this type. This is the type which naturally takes interest in construction, in machinery, and in material accomplishment and achievement. Engineering practice usually requires painstaking accuracy and exactitude. Indeed, this is perhaps more than any other one qualification fundamental for success in engineering.

THE PROFESSIONAL TYPE

166

This, then, is the composite photograph of the successful professional man: He is more mental than physical; more scientific, philosophic, humanitarian, and idealistic than commercial; more social and friendly than exclusive and reserved; more ambitious for professional high standing or achievement than for wealth or power. Unless the aspirant to professional honors has some or all of these qualifications in a considerable degree, he would better turn his attention to some other vocation where there is not so much competition. Those who have some, but not all, of these qualities would do well in other vocations, such as literature, finance, commerce, or manufacture. Many physicians become authors, inventors, or financiers; many lawyers become financiers or manufacturers; many engineers become good advertising men, manufacturers, or merchants. All such would have done better to begin in the vocation to which they afterward turned.

A good rule for the young man or the young woman to follow is to make up his or her mind to enter some other vocation rather than a profession unless he or she is markedly well qualified to outdistance the crowd of mediocre competitors and make an unusual success.

[Illustration: *Photo by Paul Thompson.* FIG. 41. Front face view of ex-Senator Root. The width of head, large, but well-formed and well-balanced features, firm mouth, chin and jaw, and expression of alertness and confident strength all indicate the unusually well qualified executive.]

[Illustration: _Copyright, by Rockland, New York_. FIG. 42. Rev. Henry Ward Beecher. A man of marked personality, shrewdness, ambition, courage, determination, self-reliance, persistence, and energy. Added to these were humanitarianism, reverence, optimism, kindliness, humor, eloquence, and organizing ability. Note high, dome-like head; prominent brows; fulness of the eyes and surrounding tissues; large, bony nose; long upper lip; firm mouth; square jaw and prominent chin; large, well-formed ears; short fingers, and shrewd, kindly expression.]

[Illustration: FIG. 43. Rufus Isaacs, Baron Reading, Lord Chief Justice of England. Keen, penetrating, alert, analytical, resolute, self-reliant, courageous, persistent, non-sentimental, practical financial. Note comparatively low, wide forehead, long upper lip, thin lips, square-set jaw and chin, long, large nose, with somewhat depressed tip, large ears, and flatness of the top of the head.]

[Illustration: _Copyright by Harris & Ewing, Washington, D. C_. FIG. 44. Hon. Elihu Root, former United States Senator from New York.

Practical, energetic, ambitious, intellectual, with courage, critical faculties, ambition, shrewdness, idealism, and a keen knowledge of human nature in excellent balance. Note high, long head; high forehead, prominent at brows, large, well-formed nose; prominent chin, general splendid balance of head and face proportions, and calm, poised, but keen and forceful expression.]

[Illustration: FIG. 45. Harland B. Howe, Lawyer. Practical, matter-of-fact, shrewd, non-sentimental, energetic, ambitious, determined, and courageous. Note wide, high forehead; prominent at brows rather square above; high head, large nose, short, thin upper lip, and square, prominent jaw and chin.]

[Illustration: _Copyright by Harris & Ewing, Washington, D. C_. FIG. 46. The late Justice Horace H. Lurton, of the United States Supreme Court. Excellent example of judicial type. Practical, matter-of-fact, comparatively unemotional, calm and poised. Note prominence at brows, comparative flatness just above temples, strong jaw and chin, calm, unwavering expression.]

[Illustration: *Photo by Pach*. FIG. 47. Prof. William H. Burr, of Columbia University. Member of Isthmian Canal Commission. A fine example of professional type. Great intellect, energy, ambition, shrewdness, determination, and constancy, with refinement, idealism, sympathy, and friendliness. Note high, full forehead; large, long, but finely chiseled, nose; high head, narrow and straight at sides; fine texture; friendly expression.]

[Illustration: FIG. 48. Hon. John Wesley Gaines, Ex-Congressman from Tennessee. A fine example of the dramatic orator and politician. Refined, sensitive, responsive, courageous, ambitious, energetic, friendly. Note high, long head, prominent nose, short upper lip, prominent chin, finely chiseled features, and spirited expression.]

CHAPTER XI

WOMEN'S WORK

This chapter is not written for the purpose of adding one whisper to the impassioned controversies at present raging over women's work. So far as it is within our power, we shall refrain from taking sides with either that army which contends that woman is in every way the equal of man and should be permitted to engage in all of man's activities on an equal footing with him, or with that other army which declares that woman's place is the home and that every woman should be a wife, mother, and housekeeper.

Doubtless there are many wholesome and needed reforms being agitated with reference to women's work. Doubtless, also, there are many pernicious changes being advocated by both the sincere but mistaken and the vicious and designing. It is not the purpose of this chapter to discuss these reforms or to favor or to oppose any of them. We shall, in this chapter, discuss the problem of vocation for women under present conditions.

BROAD SCOPE OF WOMEN'S WORK

The present day finds women at work in practically every field of human endeavor. There is no profession, business, trade, or calling which does not count women amongst its successful representatives. Nor does the fact that a woman has married, has a home and children, debar her from achievement in any vocation outside the home which she may choose. Madam Ernestine Schuman-Heinck, with her eight children; Elizabeth Cady Stanton, with her ten children; Katherine Booth-Clibborn, with her ten children; Ethel Barrymore, with her family; Mrs. Netscher, proprietor of the Boston Store in Chicago, with her family; Mary Roberts Rhinehart, with her children; Madam Louise Homer, with her little flock, and thousands of others are examples of women who have been successful not only as home-makers but also in art, literature, professional or commercial vocations.

Since this is true, it follows that, theoretically at least, woman may choose her profession in precisely the same way that man chooses his. Practically, however, this is not true in most cases. Undoubtedly, a very large majority of women have happily married, are sufficiently provided for, and are happier, healthier, more useful, and better satisfied with life in the home than anywhere else. Notwithstanding the fact that our girls, almost without exception, enter upon the important vocation of wifehood, motherhood and home-making with almost no proper training, their aptitudes for the work are so great and their natural intuitions in regard to it so true, that unquestionably, large numbers of them in the United States are happy and satisfied and have no part and no interest in all the hue and cry in regard to women's rights or women's work.

WOMEN NATURAL-BORN WIVES AND MOTHERS

The natural tendency of the majority of women for maternity and home-making must be taken into consideration. Some boys play with weapons, others with machinery, still others are interested in dogs and horses. Some boys are natural traders, others love to hunt and fish, while you will find an occasional lad curled up in a big chair in the library absorbed in a book. But practically all girls play with dolls, which is a sufficient evidence of the almost universality of the maternal instinct in women. The pity is that our educational traditions, almost without exception, are those handed down to us from schools and universities which educated boys and men only. We are therefore educating our girls to be merchants, lawyers, doctors, accountants, artists, musicians; in fact, almost anything but mothers. Twenty years ago, this was universally true. To-day, fortunately, the light has begun to break, and in many schools, both public and private, we are beginning to teach our girls domestic science, the care and feeding of infants, pre-natal culture, home management, economic purchasing, and other such important subjects.

VOCATIONS FOR MOTHERS

Occasionally we find a girl who has no talent for housework or home management. She is not particularly interested in it. She finds it monotonous and distasteful. For these reasons she probably does not do it well. On the other hand, she may have keen, reliable commercial instincts and be well qualified for a business career, or she may be educational, artistic, literary or professional in type. Such a woman has, of course, no business trying to keep house. She may have a strong love nature and ardent maternal desires. If so, there is no reason why she should not marry and become the mother of children. If she does, however, she should turn the management of the home over to someone else and seek self-expression and compensation in the vocation for which she is best fitted. This, of course, is no easy matter. Many men either have violent or stubborn prejudices against any such arrangement. Whether or not she can take her true place in the world depends upon the courage, determination, tactfulness, and personal force of each individual woman.

WOMEN AS TEACHERS

There is one occupation for women which is thoroughly established, entirely respectable, socially uplifting, and fully approved by even the most conservative and fastidious. This is teaching. The result is that the profession of teaching, for women, is overcrowded and becoming more overcrowded. The work done is, on the whole, mediocre or worse, and, as a result of these two conditions, the pay is pitifully small considering the importance of the results.

Because women can become teachers without losing one notch of their social standing in even the most hide-bound communities, thousands of women become teachers who ought to be housewives. Thousands of others struggle in the schoolroom, doing work they hate and despise, for a miserable pittance, when they might be happy and successful in a store or an office. We have met women teachers who ought to have been physicians; others who ought to have been lawyers; others, many of them, who ought to have been in business; and still others, thousands of them, who ought to have been in their own homes. And, naturally enough, we have also met women in the professions and in business and in their homes who ought to have been teachers--but not nearly so many.

The true teacher has three fundamental qualifications. First, a love of knowledge; second, a desire to impart knowledge, and third, a love of young people. Added to these should be patience, firmness, tactfulness, knowledge of human nature, facility in expression, reasoning power, enthusiasm, and a personality which inspires confidence. Can any county superintendent discover these qualities by means of the examination upon which first, second and third-grade certificates are based? Have the members of any average school board the discrimination necessary to determine the presence or absence of these qualities in any candidate who brings her certificate?

WOMEN IN BUSINESS

The business world suffers from the presence in the ranks of its workers of thousands of hopelessly inefficient girls who have no aptitudes for business, or even for the minor detailed processes of commercial activity. They take no real interest in their work. They have no particular ambition for advancement. Their one motive for condescending to grace the office with their presence at all is to earn pin-money or, perhaps, to support themselves in some fashion until they marry. It is true that some of these girls might be taught to be reliable and efficient in their work if they could be persuaded to take an interest in it, to look upon it as something more potent and more important than a mere stop-gap. Many of them, no doubt, could be trained to earn salaries which would pay them to continue in business even after marriage.

WOMEN IN DOMESTIC SERVICE

Others of these girls are utterly unfitted for office work. Some of them would succeed very well as teachers, some as artists, and others as musicians. Like so many of their brothers, however, they have followed

171

the line of least resistance--regardless of their aptitudes. Most of these girls belong in the home. They are quite justified in looking forward to matrimony as their true career. How much better if they would only earn the necessary pin-money in domestic service! From a monetary point of view, thirty dollars a month, with board, room, laundry, and many other necessities furnished, is a princely compensation compared with the five or eight dollars a week received by most girls in an office. From an economic point of view, the coming into our homes of thousands of intelligent, fairly well educated, trained, and ambitious young women would be a blessing and benefit. Socially, of course, the first young women who adopted such a radical change in custom would be pariahs. They would also, doubtless, suffer many hardships in the way of irregular hours, small, dark, stuffy rooms, unreasonable mistresses, no adequate place to entertain their friends, and other such injustices. But, with a higher and more intelligent class of household servants, doubtless these abuses would disappear.

We opened this chapter with the disavowal of any intention to advocate reform. We make this one exception. We most earnestly hope that such a reform may be consummated. At the same time, we have an uneasy suspicion that we are sighing for the moon.

THE TRAGEDY OF BAD COOKING

The whole problem of household management is just now a very serious one. When the maid is ignorant, untrained, and, as is so often the case, slack, wasteful, and inefficient, the situation is, in all conscience, bad enough. But when the mistress is only a little less ignorant than her servant, is equally slack, and perhaps even more inefficient, the high cost of living gets a terrific boost in that household, while comfort, wholesomeness, and adequacy of living are correspondingly depressed. One of the saddest elements in our consultation work is the stream of both men and women who lack courage, aggressiveness, initiative, mental focus, and personal efficiency generally because they are deficient in physical stamina. Their whole life is, as it were, sub-normal. With inherent qualifications for success, they are, nevertheless, threatened with failure because, to use the language of the ring, "they lack the punch." The trouble with nine out of ten of these unfortunates is that they are under-nourished. Not because they do not get enough food, but because their diet is not properly balanced, is served to them in incompatible combinations, is badly prepared, poorly cooked, unpalatable, and doubtless, in many cases, served in anything but an appetizing manner.

172

Napoleon is quoted as having said that an army fights with its stomach. The man who goes out to do battle for commercial or professional success from an ill-managed and inefficient kitchen and dining-room is as badly off as the army with an inadequate commissary department. Yet, while the commissary department of the modern army receives the most scientific and careful supervision, many a man must leave his kitchen in the hands of a wife who received her training in music, literature, modern languages, and classics, or in a business college, and of a servant who received what little training she has as a farm laborer in Europe.

There is no denying the truth that if housewives themselves were scientifically trained, we should have a far higher average of training and efficiency amongst domestic servants. One of the consequences of our deplorable self-consciousness in the matter of sex is that we have been too prudish frankly to train our girls to become successful wives and mothers. The result is that, when it becomes necessary for them to earn money before their marriage, instead of gaining experience in housekeeping, cooking and purchasing, they have taken up the stage, teaching, factory work, office work, and retail selling. As we have seen, a great many of them are misfits in these callings. Good food is wasted, good stomachs are impaired, and good brains and nerves deteriorate because, as a general rule, only those who are too ignorant or too inefficient for office work or factory work can be induced to take service in our kitchens.

CHAPTER XII

SPECIAL FORMS OF UNFITNESS

Place a quinine tablet and a strychnine tablet of the same size on the table before you. Can you, by looking at them, smelling of them, or feeling of them, tell them apart? Would you know the difference instantly, by their appearance, between bichloride of mercury tablets and soda tablets? Down in the basement of a manufacturing chemist's huge building, there is a girl placing tablets in boxes and bottles. They come to her in huge bins. One tablet looks very much like another. Upon her faithful, conscientious and unerring attention to every minute detail of her rather routine and monotonous work may depend the fate of empires.

In an office on the main floor of this same building sits a man directing the policy of the entire industry. Upon him rests the responsibility for the success of the enterprise a year, five years, twenty years ahead. He gives an order: "Purchase land. Build a factory for the making of carbolic acid. Equip it with the necessary machinery and apparatus. Purchase in advance the needed raw materials. Be ready to put the product on the market by the first of September." The execution of that order involves minute attention to thousands of details. Yet, if the man who gave it were to consider many of them and render decision upon them, the business would rapidly become a ship in a storm with no one at the helm.

The work of the girl in the basement, sorting tablets, may turn out to be far more important in the world's history than the work of the man in the front office, managing the business. It is just as important, therefore, that she should be fitted for her vocation as that he should be fitted for his.

GENERALS AND DETAIL WORKERS

Fortunately for carrying on the business of the world, there are many people who love detail, take delight in handling it, find intense satisfaction in seeing that the few little parts of the great machinery of life under their care are always in the right place at the right time and under the right conditions. Since there is such an incalculable mass of these important trifles to be looked after, it is well that the majority of people are better detail workers than formulators of policies and leaders of great movements. Tragedy results when the man with the detail worker's heart and brain attempts to wear the diadem of authority. He breaks his back trying to carry burdens no human shoulders are broad enough to bear. He is so bowed down by them that he sees only his mincing footsteps and has no conception of the general direction in which he is going. Nine times out of ten he travels wearily around in a little circle, which grows smaller and smaller as his over-taxed strength grows less and less.

When you put a man of larger mental grasp in charge of a wearying round of monotonous details, you have mingled the elements out of which a cataclysm sometimes comes. These are the men who, with the very best intentions in the world, fail to appear with the horseshoe nail at the correct moment. To be there, at that time, with the horseshoe nail is their duty. Nothing greater than that is expected of them. Yet, because their minds grasp the great movements of armies in battles and campaigns, they overlook the horseshoe nail and, as the old poem says:

"For the want of the nail, the shoe was lost; For the want of the shoe, the horse was lost; For the want of the horse, the rider was lost; For the want of the rider, the battle was lost; For the want of the battle, the kingdom was lost-- And all for the want of a horseshoe nail!"

Perhaps the man who bore the title of rider ought to have been charged with the duty of being there with that horseshoe nail, and the man who was only a blacksmith's helper should have ridden the horse and saved the battle and the kingdom.

INDICATIONS OF DETAIL AND NON-DETAIL APTITUDES

It ought not to be difficult for any man or woman to know whether or not he or she is qualified for detail work. The man who enjoys detail and takes pleasure in order, system, accuracy, and exactitude, down to the last dot and hairline, ought to know that he is qualified for detail work and has no business trying to carry on or manage affairs in which there is a considerable element of risk as well as many variables. Strangely enough, however, many of them do not know this, and over and over again we find the detail man wearing himself into nervous prostration in the wrong vocation.

On the other hand, the man who hates routine, grows restive under monotony, is impatient with painstaking accuracy and minute details, ought to know better than to make himself--or to allow himself to be made--responsible for them. And yet, nearly every day someone is coming to us with a complaint about the monotony of his job--how he hates its routine and how often he gets himself into trouble because he neglects or overlooks some little thing.

It ought to be easy enough to tell the difference between these two classes of workers. If you are a brunette, with fairly prominent brows and somewhat sloping forehead, a chin prominent at the lower point and receding upward toward the mouth; if your head is high and square behind; if your fingers are long and square-tipped; if your flesh is elastic or hard in consistency, then you can trust yourself to take responsibility for things in which seeming trifles may be of the highest importance. If, on the other hand, you are blonde or red-haired; if your head is round and dome-shaped just above the temples and round behind; if your nose is prominent and your chin narrow and receding at the lower point; if your flesh is elastic, with a tendency toward softness; if your fingers are short and either square or tapering, then you had better prepare yourself for some vocation where you can deal with large affairs, where you can plan and organize and direct, and let other people work out the details.

COURAGE AND RECKLESSNESS

The story is told of two soldiers going into battle. Both pushed forward swiftly and eagerly. They were rapidly nearing the danger zone. Already men were falling around them. As they went on, one suddenly looked at the other. "Why," he cried, "your face is white, your eyes are glazed, your limbs are trembling. I believe you are afraid!"

"Great God, man! of course I am afraid," replied the other. "And if you were one-half as afraid as I am, you would turn and run."

Here we have the discrimination between real courage and mere foolhardiness or recklessness. There are some vocations which require courage. There are others which require an element of recklessness. It requires courage to drive the locomotive of a railroad train at a speed of eighty miles an hour, but it also requires caution, prudence, watchfulness, and even apprehension.

In a western factory men were wanted for an important job, one in which a moment's carelessness in the handling of levers might cost a dozen fellow workmen their lives. "Find me," said the superintendent, "the most careful men you can get. I do not want anyone dumping damage suits on the company." The employment department found the very careful men, but none of them were satisfactory; they were all so careful that they made no speed, and soon had to be relieved for this reason, and because the constant nervous strain was too much for them. Here was a kind of work requiring a certain cool, calm, deliberate recklessness. Men were found with steady nerves, keen eyesight, quick reaction time, and smooth co-ordination of muscular action, together with a moderate degree of cautiousness. These men liked the work for the very tingle of the danger in it. They swung their ponderous machines to their tasks with a sureness of touch and a swiftness of operation which not only delighted the superintendent, but inspired confidence in their fellow workers.

INDICATIONS OF COURAGE AND CAUTION

If you are brunette, with small, sway-back or snub nose, narrow, rounded chin, and a tendency to disturbances of the circulation; if your head is narrow at the sides and high and square behind, look for a vocation where caution is a prime requisite, but do not get yourself into situations where you will have to fight or where there is so much risk

176

that your natural apprehensiveness will cause you to worry and lie awake nights.

Contrary wise, if your chin is broad and prominent, your head is wide above the ears, low and round behind, and rather short; especially if you are a blonde, with a large nose, high in the bridge, and a big rounded dome just above the temples, select for yourself a vocation where success depends upon a cheerful willingness to take a chance. You may blunder into a tight situation now and then, and you will occasionally make a bad guess and lose thereby, but you will not be inclined to worry and you will greatly enjoy the give and take of the fight by means of which you will extricate yourself from undesirable situations.

QUICKNESS OR SLOWNESS OF THOUGHT AND ACTION

If you are of the thoughtful, philosophical type, instead of the keen, alert, practical type, don't attempt to win success in any vocation requiring quick thought and quick decision. You like to reason things out; you want to know why before you go ahead. Your success lies in lines which require slow, thoughtful, careful reasoning, mature deliberation, and an ability to plod diligently through masses of facts and arguments.

If, on the other hand, you are of the observant, practical, matter-of-fact, scientific type, your vocation should be one calling for quick thought, quick decision, ability to get the facts and to deal with them, keen observation, and one not requiring too great a nicety of mental calculation.

If you have a small, round, retreating chin, beware of any vocation which requires great deliberation in action, because you are very quick to act. Your hands, once their task is learned, move very swiftly. You are inclined to be impulsive. If your forehead is of the type which indicates quick thinking and you have a large nose, high in the bridge, then you are of the keenest, most alert, most energetic and dynamic type. No sooner do you see a proposition than you decide. No sooner do you decide than you act, and when you have acted, you want to see the results of that action immediately. You are, therefore, unfitted for any vocation which requires prolonged meditation, great deliberation in action, and a patient, plodding willingness to wait for results.

If your chin is long, broad, and prominent at the point, your action will always wait upon your thought. If your thought is quick, as indicated by the sloping forehead, your action may follow very quickly, but never impulsively. If, on the other hand, your forehead is one which indicates reflection and slowness of thought, then you will be very deliberate, postponing action in every case until you have carefully and painstakingly thought the entire matter out. It is useless for anyone to try to rush you to either decision or action, for you may have it in you to be quite hopelessly stubborn.

THE SOCIAL QUALITIES

Some time ago a splendidly educated young man came to us for advice. "What I want to know more than anything else," he said, "is why Hugo Schultz always sells more goods than I do. I spent two years in high school, four years in a special preparatory school and four years in college. I have had eight years of fairly successful business experience. For two years I have been a traveling salesman. When I first started out my sales amounted to only about $5 a day, on an average. Within a year I had pushed them up to $1,000 a day, on an average, and now sometimes I sell $3,000 or $4,000 worth a day. With the exception of Hugo Schultz, I sell more goods than any other man representing our company. If I sell $52,000 worth in a month, Schultz sells $65,000 worth-yet Schultz has never been beyond the fourth grade in school. He is ten years younger than I am, has had practically no business experience, and has only been on the road one year."

Upon examination, we found that this young man was selling goods with a splendidly trained intellect. He analyzed all the factors in his problem carefully, even down to the peculiarities of every one of his customers. He presented his goods with faultlessly worked out arguments and appeals to the common sense and good judgment of his customers. He was, therefore, more than usually successful. In answer to our inquiry, however, he said: "No, I hate selling goods. The only reason I keep it up is because there is good money in it--more money than I could make with the same amount of effort in any other department of business. I do not like to approach strangers. I have to lash myself into it every morning of my working life, and it is very hard for me to be friendly with customers about whom I care nothing personally."

"What about Peter Schultz?" we asked. "Is he a good mixer?"

"It is his whole stock in trade. Now that you have called my attention to it, I can see clearly enough that he takes delight in meeting strangers. Why, even when he is off duty, he finds his recreation running around into crowds, meeting new people, getting acquainted with them, making friends with them. I see it all now. He sells goods on the basis of friendship. He appeals to people's feelings rather than their intellects, and most people are ruled by their feelings. I know that."

At our suggestion, this intellectual young man gave up his business career altogether and turned his attention to journalism, where he has been even more successful than he was as a salesman. Needless to say, Hugo Schultz is still breaking records on the road.

It is difficult for anyone who is not by nature friendly and social to succeed in a vocation in which the principal work is meeting, dealing with, handling, and persuading his fellow men. There is an old saying "that kissing goes by favor," and doubtless it is true that other valuable things go the same way. People naturally like to do business with their friends, with those who are personally agreeable to them. It takes a long time for the unsocial or the unfriendly man to make himself personally agreeable to strangers, or, in fact, to very many people, whether strangers or not.

If it is hard for the unsocial and unfriendly man to work among people, it is distressing, dull and stupid for the man who is a good mixer and loves his friends to work in solitude or where his entire attention is engrossed in things and ideas instead of people.

INDICATIONS OF SOCIAL QUALITIES

Notwithstanding these very clear distinctions and the seeming ease with which one ought to classify himself in this respect, we are constantly besieged by those who have very deficient social natures and who are ambitious to succeed as salesmen, preachers, lawyers, politicians, and physicians.

There is plenty of work in the world which does not require one to be particularly friendly, although, it must be admitted, friendliness is a splendid asset in any calling. Scholarship, literary work, art, music, engineering, mechanical work, agriculture in all its branches, contracting, building, architecture, and many other vocations offer opportunities for success to those who are only moderately equipped socially.

If the unsocial and unfriendly are deceived in regard to themselves, no less so are the social and the friendly. Again and again we find them in occupations which take them out of the haunts of living men, where they are so unhappy and dissatisfied that they sometimes become desperate. Why a man who likes people and likes to be with them, and is successful in dealing with them, should take himself off on a lonely ranch, twelve miles from the nearest neighbor and twenty miles from a railroad, passes the comprehension of all but those who, through experience, have learned the picturesque contrariness of human nature.

It is easy to distinguish, at a glance, between the social fellow and the natural-born hermit. Go to any political convention, or any convention of successful salesmen, or to a ministers' meeting attended by successful city preachers, or to any other gathering attended by men who have succeeded in callings where the ability to mix successfully with their fellow men is of paramount importance. Get a seat on the side lines, if possible, and then study the backs of their heads.

THE HEADS OF POLITICIANS

We attended two great political conventions in 1912. There were more than one thousand delegates at each convention. So certain were we of the type of men successful enough politically to be chosen as delegates to a national convention of their party, that we offered a prize of ten dollars to the friends who accompanied us for every delegate they would point out to us who did not have a round, full back-head, making his head appear long directly backwards from the ears. Although our friends were skeptical and planned in some detail as to what they would do with the money they expected to win from us, we attended both conventions without a penny of outlay for prizes. If you know any unfriendly, unsocial men, look at the backs of their heads and see how short they are.

There are vocations for all who have the courage, the ambition, the willingness to work, the persistence to keep ever-lastingly at it. Finding one's true vocation in life means, not finding an easy way to success, but finding an opportunity to work and work hard at something interesting, something you can do well, and something in which your highest and best talents will find an opportunity for their fullest expression.

Just as finding an unusual talent for music means years and years of the most careful study and preparation, followed by incessant practice; just as finding of a talent for the law means years of work in schools, colleges and universities; so the finding of a talent for business, mechanics, science, construction, or any other vocation involves years of study, self-development, preparation, and practice, if you are to achieve a worth-while success.

A HARD-LUCK STORY

The following incident illustrates plainly enough the mental attitude of the average fellow--the reason why he has failed, and the remedy:

A man came into our office complaining of his luck.

He was on the gray and wrinkled side of the half-century mark, somewhat bent, and slow of step.

This was the tune of his dirge:

"My life is a failure. I have never had a chance. My father was poor and couldn't give me the advantages that other young men had. So I've had my nose on the grindstone all my life long.

"See what I am to-day. While other men have made money and, at my age, are well fixed, I am dependent on my little old Saturday night envelope to keep me from starving. That wouldn't be so bad, but my employers are beginning to hint that I'm not so lively as I was once and that a younger man would fill the job better. It's only a question of time when I'll be a leading member of the Down and Out Club. Then it'll be the Bay for mine."

Our friend, whom we call Mr. Socratic, butted into the conversation right here.

"Pretty tough luck!" he said. "Know any men of your age that are doing better?"

"Sure, lots of 'em."

"What's the reason?"

"Well, they have had better luck."

"How do you mean? Investments turned out better?"

"No; I never had anything to invest."

"How, then?"

"Well, they had advantages."

"What, for instance?"

"Education."

"Why didn't you get an education?"

"Couldn't afford it."

"Had some income, didn't you?"

181

[Illustration: FIG. 49. Hon. Joseph Walker, of Massachusetts. Has good degree of balance between practical and ideal tendencies. Is shrewd, ambitious, determined, persistent, courageous, intellectual, oratorical, dramatic, forceful, social, and optimistic. Excellent planner and schemer. Note high, wide forehead, prominent at brows; keen, shrewd and determined expression; high, wide head; height of head just above temples; square jaw and chin; firm mouth; short upper lip, and well-built, prominent nose.]

[Illustration: FIG. 50. Hon. Lon V. Stephens, former Governor of Missouri, keenly observant, intensely practical, rather serious, ambitious energetic, courageous, friendly, far-sighted. A public speaker of some dramatic ability. Note great prominence of forehead at brows, depressed corners of eyes and mouth and tip of nose, high, long head, medium-short upper lip, and prominent chin.]

[Illustration: *Photo by Paul Thompson.* FIG. 51. Hon Oscar Underwood, United States Senator from Alabama. Practical, energetic, ambitious, courageous, determined, enduring. Note resemblance in profile and head shape to Figs. 48, 50, and 52, also politicians. A public speaker with considerable dramatic talent.]

[Illustration: _Copyright by Harris & Ewing, Washington, D.C._. FIG. 52. Hon. Victor Murdock, Ex-Congressman, of Kansas. Practical, alert, keen, ambitious, combative, courageous. Has considerable dramatic talent, as shown by large nose, short upper lip and long, prominent chin. Compare with Figs. 48, 50, and 51.]

[Illustration: FIG. 53. The late Robert C. Ogden, Merchant and Philanthropist. A man of keen, practical, commercial judgment, high ambition, great energy, strong determination, and strong sense of justice, together with idealism, benevolence, optimism, and kindliness. Note large development of brows; width of forehead across center; high head, domed above temples; large, well-formed nose; long, straight upper lip; straight, firm mouth, and poised, calm, kindly expression.]

[Illustration: FIG. 54. Prof. P.G. Holden, Agricultural Expert and Teacher. A fine admixture of the physically frail and bony and muscular type, hence his intellectual interest and ability in agriculture. Has ambition, energy, and great social and friendly qualities. Note height and length of head, development of brows, and size and contour of nose.]

[Illustration: FIG. 55. W. Nelson Edelsten, Insurance Special Agent. Keen, observant, alert, ambitious, energetic, courageous, refined, sensitive, emotional, enthusiastic, appreciative of approval, friendly. Note prominence of brows, high head, large, well-formed nose, chin, and ears, fine texture, high dome over temples, short upper lip, and alert, high-strung, friendly expression.]

[Illustration: _Copyright by Harris & Ewing._ FIG. 56. Dr. Beverly T. Galloway, Assistant Secretary of Agriculture of the United States. Same as FIG. 8. Note high crown large prominent nose; very full backhead.]

"Yes, but only enough to live on."

"Had time to study, didn't you?"

"No--always had to work."

"What about your evenings? Have to work nights?"

"No."

"Had a pretty good time, didn't you?"

"Oh, yes."

"Out with the fellows and the girls about every night?"

"Yes."

"Wore good clothes, smoked good cigars, hired livery rigs, took in good shows, lived pretty well, shook dice a little, risked a few dollars on the ponies now and then?"

"Oh, yes; I was no tight-wad."

"You had to be a good fellow, eh?"

"Sure, I am only going through this world once, so I have had a good time as I've gone along."

"You couldn't have put in two or three nights a week studying and still have had a good time?"

"Oh, I might have, I s'pose, but I didn't have the money to buy books."

"How much do you figure you spent, on an average, on those nights you were out with the boys?"

"Oh, I don't know; sometimes a dime for a cigar, sometimes three or four dollars for theater tickets, supper, and the trimmings."

"Well, would it average two bits?"

183

"Yes, I guess so; all of that. Maybe more."

"If you had saved that for two nights a week, it would have counted up about two and a quarter a month. Buy a pretty good book for that, couldn't you?"

"S'pose so."

"And if you had been buying books and studying them, going to night-school, or taking a correspondence course all these years, you would have had an education by now, wouldn't you?"

"Well, I don't know. Some men are born to succeed. They have more brains than others."

"Who, for instance?"

"Well, there's Edison."

"Yes; and while you were having a good time with the boys, wearing good clothes, and enjoying the comforts of life, Edison was working and studying, wearing shabby clothes and patched shoes, so that he might buy books. What right have you to say that Edison has a better head, naturally, than you until you have done what Edison did to develop his?"

"Well, if you put it that way--none, I guess."

"Then you might have been an Edison if you had sacrificed, worked, and studied as Edison did?"

"Perhaps."

"Then where does the 'hard luck' come in? While you were having a good time, Edison was having a hard time. Isn't that so?"

"Yes, and now Edison is on Easy Street and I am headed for the Bay. I see your point, Mr. Socratic. I guess it isn't luck, after all. It's my fault. But knowing that won't make it any easier for me when I get canned."

"What's the use crossing the bridge before you get to it? I read the other day of a man who studied law, was admitted to the bar, and made money on it, all after he was seventy years old."

"Think there's any chance for me? Can I learn anything at my age?"

"You learned something just now, didn't you?" asked Socratic.

"Yes, I guess I did."

"Well, if you can learn one thing, you can learn a hundred, can't you?"

"Guess so."

"Will you?"

"I sure will."

If you are a worker and not a shirker--if you are a lifter and not a leaner--if you have done your best to succeed in your present vocation, and are still dissatisfied, and feel that you could do better in some other line of work, we hope that this book has been of some assistance to you in determining your new line.

If, however, you have never attempted your best--if you have never worked your hardest--if you have grown weary, and laid down your burden in the face of difficulties and obstacles--if you have neglected your education, your training, your preparation for success, then, before you make a change, before you seek vocational counsel, do your best to make good where you are. It may be the one vocation in which you can succeed.

PART TWO

ANALYZING CHARACTER IN SELECTION OF EMPLOYEES

CHAPTER I

THE COST OF UNSCIENTIFIC SELECTION

People used to thank God for their sickness and pain--at the same time naively praying Him to take back His gift. This inconsistency was due to a combination of ignorance and the good old human foible of blaming some one else. Folks did not know then, as well as they do now, that they had the stomachache because they were too fond of rich dainties. The cause of the pain being mysterious, they went back to first principles and blamed (or thanked) God for it. They believed that God afflicted them for their good and His glory, but their belief was hardly practical enough to keep them from praying Him not to do them too much good or Himself too much glory.

Bodily ills are no different from our other troubles. In case of doubt as to their origin, it is far more convenient to blame some supernatural source for them than to take the blame upon ourselves. In support of this, take the attitude of employers toward strikes and lockouts, their most outbreaking and violent troubles. These are named in all of our contracts along with lightning, tornadoes, floods, and other "acts of God," if not directly, at least by inference It is plain enough, at any rate, that those who draw up the contract consider strikes and lockouts as wholly outside of their control, as they do the elements. It is the same old ignorance, the same desire to shift the blame.

WHO IS TO BLAME?

Modern business common sense counts strikes and lockouts among preventable industrial diseases, just as the modern science of medicine classes smallpox, diphtheria, typhoid fever, the plague, tuberculosis, and the hookworm amongst preventable bodily diseases. The strike is a violent eruption, according to those who have made the closest study of the situation, resulting from long-continued abuses of bad management, bad selection, bad assignment of duties, and other vicious or ignorant practices. So a fever is a kind of physical house cleaning for the removal of debris of months or even years of foolish living.

But persistent violation of the laws of health does not always lead to acute disease. Seated in the office of a prominent and successful physician in a Western city one day, we were discussing with him the true nature of disease. "My patients," said he, "many of them are now lying on beds of pain, burning with fever. They are called sick people. The folks walking along the street out there are called well people. The terms are inaccurate. Fever is the effort of nature to throw off poisons, poisons which have been accumulating in the system for years as the result of wrong ways of living. Many people suppose that fevers are caused by germs. This is not true. No germ can harm or disturb a healthy body. It is only when the body is depleted in vitality that its defenses come down and germs find a ready soil in which to propagate. People who have fevers, therefore, are only taking a violent manner of getting well, and, if wisely treated and intelligently nursed, they do get well. As you know, it is a very common experience for a person to feel far better after recovery from a spell of sickness than he has for years previously. Now, nine out of ten of the people going along the street who call themselves well are not well. The majority of them are probably only 25 per cent, efficient physically. They are loaded up with the debilitating consequences of their own recklessness or ignorant manner of living."

A PROLIFIC CAUSE OF INEFFICIENCY

In the same way, there are latent illnesses and inefficiencies in many commercial organizations which never reach the point of strikes and lockouts. For some reason or other that lively germ, the walking delegate, fails to get a foothold. Perhaps there would be a beneficial house cleaning if he did. Discontent, dissatisfaction, unrest, and constant changes in personnel load the body up with wastes, inefficiencies and unnecessary expenses. Any employer who thinks at all, and who has any basis for judgment as a result of observation, knows that what he desires to purchase, when he pays wages, is not a prescribed number of days and hours, is not a standard number of foot pounds of physical energy, but rather human intelligence and human willingness and enthusiasm in the use of that intelligence in his service. It is true that most employees do a certain amount of physical work, but it is also true that the value of that work depends entirely upon the amount of intelligence and good will the employee puts into it. The employee who is doing work for which he is not fitted and is unhappy and discontented is doubly inefficient. He is inefficient because he is not well fitted for the work and could not do his best even if he were perfectly satisfied and happy. And he is inefficient because he is in a bad psychical state. With his mental attitude, he could not do good work even if he were in the place for which he was best fitted.

Efficiency experts maintain that the average employee in our industrial and commercial institutions is only from twenty-five to thirty-five per cent, efficient. Sixty-five to seventy-five per cent, loss in productive power on the part of the forty million workers in this country constitutes an almost incalculable sum.

Who is to blame for this loss? Are we not too intelligent, too well versed in the laws of cause and effect and too courageous to try to blame the Almighty for it or to lay it to the public schools or to hold the employee accountable? As a matter of fact, no matter how we may try to shift the blame, those of us who are executives know only too well that our board of directors and stockholders hold us strictly responsible for results. What they want is dividends, not excuses. They do not care to hear how hard it is to find good men. They are not interested in the stories of employees who are so ungrateful as to leave just when they have become most useful. They will not permit you to shift any of the blame upon the shoulders of the employee. They expect you to use methods in selecting and assigning employees and handling them after they are selected that will yield the largest possible permanent results.

HIGH COST OF HIRING AND FIRING

Employers who will take the trouble to study their records for some years past, will, unless they are very exceptional, find that the average length of service in their organization is much shorter than they would be prepared to believe unless the actual figures were before them. We have the word of its manager in regard to a certain foundry in the Middle West that the average period of employment for any one man in that foundry is only 30 days. We know a large steel mill employing 8,000 where the average length of service per employee is a few days more than four months. These figures were given to us by the employment manager of the mill. The head of the employment department of a large electrical manufacturing company stated to us that the average length of service per employee for his organization was one year or a little less.

From "Current Affairs," Boston, we quote the following significant editorial:

"Do employers realize the waste and extravagance and actual money loss due to haphazard hiring and firing?

"Twelve typical factories were recently investigated as to their employment records by Mr. M.W. Alexander. He chose the normal industrial year of 1912. He chose representative factories, big and little, in several States. The results of this inquiry were reported in an address before the National Association of Manufacturers.

"Mr. Alexander found that this group of factories had 37,274 employees at the beginning of 1912, and 43,971 at the end of the year-- a net increase of 6,697 workers. But the books showed that the factories had actually hired 43,571 new hands, 35,874 having been dropped during the year Of course, not all were fired. Some were absent because of sickness, some died, some left voluntarily; but these were only a small proportion. And the fact remains that in order to increase their working force by 6,697 these twelve industries had to break in 42,571 new employees and suffer the consequent extra expense of instruction cost, reduced production, and beginners' spoiled work. Making liberal discounts for the workers unavoidably withdrawn, it is estimated that these twelve factories suffered a definite money loss of more than $831,000 during the year on account of reckless hiring and firing.

"The conclusion seems justified: 'The highest grade of judgment in the hiring and discharging of employees is needed. The employment "clerk" of to-day will have to be replaced by the employment "superintendent" of to-morrow, not merely by changing the title and salary of the incumbent of the office, but by placing in charge of this important branch of management a man whose character, breadth of view, and capacity eminently qualify him for the discharge of these duties.'"

It is probable that most executives and employers do not know because they have not fully considered what this rapid ratio of change costs. This cost, of course, varies over a very wide range, according to the kind of work to be done and the class of employees. The sales manager of one organization told us that it cost his concern $3,000 to find, employ, train, and break-in to his work a new salesman. The employment manager of one of the largest corporations in the world informs us that it costs him $10,000 in actual money to replace the head of a department. The employment manager of a large factory employing people whose wages ran from $5 a week up, told us that the records of his department showed that it cost $70 to get the name of a departing employee off the payroll and to substitute thereon the name of a new permanent employee to take his place. But these are only costs that can be computed. There are other costs perhaps even greater, records of which never reach the accounting department or the employment department. Let us tell you a story:

A COMMONPLACE STORY

Joe Lathrop, foreman of the finishing room, had a bad headache. It had been along toward the cool, clear dawn of that very morning when, having tearfully assured Mrs. Lathrop for the twentieth time that he had taken but "one li'l' drink," he sobbed himself to sleep. His ears still range disconcertingly with the stinging echoes of his wife's all-too-frank and truthful portrayal of his character, disposition, parentage, and future prospects. His heart was still swollen and painful with the many things he would like to have said in reply had he not been deterred by valor's better part. It was a relief to him, therefore, to take advantage of his monarchical prerogatives in the finishing department and give vent to his hot and acrid feelings.

With all his flaying irony and blundering invective, however, Joe Lathrop never for a moment lost sight of the fact that there were some men upon the finishing floor whom it was far better for him to let alone. With all his truculence, he was too good a politician to lay his tongue to the man tagged with an invisible, but none the less protective, tag of a man higher up. And so Joe Lathrop let loose his vials of wrath upon those whose continuance upon the payroll depended upon merit alone. One of these was Robinson.

HATED FOR HIS EFFICIENCY

Robinson had been finishing piano frames upon this floor for twenty months. He was a young married man, in good health, ambitious, faithful, loyal, skilful, and efficient. He was a man who worked far more with his brains than with his hands. He understood the principles of piano construction, and was, therefore, no rule-of-thumb man. He had studied his work and, as a result, had continually increased both its quantity and quality Robinson was not self-assertive, perhaps a little taciturn, but there was something about him which made people respect him. Over the dinner pails at noon there had been many a conjecture on the part of Robinson's fellow-workers that he was in line for promotion and that he might be made assistant foreman at any time.

Joe Lathrop knew that Robinson's quiet efficiency and attention to business had not escaped the superintendent's eye. He felt that the day might come almost any time when, on account of his "just one li'l' drink," or its consequences, he might have to yield his scepter to the younger man.

DISCHARGED WITHOUT CAUSE

Along about nine o'clock of this particular morning, Lathrop was brow-beating one of the men for some fancied fault near the place where Robinson was working. Seeing Robinson quietly doing his work, paying no attention to the wrangle so near him, only further irritated the suffering foreman.

"Robinson," he yelled. "You have been here long enough to know better than this. What do you mean by standing there like a wooden post right beside this man and letting him make such a botch of these frames?"

Robinson, of course, being a wise man, kept his own counsel, and went on with his work. He could not acknowledge himself at fault when he was not at fault. His manhood revolted. His business was to concentrate upon his own work. Since he could not acknowledge the fault, he therefore said nothing. This, of course, was just what Lathrop did not want.

"Speak up," he bawled, "explain yourself."

"I have my own work to attend to, Mr. Lathrop, as you know," he said quietly.

"I'll have no back talk from you, you sulky dough-face," roared Lathrop. "Get to hell out of here. Go to the office and get your time."

Robinson knew better than to protest. He even hesitated to go to the

190

superintendent, but finally decided to do so.

"It's a shame, Robinson," admitted the superintendent, "but Joe is an awfully good man when he is right, as you know, and as long as we keep him in our service we have to stand behind him in order to maintain discipline." And so Robinson walked out with half a week's pay in his pocket.

THE BEGINNING OF LOSSES

Let us estimate roughly what Joe Lathrop's "one li'l' drink" and his suspicious jealousy cost the piano company.

Of course, his first cost was the loss of time in the finishing room while Robinson's place stood empty. It is fair to suppose that the company was making some profit on Robinson. It, therefore, lost the profit of those two days. Besides this, the machinery and the equipment Robinson operated stood still for two days eating up, in the meantime, interest on investment, rental of floor space, depreciation, light, heat, and all other overhead charges that it ought to have been making products to pay. In addition to all the overhead charges, the machinery ought also to have been making a profit for the piano company.

But there were other losses. Robinson's absence disorganized the shop routine. There were delays, conflicts, piano parts piled up in one end of the room while other departments clamored for finished frames at the other end of the room. Then, at least one-half a day of Joe Lathrop's valuable time went to waste while he was out trying to find some one to fill Robinson's place. His first attempt was made at the gate of the factory, where the sea of the unemployed threw up its flotsam and jetsam. But finishing piano frames is rather a fine job and none of the willing and eager applicants there could fill the bill. Joe then made the round of two or three employment agencies who had helped him out in previous similar emergencies. This time, however, they seemed to be without resource, so far as he was concerned. Being in considerable perspiration and desperation by this time, he was probably gladder than he ought to have been to receive a summons to appear at the court of Terrence Mulvaney. Terrence, who sat in judgment in the back room of his own beverage emporium, the place where Lathrop secured his "li'l' drinks," had heard, in the usual wireless way, that there was a finisher needed at the big factory Lathrop still owed Terrence for a good many of his "li'l' drinks." Furthermore, Terrence, by virtue of some mysterious underground connection, pulled mysterious wires, so that an invitation from him was a command. For these reasons, also, Joe Lathrop found it discreet in his own eyes to engage on the spot Tim

Murphy, a very dear friend of Mulvaney and, according to Mulvaney's own impartial testimony, a very worthy and deserving man.

BREAKING IN AN INCOMPETENT

Valuable hours and moments of the company's time were consumed in initiating Tim Murphy into the employ of the company. There were certain necessary processes in the paymaster's department, the accounting department, the liability department, the tool room, and the medical department.

Now, while Murphy had had some experience in finishing piano frames, he was utterly unfamiliar with the make of piano produced in this factory. Likewise, he was ignorant of the customs, rules, and individual methods which obtained in the factory. This meant that his employers paid him good wages for five or six weeks while he was finding his way around. It was good money spent without adequate return in the way of service. In fact, during these weeks, the company would probably have been better off without Tim Murphy than with him, for he spoiled a good deal of his work, took up a great deal of his foreman's time which ought to have been applied in other directions, broke and ruined a number of valuable tools and otherwise manifested those symptoms which so often mark the entrance into an organization of a man propelled by pull rather than push.

The trouble in Tim Murphy's corner continued to halt and disorganize the work in the department so that there were still further delays and losses up and down the line. All this was bad enough, but by the end of five weeks of Murphy's attachment to the payroll he had demonstrated that he was not only incapable, indolent, careless, and unreliable, but that he was a disorganizer, a gossip, and a trouble maker.

BAD EFFECT UPON OTHER EMPLOYEES

Finally the superintendent, who in some mysterious way had managed to escape the entanglement of underground wires running from Terrence Mulvaney's saloon, issued a direct, positive order to Foreman Lathrop, and Murphy's place in that factory knew him no more. Nor was Murphy astonished or disappointed. He had been expecting this very thing to happen, and was prepared for it. So when he walked out, two skilful, but easily influenced companions, walked out with him. Thus Joe Lathrop had, added to one of his frequent early morning headaches, the serious trouble of trying to find three men to fill yawning vacancies. The company was faced with a new series of losses even greater than those which had followed the discharge of Robinson.

Furthermore, there was trouble and disorganization among the men still remaining in the department. Every man there had liked and respected the competent young worker, Robinson. They all knew that he had been discharged largely because Joe Lathrop was jealous and somewhat afraid of him, and because Joe had had a bad headache and grouch. They resented the injustice. Their respect for their foreman dropped several degrees. Their interest in their work slackened. "What is the use," they thought, "to do our best when superior workmanship might get us thrown out of here instead of promoted?"

And so Joe Lathrop's series of "li'l' drinks" finally resulted in decreasing the efficiency of his department to such an extent that the superintendent was obliged to discharge him. Then the superintendent was in for it. He had to find a new man. He had to take the time and the trouble to break the new man in, and the company had to share the losses resulting from disorganization until the new foreman was installed.

This is not a fanciful story, but was told to us by a man who knew the superintendent, Joe Lathrop, Robinson, Terrence Mulvaney, and Tim Murphy. Nor is it an unusual story. Just such headaches, discharges, troubles, and losses are occurring every day in the industrial and commercial institutions of this country.

This story illustrates not only the high cost of constant change in personnel, but also the high cost of leaving the important matter of hiring and firing to foremen. Where this is done, discharges without cause, the selection of incompetents, grafting on the payroll, inside and outside politics, the indolent retention on the payroll of those who are unfit, and many other abuses too numerous to mention, are bound to follow.

ONLY ONE LEGITIMATE REASON FOR HIRING

There is only one legitimate reason for putting any man or woman on the payroll, namely, that he or she is well fitted to perform the tasks assigned, will perform them contentedly and happily and, therefore, be a valuable asset to the concern. But with foremen, superintendents, and other minor executives selecting employees, for any reason and every reason except the legitimate reason, it is small wonder that employees grow discontented and leave, are demoralized and incompetent so that they are discharged. For these reasons it is an unusual organization which does not turn over its entire working force every year. The average of the concerns we have investigated shows much more frequent turnover than this.

Under these circumstances, it should be easy to understand why our efficiency engineers and scientific management experts find the average organization only 25 per cent efficient. And this is not the only trouble we make for ourselves as the result of unscientific selection in the rank and file. In many cases we use no better judgment in the selection of even our highest and most responsible executives. If it is true, as has been so often stated, that a good general creates a good army and leads it to victory, and a poor general demoralizes and leads to defeat the finest and bravest army, then it is more disastrous for you to select one misfit executive than a thousand misfits for your rank and file.

In our next chapter we shall attempt to show some of the troubles which overtake a man who selects the wrong kind of executives.

CHAPTER II

THE SELECTION OF EXECUTIVES

The President and General Manager of a large manufacturing and sales company, who, for the purpose of the present narrative, shall be called Jessup, was making a trip from Chicago to New York on the Twentieth Century Limited. In the smoking room of his car he met a gentleman whose appearance and manner attracted him greatly. Acquaintanceship was a matter of course, mutual admiration followed swift upon its heels, and friendship soon began to crystallize in the association. As the train sped on through the night, the Big Executive became more and more delighted with his new-found acquaintance. The man agreed with him in many of his sentiments; belonged to the same political party; was a member of the same fraternal order; wore the same Greek letter society pin as his oldest son; and, what was, perhaps, more important, entertained what seemed to him intelligent, clean-cut, forceful, progressive ideas in regard to business.

As their talk proceeded, President Jessup found that the gentleman was a Mr. Lynch, advertising manager of a firm manufacturing jewelry, located in Providence, Rhode Island. He had been in this position for five years and during that time had planned, assisted in designing, and sold to a national market several profitable jewelry specialties. Lynch's graphic story of how these advertising campaigns had been planned, executed, and carried through to success fascinated the President of the western concern. To his mind, his own enterprise, the manufacture and sale of steam and hot-water heating plants, had long been in the doldrums. He himself had spent many sleepless nights trying to plan some way of extending its business; of opening up new markets; of creating a wide new patronage; of manufacturing something which would bring in more profits than their regular line, and finding a successful sale for it. It now seemed to him that he had found just the man to assist him in carrying out these vaguely formed plans, which as yet were little more than dreams. He told Lynch something of his ideas and ideals, and, as the two men parted for the night, he said:

"I have just a glimmering of an idea, Mr. Lynch, that we might be able to make an arrangement whereby you would be greatly profited in increased opportunities and bigger income, and perhaps we also would reap an advantage in increased business. Think it over."

SELECTION BY PERSONAL PLEASURE

Long after he had retired, President Jessup pondered over the situation, and the more he pondered, the more he became convinced that he had found just the man he wanted. True, he had not had in mind, during any of his midnight vigils, the taking on of any new help--his payroll was already heavy enough. He had a good advertising manager and a good sales manager, men who were competent to take care of the business of the concern. In response to their efforts, patronage was growing, not rapidly and spectacularly, yet steadily and substantially. Now, however, he saw an opportunity to produce something which would be different enough from the product of any of his competitors to warrant him in undertaking a national advertising campaign. Up to the present he had had only a local business. A few hundred miles from his factory in all directions could be found all the heating plants which he had manufactured and sold. His dream was to produce some special form of apparatus which would sell wherever there were homes, stores, offices, churches, theaters, and schools to be warmed. Mr. Lynch was just the man to study their business carefully, decide upon some such product, help to design it, and plan and execute the national advertising campaign which would develop a local into a national business. Jessup dropped to sleep with his mind made up.

Next morning, as the train sped along between the Catskills and the Hudson, the two men, over the breakfast table, began negotiations. Jessup was surprised, and somewhat disappointed to find what a large salary his new friend was drawing in Providence. He was still more surprised and disappointed to find that Lynch's future prospects in the jewelry business were so bright that it would take a considerably larger salary to entice him away. The Westerner's mind, however, was made up and the future profits he saw arising from a national business were so attractive that he finally threw aside caution and offered Lynch twelve thousand five hundred dollars a year and moving expenses to the western city where his factory was located. This offer was finally accepted, the two men shook hands, and arrangements were made for Lynch to report for duty in the West within thirty days.

THE NEW MAN IN A QUANDARY

Now, President Jessup had no intention of dismissing his advertising manager and his sales manager. Each knew the business from beginning to end; each was thoroughly familiar with the trade already built up and personally acquainted with many dealers who handled the products, and could be depended upon not only to hold the present trade, but to increase it. Therefore it seemed good judgment to retain these two men on the local trade while turning Lynch loose upon the campaign for the securing of a national market. So it was decided to retain both of the old men and to give the newcomer the title of sales promotion manager. There were some heart-burnings on the part of those already in the office when the new man came in and took charge. It was not pleasant for men who had been with the business for years and served it faithfully and helped to build it up, to have a man placed over them who knew nothing about it and whose salary was more than their two salaries combined. However, Lynch's personality was so pleasant and he was so tactful and agreeable that this little feeling of inharmony seemed soon to disappear. Presently all were working together in the happiest possible way toward the inauguration of the new policy of the concern.

As time went on, however, Lynch began to show signs of restlessness and uneasiness. Being a man of keen, alert mind and quick intelligence, he had quickly grasped the fundamentals of the heating business. He was soon able to talk with the firm's designers and engineers in their own language. But the more he studied boilers and radiators, the less interest he took in them. He had sense enough to know that the only thing that would win in the plan he had in mind was a radical change in design which would increase the amount of heat delivered in proportion to the amount of fuel burned, or the amount of heat delivered in proportion to the cost of fuel burned, or would reduce the amount of supervision required, or would do away with some of the long-standing sources of trouble and annoyance in heating apparatus. Long and hard he thought and conjectured, and studied statistics, and followed reports of experiments, but for the life of him he could not take any interest in any such line of research. He hated the gases, ashes, soot, smoke, and

196

dirt generally. Huge rough castings of steel and iron seemed gross and ugly to him, and the completed product seemed coarse and unfinished. The only improvements he could think of were improvements in beauty of line, in refinement of the design, in added ornamentation, and other enhancements of the physical appearance of the product. In these he took some interest, but he had the good sense to know that no change of this kind would accomplish what they wished in the matter of going after a national market.

THE HIGH-SALARIED ONE FAILS

For a while President Jessup waited patiently; then, as the big salary checks came to him to be signed month after month, he began to grow restless. No result had yet been announced and in his conferences with Lynch, he could not determine that any hopeful progress was being made. Finally, in desperation, he called his engineers and designers together. For three weeks he worked with them night and day, studying, analyzing, making records, and computing results. They took cat-naps on benches in the laboratory while waiting for fires to burn a standard number of hours; ate out of lunch-boxes; and finally, unshaven and covered with soot and ashes, they triumphantly produced a fire-box and boiler which would burn the cheapest kind of coal screenings satisfactorily, with but little supervision and a high degree of efficiency. This was the best thing they had ever done in the laboratory. This was the attainment which he had so long desired. This, properly advertised and handled, certainly ought to revolutionize the steam and hot-water heating business. But it was not one of Lynch's brain-children. However, Lynch would now have an opportunity to prove his value and return to the concern large profits for the amount they had spent and would spend upon him. At any rate, he knew how to plan and conduct an advertising and selling campaign.

Lynch, intensely relieved by the solving of this problem, the utility of which he very readily saw, threw himself, heart and soul, into the construction of the advertising campaign. As this work progressed, Jessup began to have some misgivings. While the advertisements, circulars, catalogues, and other literature were beautiful; while the English in them was elegant, and the form of expression refined, somehow or other, they seemed to lack the necessary punch or kick which Jessup knew they ought to have. The two big things about the new product were, first, economy of fuel; second, ease of operation and small demand for supervision. These points were not brought out clearly enough. They did not grip. They did not get home as they should. There was a good deal of talk in all the advertising about the

197

beauty of the new apparatus; about the refinement of its finish; about its workmanship, and many other things which, to Jessup's mind, detracted from the main issue. The one thing he wanted to hammer into the minds of the readers of his advertising was the fact that here was a heating apparatus for which fuel could be purchased in the usual quantities and at half the regular price. What he wanted to do was to make them actually see the dollars and cents saved, not only in fuel, but also in the cost of operation. He wanted suburbanites to see the fact that they could attend to their furnaces each morning before going to town, and that the fires would not need any further attention until the following morning; but, somehow or other, the advertising did not seem to picture this clearly enough. The statements were made, yes; there was plenty of evidence produced to show this; but it was done in a way which, somehow or other, did not produce an intense conviction.

Jessup had secured from his board of directors an appropriation of fifty thousand dollars for a national advertising campaign. Upon the result of his first attempt would depend his securing a further appropriation for such a campaign as he had planned and as he wanted to execute. This being the case, he did not feel that he was justified in permitting Lynch's advertising to go out as it was. The result was that, just before the time came when copy must be sent to the magazines, newspapers, and street-car advertising companies, Jessup called his old advertising manager into conference and for a week they struggled together, revising the copy, rewriting the selling argument, and placing emphasis in clear, strong, unforgetable figures where it would do the most good.

WHY THE "GREAT FIND" WAS A DISAPPOINTMENT

The result of all this was that Lynch, seeing the writing on the wall, tendered his resignation--which was all too gladly accepted. In offering his resignation, however, Lynch had stipulated that he was to receive four thousand dollars out of the six thousand five hundred still due him on his year's contract. President Jessup's error in selecting an employee had cost him ten thousand dollars in salary. Besides this was the still larger sum in expenses, in wasted effort, and in the disorganization of his entire factory and selling force as the result of the introduction of a man who did not belong there.

His mistake was due to two fundamental errors. In the first place, the facts that a man is personally agreeable, that he belongs to the same political party, that he belongs to the same lodge or fraternity, that his ideas and opinion on matters outside of business agree with his employer's, are merely incidental and by no means adequate reasons for

198

employing him. Nor is the fact that he has made a good record, even an extraordinary record, in some other line of business a good reason for employing him. Perhaps, on the other hand, the fact that his record is made in a totally different business is a good reason for not employing him. It certainly was so in this case.

In the second place, President Jessup did not take into consideration the natural aptitudes of his man, natural aptitudes which he might very easily have determined with a moment's casual observation. Lynch was exceedingly fine in texture; his hair, his skin, his features, his hands, and his feet were all fine and delicate. He, therefore, loved beauty, refinement, small articles, fine lines, elegant designs. These things appealed to him strongly, and because of this he was able to make them appeal to others. Anything which was heavy, rough, coarse, crude, uncouth, or ugly repelled him. He could not take an interest in it except in the most theoretical way. For this reason he could not interest others in it. He had an unusual knack for selling things to people which would appeal to their love of the beautiful and their desire for adornment; in short, to their vanity; but he had no qualifications for selling to people on a purely commercial basis, and especially selling something which was so matter-of-fact and commonplace in its character as the saving of coal and the freedom from necessity of frequent attention.

A WEAK MAN AND HIS TEMPTATION

In the winter of 1914-1915, the people of New York were shocked at the downfall of a man who had held a very high social, church, and business position. He had a wife and two or three beautiful children; he occupied a very prominent place in church and Sunday-school; he was well connected socially; he was a prominent member of one of the more popular secret fraternal organizations; he had a good position at a large salary, and enjoyed the complete confidence and respect of his employers and business associates. Like a bolt out of a clear sky, therefore, came the revelation that he had robbed his employers of more than a hundred thousand dollars. This money he had lost in speculation.

It was the old, old story. He had begun speculating with his own reserve; this was quickly wiped out. Then, in order to win back what he had lost, he had begun to borrow, little by little from his employer. He would win for a little while; then he would lose, and, as a result, would have to borrow more in an attempt to make good his losses and repay what he had borrowed.

This man's employers had to make good a loss of about one hundred and twenty-two thousand dollars. In addition to this, they lost time, money, service, energy, and physical well-being because of the upset in their business and the bitter disappointment to them in the defalcation of their trusted employee. They also spent money tracing him in his flight and bringing him back to face trial and receive his penalty. More money was spent trying to discover whether he had concealed any of the funds he had stolen, so that they might be recovered. All of this might have been saved and the man himself, perhaps, might have been protected from the fate which overtook him, if, instead of judging him by his church record and his pleasing personal appearance and manner, they had taken the trouble to learn something about the external evidences of weaknesses which this man possessed in such a marked degree.

WHY HE GAMBLED AND STOLE

If they had learned some very simple principles, they would have been able to determine at a glance at his curly blond hair; by his secretively veiled eyes; by his large, somewhat fleshy nose, not particularly high in the bridge; by the weakness and looseness of his mouth, and the small and retreating contour of his chin, and by other important indications, that he was selfish by nature, grasping, extravagant, too hopeful, too optimistic, too fond of money, too self-indulgent; that he lacked conscientiousness; that he lacked caution; that he lacked foresight; that he lacked any very keen sense of distinction between what was his and what belonged to others; that he lacked firmness, decision, self-control, will-power. Notwithstanding his lack of all these things, he had made a success for himself, up to the time of his defalcation, by means of a keen, penetrating intellect, excellent powers of expression, the ability to make himself agreeable, ease in mingling with strangers, a natural talent for piety and pious profession, and considerable financial and commercial shrewdness.

A man of this type is nearly always a gambler if he has an opportunity; but he ought to be placed in a position where there will be no temptation to him to rob others to satisfy his gambling proclivities. He is one of the last men in the world who ought to be placed in a position of responsibility, trust, and confidence. For the protection of others and for protection against himself, he ought to be under the most careful supervision. His intellectual powers, his suavity, his ability to meet and handle strangers, his commercial and financial shrewdness, ought all to be given full scope by his employers, but any opportunity to handle money or help himself to the funds of others should be carefully shut away from him.

AN ENGINE WITHOUT A BALANCE WHEEL

Some years ago we had an opportunity to look into the affairs of a mail-order house which had just failed for a large sum, so that its creditors, in the final adjustment, received about eleven cents on a dollar for their claims. The business had been established by a capitalist of considerable wealth, who had made his money in an entirely different line. For some years it was operated in a conservative way by a man who had had years of experience in the mail-order business. The man was well along in years and rather old-fashioned in his ideas. While his management was safe and sane, it had not produced a very large return upon the capital investment. For this reason, the owner determined to engage, as advertising manager, a young man who had several years' successful experience in advertising, but no first-hand knowledge of the mail-order business. The young man did brilliant work. The business of the house began to grow, dividends began to come in, and the owner was delighted. But the new advertising manager and the old general manager did not get along well together. The young man was progressive, optimistic, had ideas of expansion and growth, while the old man was conservative, careful, and somewhat out of date in his ideas as to business.

There could be no result of such a combination except the final resignation of the old general manager. This was only too gladly accepted, and the young man who had come in as advertising manager was placed in full charge. Following his appointment there was a period of rapid expansion. Many new lines were added; the concern rented two more floors in the building where it was located, and eventually purchased ground and built a fine new building. The payroll doubled, then trebled, then quadrupled. All these things, of course, took more capital, and the owner was compelled to add many thousands of dollars to his original investment, first, for permanent improvement; then, from time to time, for working capital. He was glad to do this, because the business was growing. There seemed to be every prospect that in the near future there would be profits far in excess of anything the owner had ever dreamed of under the old management.

SUPERSTRUCTURE WITHOUT FOUNDATION

Then came a time when other ventures of the owner compelled the use of all of his spare capital. He could no longer add to the funds invested in his mail-order business. He called his new general manager in and said: "I have put a great deal of money into this mail-order business. You have your beautiful new building; you have a goodly amount of working capital; you have expanded and added new lines; and I think the time has come when you ought to be able not only to run along without any more investment on my part, but very soon to show me a nice little profit. I assure you that it will come in exceedingly handy in the new venture which I have undertaken."

"Oh, certainly," the young man said, "there is no doubt that we shall soon be paying you larger profits than any other enterprise you control, with the new business we have secured and the splendid profits on all lines we are now handling. There is no reason why we should need any more capital, and I do not think it will be very long before we will have repaid you in dividends for every penny of money you have recently put into the business."

And so the owner turned his back on his mail-order business and gave his time, thought, and energy to his other ventures. Reports, of course, reached him regularly, but he had full confidence in the manager, and he was very busy, so he paid but little attention to them.

THE INEVITABLE COLLAPSE

A little more than a year had passed when the capitalist was profoundly astonished and dismayed to have one of his best business friends call upon him and request: "Charlie, I wish you could do something for me on that account. It's long past due and it's getting altogether too large for me to carry as business is now."

"Why, what account is that? I didn't know I owed you a cent."

"Why, for that mail-order business of yours. They've been ordering goods from me for over a year now, and what they have ordered during the last six months has not been paid for. I knew that you were good, of course, and so was perfectly willing to extend the credit. But you know, as a businessman, that there is a limit to such things, and I think it has about been reached. I hope you can take care of it immediately, as I can very readily use the funds."

"Why, how much is this wretched account of mine, Will? I didn't know I owed you a cent. It can't be very much."

"Well, it all depends upon what you call very much. It's something like thirty-five thousand dollars."

"Thirty-five thousand dollars! Why, man, you must be dreaming," and the capitalist turned to his telephone and called up the general manager of his mail-order business.

202

"Why, yes," came back the cheerful, confident tone of the optimistic young manager, "we do owe them around thirty-five thousand, I think. I supposed, of course, you knew all about it. I've been sending my reports in every week."

"But why haven't you paid it? Certainly your sales are big enough and your income from them good enough for you to pay your bills."

"Well, I'll tell you; it is taking us just a little longer for us to get on our feet than I had expected. Then, after your decision not to put any more money into the business, I found it necessary, in order to round out and complete our line, to add some new items which cost us quite a little. But we are in good shape now and the sales are increasing. We shall soon be able to take care of all of our outstanding obligations."

"How much are your outstanding obligations?" asked the capitalist, with a sinking heart.

"Well, about two hundred and fifty thousand dollars, I should say. But it won't take us long to clean that up now that we've squared away."

"You'd better come right over here and bring your books with you. I want to go into this thing."

WHY HE FAILED

It took only a few hours' investigation of the books to convince the capitalist that his mail-order business was hopelessly insolvent. It took expert accountants to find out why it was insolvent. The trouble was that the young manager had proceeded with only the vaguest and roughest kind of an estimate of cost, based, not upon facts, but mostly upon his own superb guesswork. New business had been brought in by reducing prices. "Low prices" had been one of the slogans of the young man's campaign, and he had cut under all of his competitors. On the other hand, there had been the slackest kind of management inside. Overhead expenses had mounted and mounted. The young man had been altogether too easy and generous in fixing salaries, granting promotions and increases, and in giving positions to those who applied. He was really a splendid young fellow, with a sympathetic heart and a generous hand, and it was very difficult for him to turn away anyone who could tell an artistic hard-luck story. Expensive equipment had been purchased which had far greater capacity than the needs of the business required; therefore, many machines and other fixtures had stood idle seventy-five per cent of the time, eating up money in interest charges, depreciation, space, light, heat, and other expenses. In addition to these out-and-out expenditures, there were dozens of little leaks in all the departments of the business, all busily draining away not only possible profits, but the working capital, and, finally, the limit of the concern's credit.

As a result of this kind of management, the final accounting showed the liabilities of the concern to be in the neighborhood of four hundred thousand dollars and its assets only about forty-five thousand. No one could be found to take the business, even as a gift, and assume its obligations. The owner himself had his capital so tightly involved in other ventures that he was unable to save this concern, and it was therefore sold under the hammer. The creditors received their little eleven cents on the dollar. The owner's capital investment was, of course, a total and complete loss.

This man made his mistake in placing a business in which there is a multitude of detail and a necessity for the closest possible scrutiny of every cent of expenditure--a business which must be done upon the smallest possible margin in order to be successful--in the hands of a man who could look only outward and forward and upward. The young man was, indeed, a splendid business getter. He was a natural-born advertiser, salesman, and promoter. His personality was forceful, pleasing, and magnetic. In his intentions and principles he was honest and highly honorable. He was keen, positive, quick in thought, quick in action, progressive, eager, buoyant; he had a splendid grasp of large affairs, principles, and generalities. But he had no mind for details; he rather scorned them. He was perfectly willing to leave the details to someone else, and even then did not care to hear any more about them himself. He never ought to have been placed in charge of a business involving such minute carefulness as the mail-order business. He was dangerous in any position of responsibility without a partner or an auditor and treasurer competent to look after the finances and all of the details of the accounting and administration. This young man's function was getting in the business, but he was not equipped by nature or by training to take care of the business after it came into the house or to administer the funds which came in with it. The capitalist would have known, if he had exercised one-half the care in choosing a general manager that he did in selecting a driving horse, that the young man was unfitted for the work he was expected to do.

A COMMON TYPE

He would have known that anyone as blonde in coloring and as round-headed as this young man was unfit for a position which required the minutest and most careful scrutiny of every detail of administration. He would also have noticed his wide-open, credulous, and generous eye; the narrowness of his head just behind the ears, indicating his inclination to side-step anything in the nature of a disagreeable contest or combat. The high dome of his head just above the temple and the turned up tip of his nose, both indicating extreme optimism; his very short fingers, indicating dislike of detail and the inability to handle it; his rather soft-elastic consistency of hand, showing inability to bear down hard and firm in cutting expenses and holding down salaries.

This young man's type is very common. We meet it constantly in business, and wherever we have met it, we have always found that, unless it was associated with a man of dark complexion, hard consistency, keen, shrewd eyes, the ability to fight and to stick, a sort of bull-dog tenacity, it simply ran away in over-optimistic ventures, dissipated its earnings, and ended in dismal failure.

[Illustration: FIG. 57. Conical hands, with conical finger tips. Indicate refinement, responsiveness, sentiment, love of beauty in music and art, and an emotional nature. This hand, however, is not very practical, and is not the typical hand of the musical performer or creative artist. May be the hand of an actor or singer.]

[Illustration: FIG. 58. Back and front view of hand of Mrs. Flora E. Durand, of Libertyville, Illinois, Pianiste and Pipe Organist. Mrs. Durand is a performer of unusual skill and artistic feeling. Note squareness of entire hand and of finger tips.]

[Illustration: FIG. 59. Back and front view of hands of financier and administrator. Very practical, matter-of-fact, and sensible; not particularly fond of detail, but can compel himself to do it. Note square hands and finger tips and moderately short fingers.]

[Illustration: FIG. 60. Front and back view of hands of a mechanical and electrical engineer of some prominence. He is not only highly qualified, intellectually, for engineering work, but is a mechanic of great expertness and skill. All his work is beautifully finished and marvellously accurate. Note long, square hands and fingers.]

[Illustration: FIG. 61. Long fingers, indicating a tendency to capacity for details.]

[Illustration: FIG. 62. An example of narrow head, indicating mildness of disposition--an inclination to win way and secure ends by intellect, tact, and diplomacy, rather than by direct conflict.]

[Illustration: _Copyright Ernest H. Mills._ FIG. 63. Sir Henry Fowler.

A splendid example of fine, enduring physical balance with excellent intellectual equipment. Note large, long nose, ears, and chin; long, straight upper lip; long, rather lean lines of cheeks and face in general, flat-topped head; prominent brows, and square jaw, These are all typical indications of calmness, practical judgment, prudence, shrewdness, moderation, and, as a result, longevity.]

[Illustration: FIG. 64. Reginald D. Barry, Engineer and Scientific Experimenter. Interested in mechanics and engineering in an almost purely intellectual manner. Ambitious, determined, optimistic. Note especially height and width of upper part of cranium, with slender lower face; also rounded dome above temples, and width and fulness back of upper corners of forehead.]

[Illustration: FIG. 65. Colbert E. Lyon. Note especially high dome of head above temples, indicating optimism, faith, hope, sympathy, generosity and humanitarian leanings. Note also fine texture, indicating love of beauty, refinement, and responsiveness. Practical judgment, energy and determination are shown by prominent brows; large, high nose; and strong chin; fine powers of expression by prominent eyes.]

[Illustration: FIG. 66. Dr. V. Stefansson, Explorer. Of the active, restless, eager, pioneering type, capable of enduring hardship. Note square jaw, large nose, convex profile, blond color, high, wide cheekbones, strong chin, and coarse texture.]

[Illustration: FIG. 67. High, square head, indicating conscientiousness, prudence, carefulness, dependability, and constancy.]

[Illustration: FIG. 68. High, round head, indicating ambition, love of adventure, and a certain degree of recklessness, carelessness, and irresponsibility.]

ROOSEVELT AND TAFT CONTRASTED

When Mr. Roosevelt was about to end his term as President of the United States in 1907, he and his more prudent advisors did not consider it good political judgment for him to seek at that time nomination for what would have been, in effect, a third term. He therefore began to cast about to find a successor who would carry out his policies. As President, he had inaugurated certain policies of administration which he regarded as being of the highest possible importance to the country, and to the world at large. We are not here discussing the common sense, wisdom, and statesmanship of those policies. The fact to which we are calling attention is that Mr. Roosevelt wished to use his influence as President and as the leader of his party to have placed in nomination, as his successor, a man upon whom he could rely to continue to administer the office of President according to the policies he himself had inaugurated.

Mr. Taft had long been a member of Mr. Roosevelt's cabinet and had also been a very close personal friend. As Governor of the Philippines, and as Secretary of War, he had made a splendid record and was considered to be one of the most loyal and able of the President's official family. Accordingly, he was selected by Mr. Roosevelt as his successor. In his campaign for election, and in his inaugural address, Mr. Taft repeatedly gave assurance to the voters that it was his intention to carry out the Roosevelt policies. There is practically no one, even those who disapprove most heartily of Mr. Taft's record in the Presidency, who thinks that he was anything but sincere and honest in making these promises to the voters.

HOW IT WORKED OUT

Now, without discussing for a moment Mr. Taft's administration as President from the standpoint of its true value to the country, or the actual quality of his statesmanship, there is no question in the mind of anyone that he signally failed to carry out the Roosevelt policies. In fact, he became the titular leader of that faction of the Republican party, before the end of his administration, most violently opposed to the Roosevelt policies. He has subscribed to and preached a totally different political doctrine from that of his former friend and chief ever since. This course of action may have been right; it may have been wrong; it may have been wise, or it may have been unwise. It may have been fully justified, or it may not have been justified. These are not questions which interest us here.

The point is that Mr. Roosevelt, in all good faith, and believing in the wisdom of his choice, selected Mr. Taft to carry out his policies in the government, and that Mr. Taft, no doubt with the best of intentions, failed to carry out those policies. The result was a split in the Republican party, the election of a Democratic President and Congress, and other far-reaching consequences, the full meaning of which we have not yet begun to see. They may be good; they may be unfortunate. That is not the question at issue. The question is, could Mr. Roosevelt, if he had had a scientific understanding of human nature, have foretold Mr. Taft's course of action?

INDICATIONS OF DIFFERENCES IN CHARACTER, IDEAS,

IDEALS, AND ACTIONS

The Roosevelt policies were aggressive and bold, cutting across traditions, flinging down the gauntlet, and throwing defiance into the faces of powerful political and business interests. They assumed for the executive office at least all of the powers which, according to the Constitution, belong to it, working in harmony with a group of men who had interested themselves in a number of progressive--perhaps some might say radical--reform measures. Furthermore, these policies were a perfectly natural expression of Mr. Roosevelt's personality.

Do Mr. Taft's physical characteristics, as easily observable indicate that he is of a character, temperament and aptitude to continue such policies as these. A comparison of the two men should give us the answer.

Mr. Taft is very much lighter in color than Mr. Roosevelt. As a general rule, the lighter blond coloring is an indication of mildness of disposition, instead of the fierceness and eager determination to dominate of the man who is as ruddy as Mr. Roosevelt.

Mr. Taft's forehead is very much more practical in type than Mr. Roosevelt's. He is, therefore, far more interested in the practical application of such principles as he has than in theories, hypotheses, and reform.

Mr. Taft's nose, by its roundness and softness of contour, indicates mildness, good nature, refinement, and delicacy of feeling, while Mr. Roosevelt's is the large-tipped, bony-bridged nose of aggressiveness and combativeness.

Mr. Taft's mouth is a good-natured, smiling, laughing, jovial mouth, instead of the grim, hard, fighting mouth as shown in Mr. Roosevelt's type.

Mr. Taft's chin is of the rounded and rather retreating type, an indication that he is probably far better qualified by disposition to follow a strong and aggressive leader than to take the aggressive, dominating, fighting leadership himself.

Mr. Taft is a very much larger man than Mr. Roosevelt. This, while not particularly important, is just one more indication of his good nature and his dislike for a hard, grueling fight. It is an interesting fact that almost all of the great fighters of the world have been little men. Alexander, Caesar, Napoleon, Grant, Lord Roberts, Sheridan, Sherman, Wilhelm II, and many others have been below medium in stature. Of the others, Kitchener, Wellington, Frederick the Great, Washington, and von Hindenberg have been men of not more than medium size. It is almost unprecedented to find a fighter in a man of Mr. Taft's huge size.

In structure, Mr. Taft is essentially of the judicial type. This type is always a defender of property, an upholder of the Constitution, a strong advocate of making the best of things as they are, rather than plunging into violent innovations, the results of which are unknown and may very easily prove to be disastrous. On the other hand, Mr. Roosevelt is of restless, active, pioneering structure--the bony, muscular type of man who has always led reform movements and led in fighting for changes he thought would add to the freedom of humanity.

Mr. Taft's texture is finer than that of Mr. Roosevelt. He is, therefore, more interested in the refinements, the luxuries, and the delicacies of life than is Mr. Roosevelt. He is also less vigorous, less virile, and less insistent upon reform and the right of the people to rule. It is an interesting fact that most of the great friends of the people, most of those who are eager in demanding the rights of the proletariat, are men of medium or coarse texture.

Mr. Taft is soft elastic in consistency of fiber, while Mr. Roosevelt is hard elastic. This indicates more impressionability or amenability to influence, more desire for finding an easy and pleasant way to accomplish his end on the part of Mr. Taft than on the part of Mr. Roosevelt.

In Mr. Taft the vital element leads--in Mr. Roosevelt, the motive. The vital element conduces to putting on of flesh, enjoys the good things of life, loves an easy time, and naturally inclines to make the best of things as they are. On the other hand, the motive element demands outdoor activity, freedom, liberty of movement, and not only liberty for itself, but liberty for everyone else.

Mr. Roosevelt's jaw is square and determined, which shows an inclination to push things through regardless of obstacles; to pursue his ends no matter what difficulties stand in the way. Mr. Taft's jaw is rather rounded and not so prominent. This indicates less determination, less perseverance, less persistence in pushing against obstacles and difficulties.

Note the difference in width between Mr. Roosevelt's and Mr. Taft's head just above the ears. Mr. Roosevelt is very wide-headed. This indicates energy, aggressiveness, impatience, a certain amount of destructive tendency. It is this which not only makes Mr. Roosevelt an aggressive, eager, fighting, dominating politician and statesman, but also a mighty hunter.

On the other hand, Mr. Taft's head is medium narrow just above the ears. This indicates mildness, an inclination to use diplomacy rather than force, and a tendency to take things as they are rather than to push ahead aggressively and make radical changes.

Mr. Roosevelt's head is high in the crown. Mr. Taft's head is low in the crown. A high crown indicates firmness, decision, love of power, love of authority, a demand to rule, and great ambition. A low crown, on the other hand, indicates amenability to authority, a willingness to compromise, and a lack of domineering quality.

Compare the expression of the two men. Mr. Roosevelt's expression is intense, vigorous, and almost belligerent. Mr. Taft's expression is mild, calm, judicial, good-natured, and jovial.

By what stretch of the imagination could anyone suppose that a man of Mr. Taft's character and aptitudes, as shown by the indications pointed out in the foregoing, could even begin to carry out the policies of a man of Mr. Roosevelt's character, as shown by the indications we have pointed out? And yet, all of the political history of the United States since 1909 has been completely changed as the result of Mr. Roosevelt's lack of knowledge of the plain facts of the science of human nature. Indeed, the result of Mr. Roosevelt's choice of a successor is found in Mexico, in Germany, in England, in France, and, in fact, throughout the world.

IF NOT SCIENTIFICALLY, HOW?

Woodrow Wilson has been criticized, perhaps, as severely for his selection of men for various posts in his administration as for any other cause, if reports are to be believed. He has probably suffered far more from unfortunate selection of lieutenants and of men for special tasks, and has more deeply regretted his mistakes of this nature, than any other thing in his administration up to the time that these lines are written.

The few examples we have given in this chapter of men who gave excellent promise and then failed to live up to their expectations are typical. They are occurring every day in every line of business and industry, as well as in politics and government. We are told by some who have made a study of this subject that the only way to find out what a man can do, what his aptitudes are, what are his abilities, his capacities, his type, and what his performances will be, is to put him in a place where he will have an opportunity to show what there is in him.

If this is the best that science can do for us, we are, then, groping in darkness through a tangled maze of pitfalls. We have nothing left but to go on using disastrous and impracticable methods in the selection of men for commerce, for industry, for financial responsibility, and for the highest positions of honor, responsibility, and power in the gift of the people.

CHAPTER III

THE REMEDY

True, we can determine a man's fitness by giving him a trial. But, if he is a failure, and we learn nothing by experience, the next incumbent may be a hundred-fold worse. Furthermore, in many places, selection by trial is an impossibility, as in marriage, in the presidency of a bank, or in a general to lead a forlorn hope. There must be some better way.

Some years ago we were asked to make an investigation at a printing and publishing house. Two years before this time the proprietor had ceased to receive any profits from the enterprise and, at this particular time, complained that for months he had been putting money into the business in order to keep it going. He himself was not a practical printer and was not in immediate management of the concern. His manager, however, was an able man, a good printer, and was considered to be a good business man.

At the very outset of our investigation, we found that the foreman of the composing-room purchased type, leads, and slugs, furniture, cases, and all of the other materials used in his department. The foreman of the press-room purchased paper, ink, rollers, twine, and other things. The foreman of the shipping-room purchased packing-cases, wrapping paper, twine, nails, hammers, marking ink, and other materials he used. The foreman of the bindery purchased glue, cloth, leather, boards, paper, and wire. The office manager purchased typewriter ribbons, carbon paper, clips, paper fasteners, pins, mucilage, rulers, pens, and pencils. The foreman of the electrotyping department purchased copper, acids, metal, and tools. We were rather surprised to find that the coal and lubricating oil for the engine room were purchased by the manager himself, but not at all surprised to learn that he had never heard of such a quantity as a British Thermal unit and that he had absolutely no records to show the kind of coal most efficient under his boilers. A little further investigation showed that each head of department had charge of the stores of materials and supplies for his department and gave them out to employees upon a mere verbal request. We were not long in discovering that the foreman of the composing-room received "tokens of regard" from salesmen; that the foreman of the press-room was regularly on the payroll of several companies furnishing inks and rollers, and had a brother-in-law running a little print shop around the corner and spending very little money for ink, paper, and other such materials. Each head of a department also had full power to "hire and fire," as he called it. The foreman of the composing-room said to us, when we questioned him in regard to this matter, "Why, if I didn't have the power to hire and fire I could not maintain discipline in my department; rather than give that up, I would resign my position."

As a result of this state of affairs, we found a brother of the foreman occupying an easy position in the composing-room, a brother-in-law, two nieces, two nephews, and a son occupying easy positions at good salaries in the press-room and various other nephews and other semi-dependents working away under foremen who were related to them in the various departments. In the composing-room, also, we found, upon careful investigation, that several of the employees were very heavily overpaid at times and that they divided the surplus in their pay envelopes with the foreman.

When we called these things to the attention of the manager, he was deeply surprised and pained. "Why," he said, "every head of a department in this printing and publishing house is a personal friend of mine. I have the highest regard for them and have held their honor and uprightness so high in my estimation that it has never occurred to me to investigate their administration in their several departments. You know, of course, that this is the usual procedure in the printing business. The foremen regard these prerogatives as being especially theirs and would very deeply and bitterly resent any attempt on the part of the management to take them away." The manager was only partly right. It is true that these practices have been followed in many printing and publishing houses; that they are followed in some even to-day; but even in his time the most progressive and successful had long ago abolished this inefficient and dishonesty-breeding system.

SCIENTIFIC PURCHASING ENDS ABUSES

To-day in every well-managed printing office, as well as every other industry, there is a purchasing department. Materials are purchased, not through favors, or on account of bonus from the salesmen, but upon exact specifications which are worked out in the laboratory. Materials

212

are accepted and paid for only after a laboratory analysis to ascertain their true worth. Materials are kept in a stores department and are issued only upon written requisitions. Requisitions are carefully checked up, records kept to show that each department is using only its proper quota of materials and supplies of all kinds.

While the purchasing of mere inanimate material, which after all is only secondary in importance, has thus been reduced to science and art in charge of specialists, the methods of selection, assignment, and handling of employees in nearly all industrial and commercial institutions continues to-day on the same old dishonest basis as that which we found in the printing and publishing house described. Foremen, superintendents, and heads of departments still guard jealously their prerogatives of hiring and firing. So deeply rooted is this prejudice in the minds of the industrial and commercial world, that many managers have said to us in horror, "Why, we can't take away the power to hire and fire from our foremen. They couldn't maintain discipline. They would not consent to remain in their executive positions if they did not have this power of life and death, as it were, over their employees."

Incidentally, we may say, that we have had almost no trouble in securing the enthusiastic and loyal co-operation of foremen and superintendents where employment departments have been installed.

SCIENTIFIC EMPLOYMENT THE REMEDY

It is becoming increasingly clear to employers that, only by following the example of the purchasing department, can industry and commerce cure the evil which we have briefly described and exemplified in the two preceding chapters. We find that employment, instead of being left to the tender mercies of foremen, Tom, Dick, and Harry--who may or may not be good judges of men, who may or may not be honest, who may or may not indulge in nepotism, who may or may not pad the payroll; who may or may not be unreasonable, tyrannical and otherwise inimical to the best interest of the concern from whom they draw their living--selection of help is now delegated to specialists and experts. Employment departments are now established with more or less complete control over the selection and assignment of men and women in the organization. In some of these departments complete records are kept. Exact and painstaking care is used in securing data, hunting up applicants, watching the actual performances of those who are put to work, determining whether or not they live up to their opportunities. In other employment departments this system is very loose and the departments exist principally for the purpose of securing applicants who are then turned over without recommendation to the foreman who still has the power of employing and discharging.

The remedy for which we have been looking is to be found in an employment department, organized with a carefully selected personnel, which will perform the same careful, analytical research and record-keeping functions as a scientific purchasing department. Perhaps, for the sake of clearness, it would be well for us to describe rather in detail the work of such a department.

ORGANIZATION

The organization of such a department depends entirely upon the number of applicants and employees with which it must deal and the character of the work to be done. Suppose, for example, we have a factory with two thousand employees, seventy-five per cent of them skilled, fifteen per cent of them unskilled, and ten per cent office employees. The work of such a department could be very well carried on by one employment supervisor, one assistant supervisor, one clerk and record-keeper, and part of the time of one stenographer. The employment supervisor is a staff officer. His position in the company is that of a member of the staff of the general manager or president. His work should be subject to oversight by the president or general manager alone, and he should not be answerable to any other officer or member of the corporation. It is the function of the employment supervisor to direct the work of his department, to conduct its relations with all other departments of the business, to interview, analyze, and recommend for employment all executives and employees of more than ordinary importance; to hear and adjudicate all cases of complaint or disagreement between executives or between executives and their employees and also to review cases heard by his assistant in which there is any degree of dissatisfaction with the settlement proposed.

It is the duty of the assistant employment supervisor to interview and analyze, select, and recommend for employment all applicants for minor positions in the factory and office. It is also his duty, under direction of the supervisor, to number and carefully analyze every position in the organization, determining its requirements, and, having made a careful list of these requirements in a card index, to keep it in the files of the department where it can be readily consulted. It is the duty of the clerk and record-keeper to make out all reports, to record all reports sent from heads of departments, to keep the files, to make out notifications to the paymaster and to other officers as occasion requires,

214

and in general to keep the records and files of the department in a neat, orderly condition, up to date every moment of the day, and so managed as to yield readily and instantly any information desired.

It is the duty of the stenographer to attend to all correspondence of the department, including dictation from the supervisor and the assistant supervisor.

FUNCTIONS OF AN EMPLOYMENT DEPARTMENT

Briefly, it is the function of the employment department to secure, interview, analyze, select, and recommend for employment men and women who will pre-eminently fit into the various positions in the organization; by competent counsel, upon request, to assist the line executives in the management of employees, and, in all its activities, to act in the capacity of expert in human nature, conducting all phases of relationship between the corporation and its employees.

In detail, however, the functions of a well-organized and efficient employment department are these:

ANALYSIS OF POSITIONS

1. Theoretically, the first function of an employment department is to analyze carefully every position in the organization, listing its requirements, noting the environment and other conditions which surround it; in short, painting what will be to the members of the department a clear and easily recognizable word-picture of the aptitudes and character of the man or woman best fitted to fill that position. While this is the theoretical first function of the department, in actual practice certain conditions may arise which will make this inadvisable. But it ought to be done as quickly as possible, and the records tabulated on cards in a convenient way in a card file. These are the specifications for the human material needed in each place. The method of making this analysis varies under different circumstances.

ANALYSIS OF EXECUTIVES

2. The next step in the work of an employment department is the analysis of all executives. Each executive is interviewed and carefully analyzed for two purposes; first, to find whether he is indeed the right man in the right place; second, to observe his characteristics, his peculiarities, his personality, and to learn from him his preferences. All of these are carefully listed, and, in selecting employees, care is taken to select only those who will work harmoniously and happily with the executives under whom they are placed.

ANALYSIS OF EMPLOYEES

3. Employees in the organization at the time of the installation of the employment department are analyzed as opportunity offers. In this way the supervisor determines whether or not they are well placed as they are, or whether they have talent and abilities which would make them far more valuable in some other part of the institution. The analysis of each employee is made out either completely and in detail or in a general way, according to his importance, his future possibilities, his probable length of service with the institution, and other conditions. Clearly a great deal more time would be spent and a great deal more careful analysis made in the case of an important executive, than in the case of a day laborer engaged as a member of a temporary shoveling gang.

These analyses, after having been written out, are filed in folders. Each employee has a folder of his own, and in this are placed not only his analysis, but a sheet for the keeping of his record and all letters and papers referring to him.

SECURING OF APPLICANTS

4. Inasmuch as every live organization is always growing and, therefore, taking on new employees, and inasmuch, also, as there is a state of flux in every organization, vacancies occurring for one reason or another, it is a function of the employment department to secure as many of the most desirable applicants possible for all of the positions in the enterprise. Some of these applicants come to the employment department in the natural course of events, others come as the result of advertisements; still others because the employment supervisor and his assistant take means to ferret them out and send for them. Promising young men in schools and colleges and in the employ, perhaps, of other organizations are kept under careful observation. Data in regard to them is listed in the reserve file, and their records, as they come in various ways to the employment supervisor, are filed with them.

5. Applicants having been secured in these ways, the next step is carefully to analyze them. Under ideal conditions this analysis is made by observation, unknown to the applicant, during a pleasant interview. He may be asked certain questions, not chiefly for the sake of bringing out direct information, but for the sake of observing the effects of the interrogations upon him.

In some large organizations, in the rush season, 100 new employees may be added every day. In order to select this number, perhaps several hundred applicants may be interviewed. Obviously, a detailed and thorough analysis of each cannot be made. Under such conditions, however, the work is usually of such a character that the most casual observation on the part of a trained interviewer will reveal at once the fact that the applicant either is or is not fitted for the work to be done.

As a result of the analyses made by the employment supervisor and his staff, applicants are recommended to foremen who have made requisitions for the filling of vacancies. Bear in mind, it is not the function of the employment department arbitrarily to employ. When a desirable applicant has been found, he is sent, with a recommendation, to the head of the department which has made requisition for an employee. Then the foreman or superintendent or the manager either rejects or accepts the applicant. In case of rejection, the executive returns the applicant to the employment department, stating his reason for his action.

When an applicant is accepted, the employment department notifies the paymaster, also places a folder for a new employee in the file. It is often highly desirable, also, before sending an employee to a foreman to inform him fully and in detail as to the work he is expected to do, the conditions under which he will be expected to work, the rate of pay he will receive, the opportunities for advancement, and all other information which may decide the applicant for or against accepting the position if it is offered to him.

REPORTS AND RECORDS

6. The employment department organizes methods for receiving regular and complete reports upon the performance and deportment of every employee in the organization. These reports include punctuality, attendance, efficiency, special ability, deportment, home environment, and habits, companions, and other necessary and valuable information. Every employer who has the good of his employees and their advancement at heart ought to know these things. Reports are received from foremen and superintendents, also from others who are especially assigned by the employment supervisor to secure the information.

RECOMMENDATION FOR TRANSFER, PROMOTION AND INCREASE

7. As a result of these reports and of its own analysis, the employment department recommends for transfer from one department to another, or for promotion, or for increase of pay, such employees as merit these changes in their positions and relationship with the company. In cases

where necessity seems to demand it, the employment department may also recommend the discharge of an employee.

CONSULTATION ON RATES OF PAY

8. In co-operation with properly constituted authorities, and as the result of careful, scientific study of the whole situation, the employment department assists in establishing rates of pay commensurate with the work done, with the conditions in the industry, and with their probable effect upon the loyalty, happiness, and consequent efficiency of the employees.

SPECIAL INFORMATION TO MANAGEMENT

9. Upon request of the general manager or any other executive in the organization, the employment supervisor may furnish complete information as to any employee in the organization when that information is legitimately required. Oftentimes, also, there will be a call made upon the employment department for some one with special ability to undertake a certain task. It may be that the employment department has had under its observation for months or even years some man already in the employ of the company who will exactly fill the new position or the vacancy just created. Or it may be that, upon consultation of the records, the employment department will find just the man it is looking for. In case neither of these things happen, then the right man may be found listed and described in the reserve file.

TRANSFER AND DISCHARGE

10. When a foreman or other executive can no longer use any man in his employ, he does not discharge him, but sends him instead to the employment department with a report and recommendation. Oftentimes the employment supervisor or his assistant can adjust the matter and return the man to his position, better fitted than ever to perform his task. It may be that the executive and not the employee is at fault. On the other hand, it is often the case that the employment department can take the man so returned and place him in another department, where he will be happy and efficient. It may be that the work that he has been doing is suited to him, but that his executive is not the right kind of personality for him. Whatever the employment department finds in regard to the man, action is taken in accordance therewith. In case there is real cause for it, the employee is paid off and dropped from the rolls of the company.

AID IN MANAGEMENT AND DISCIPLINE

11. Owing to his peculiar knowledge of human nature, it is often possible for the employment supervisor or his assistant to aid executives in discipline in their several departments. It has been our experience that an efficient employment department is not in existence very long before many executives begin to come in for consultation and to ask the employment supervisor or his assistant what course to pursue in reference to some particular man or some particular set of circumstances. This has been found to be one of the most valuable functions of an employment department.

SETTLEMENT OF DISPUTES

12. Also because of his expert knowledge of human nature, the employment supervisor or his assistant is often called upon to adjudicate between executives, between fellow-employees or between an executive and his subordinate. Disputes and differences of opinion usually arise because people fail to understand each other. The employment supervisor, understanding both parties in the quarrel, is usually able to point out some basis of amicable adjustment and the restoration of friendly relationship.

EDUCATION OF EMPLOYEES

13. Employers are learning that the finest and most valuable assets in their employees are not their bones and muscles; not their intelligence, training, and experience when they enter the organization; but, rather, the possibility of development of their intelligence, talents, and aptitudes. Educators now almost entirely agree that the best and most serviceable education possible is that afforded by work, provided the work is intelligently directed and constantly used by those who direct it as an educational force. Employers are also grasping the great possibilities for them in this theory. Corporation schools, night schools, special classes, and many other forms of education inside the walls of commercial and industrial enterprises are being used to good advantage. In an ideal economic system, every factory, every store, every shop, every place where men and women are gathered together for employment should be, in the higher sense of the word, a school for the development of the very best human qualities.

Since this is true, who is better qualified by training, by education, and by experience to conduct this education than the employment supervisor and his assistants? If he is properly chosen for his work, he has a special scientific knowledge of human nature; he knows not only the talents and aptitudes of every member of the force, but also knows the best way for developing and bringing out these talents and aptitudes. He knows for just what vocation each one under his tutelage is suited. He knows just what study and training each one ought to pursue in order to best fit himself for that vocation.

WELFARE WORK

14. Because of its peculiar relationship to all the employees in the organization, there is no department better fitted to undertake all of that activity in connection with industrial life, which is known as welfare work or social betterment, than that entrusted with employment.

ADAPTABILITY

The organization and plan of an employment department, as we have outlined it, is, as we have said, for an institution employing two thousand men and women. For larger organizations, of course, the employment supervisor must have more assistants, there must be more clerks and stenographers, according to the number of employees handled and the character of the work to be done. There are some organizations in which there is very little fluctuation in the personnel. In such cases a small employment department is all that is necessary, even although a large number of employees may be on the payroll. In other kinds of work there is a very large fluctuation, under ordinary conditions, and in such cases it is necessary to have more help in the employment department. In the case of small business, such as retail stores, the employer himself is oftentimes the entire employment department, except for such assistance as he may obtain from a clerk or stenographer. In such a case, also, the records do not need to be so complete and so voluminous, since the proprietor can carry a great deal in regard to each one of his employees in his own mind. We know many executives in large organizations, where employment departments have not been established, who constitute, in themselves, employment departments for their own little corner of the industry. They may have only five or six employees under their care, but they handle them according to scientific principles, analyzing them and their work with just as great care as if there were hundreds of them.

The method, after all, is unimportant. It is the spirit of the work that is all important. It does not matter whether you have a huge force of clerks, assistants, interviewers, and stenographers, or whether you yourself, in your little corner office with your three or four retail clerks as a working force, constitute the whole organization. The spirit of scientific analysis and the fitting of each man to his job in a common sense, sane, practical way, instead of according to out-of-date methods, is the important consideration in the remedy which we present.

CHAPTER IV

RESULTS OF SCIENTIFIC EMPLOYMENT

In a lecture to the students of the New York Edison Company Commercial School, on January 20, 1915, afterward also presented at the Third Annual Convention of the National Association of Corporation Schools at Worcester, Mass., on June 9, 1915, Herman Schneider, Dean of the College of Engineering of the University of Cincinnati, in discussing "The Problem of Selecting the Right Job," made the following statement:

"2. Physical Characteristics.

"This seems to be a development of the old idea of phrenology. It is claimed in this system that physical characteristics indicate certain abilities. For example, a directive, money-making executive will have a certain shaped head and hand. A number of money-making executives were picked at random and their physical characteristics charted. We do not find that they conform at all to any law. Also, we found men who had physical characteristics that ought to make them executives, but they were anything but executives. A number of tests of this kind gave negative results. We were forced to the conclusion that this system was not reliable."

It is of exceeding great importance for us to know whether the conclusion of Dean Schneider is to be accepted as final. He is a man of high attainment and has done some most remarkable and highly commendable work in connection with continuation schools in the city of Cincinnati. His opinion and conclusion, therefore, are worthy of the most careful consideration.

At first glance, Dean Schneider's method of investigation seems sound and his statement, therefore, conclusive. He examined actual cases; he collected evidence, and he found that physical characteristics were not a reliable guide to aptitudes and character. It is well for us, however, to remember in discussing problems of this kind, that every new scientific discovery has always been rejected by many recognized authorities after what they considered to be careful and convincing tests. Harvey nearly died in trying to maintain his theory of the circulation of the blood; Darwin's theory was insistently repudiated and rejected by many scientific men of his day; Galilo, Columbus, Boillard, the discoverer of the convolution of Broca, and Stevenson, the inventor of the steam locomotive engine, failed to convince the recognized authorities of their times. Gall, who localized the motor functions of the brain, a

221

discovery universally accepted by all brain physiologists today, was laughed out of court by men of the highest scientific authority, who, by experiments, "proved" that he was wrong. So great a mathematician and scientist as Professor Simon Newcomb made the emphatic remark that the dream of flight in a heavier-than-air machine was absurd and would never be realized. The difficulty with all these conclusions lay in the fact that the much-vaunted "proof" was negative in character. Nothing is easier--or more fallacious, logically--than to "prove" that a thing is *not* so. The difficulty lies in proving that it *is* so; therefore, logically sound.

According to logicians, conclusions based upon negative premises are inherently unsound. In order to reach reliable conclusions, we must first have *all* of the essential facts in the case. We question seriously whether this was possible in the course of such a brief investigation as Dean Schneider made. Scientific selection of employees according to the science of character analysis by the observational method was first proposed in the summer of 1912, so that Dean Schneider has had only three years, during which he was much occupied with other duties, in which to make his observations. We only wish here to raise the question as to whether, in that short time, he could obtain all of the facts necessary for reaching a final conclusion. At any rate, other scientists have spent at least fifteen or twenty years in the examination of the same facts before reaching their conclusions.

The method employed as outlined in the paragraph quote does not seem to fulfill all of the necessary requirements of a careful and complete scientific investigation. Take, for example, the test of "directive money-making executives." Would Dean Schneider, or any other engineer, permit a layman, no matter how well qualified otherwise, to examine twenty or thirty different pieces of engineering work for the purpose of determining whether or not they "conform to any law." We acknowledge Dean Schneider's ability as an engineer and as an educator, but until he has submitted proof, we must question his ability and training as an observer of physical characteristics as indicative of character and aptitudes.

Again, take the test of those who have "the characteristics that ought to make them executives." We should like to know what these physical characteristics were. We should also like to know what other physical characteristics these men had. Perhaps there were some which interfered seriously with their becoming successful as executives.

Still further, it would be illuminating to know whether the men so examined had ever been properly trained for executive work; whether they had had opportunities to become executives or whether some or all of them may not have been misfits in whatever they were doing. Obviously, a sound, scientific conclusion cannot be reached until all of the variables in the problem have been adequately studied and brought under control. There is no evidence in the paragraph that we have quoted that Dean Schneider had done this.

But, after all, we shall proceed very little, if any, with our inquiry as to the reliability of Dean Schneider's conclusions if we content ourselves merely with criticizing his methods of research and reason. Even if we could prove beyond a doubt that the methods used were unscientific and the reasoning unsound, we could go no further toward establishing the contrary of Dean Schneider's conclusion than he has in establishing the unreliability of determining mental aptitudes and character by an observation of physical characteristics. The main question is not, "Is Dean Schneider right or wrong?" but rather, "Is an employment department, conducted along the lines laid down in the preceding chapter, a profitable investment, and, especially, is it possible to determine the right job for any individual by observing his physical characteristics?"

BUT IT IS BEING DONE

Fortunately, this question is no longer academic. There is no need for the bringing up of arguments, the stating of theories, the quoting of authorities, or any such controversial methods. Employment departments *have* been established in a number of commercial and industrial organizations, some very large--some small--and *are* being conducted, with some variations, according to the plan outlined in the preceding chapter. The science of character analysis by the observational method *is* the basis of their work. In addition, this science is the basis of employment work in several hundred other employment departments, large and small, where the Blackford plan has not been adopted in its entirety. The plan referred to was formulated in 1912. The fact that this method has been in actual commercial use under widely varying conditions and in the hands of many different individuals, for more than three years, is, on the face of it, a reasonably fair presumption of its reliability. At any rate, it is fully as convincing as Dean Schneider's purely negative "proof."

The question remains as to whether the commercial applications of this method are successful; whether the results obtained are reliable; whether the inefficiencies and losses, to which we have referred in

223

previous chapters, are appreciably remedied by its use.

SOME PRACTICAL RESULTS

In one of the first organizations where the Blackford Employment Plan was installed there were employed about 2,500 men and women. At the time of the adoption of this plan the various foremen and superintendents in the plant were hiring about 6,600 new employees each year in order to maintain their regular working force of 2,500. Within six months new employees were being taken on at the rate of only 4,080 a year--and this notwithstanding the fact that many changes were necessitated by sweeping reorganization and adoption of new methods of manufacture in the industry.

Excellent results were obtained in reassignment of executives as the result of a careful analysis of those holding positions when the department was installed. One executive instantly recognized as being clever, designing, and essentially dishonest was replaced by another of a reliable, efficient type. Under the new executive, the department more than doubled its output, at the same time cutting the payroll of the department down to 43 per cent of its former size. Still another executive, holding a position of highest trust and responsibility, was reported upon adversely after analysis by the employment department. An investigation made as the result of this report revealed serious irregularities covering a long period of months. Another man properly qualified for the position was selected by the department, and immediately began to effect noticeable savings, as well as greatly increasing the value of the department's work in the institution. Still another executive selected by this department increased the output of one of the shops by 120 per cent, with a very slight increase in the payroll. In another organization, careful records showed that among employees selected according to this plan, 90 per cent were efficient, satisfactory, and permanent; 8 per cent fairly satisfactory but not permanent; and 2 per cent unsatisfactory and discharged.

AN UNUSUAL HARMONY OF JUDGMENT

But these results, while desirable, are not wholly convincing. It is easy enough to explain them on the ground that any man or woman of common sense, keen observation and good judgment, devoting all his or her intelligence and time to employment problems, might have gained the same results without using a method for determining aptitudes and character from an observation of physical characteristics.

More specific and more convincing evidence may be found in a series of incidents which occurred in connection with an employment department established in a textile factory, employing twelve hundred men, located in New England. The supervisor of this department is a young man who has been a student and practitioner of this method in employment work since August, 1912. Previously to taking up this work, he had taken an engineer's degree and had some experience as an executive, in a large factory.

In January, 1915, the supervisor analyzed carefully twenty executives then at work in the plant, carefully wrote out the analyses and submitted them to the management with recommendations for transfers and readjustments of rather a sweeping nature. The management, wishing to make an experiment, agreed to make the changes, provided we were also to analyze the executives in question, submit our analyses in writing, and show agreement as to the character and aptitudes of the men. We accordingly proceeded to the factory, and there, without consultation with the supervisor or his report, proceeded to analyze the twenty executives independently. It would not be fair to the executives in question to publish all of these analyses in full, but a comparison of the essential points in a few of them will be instructive:

Supervisor says of No. 1: "Sociable, scheming, secretive; poor judge of men; lacking seriously in executive ability; decidedly a 'one-man-job' man; does not plan ahead; clannish, narrow-minded; very low intelligence for a foreman. Any organization he builds will be close-mouthed, unreliable, and selfish in structure. Because of the technical knowledge of the business which he has gained, and which can be gained only by long experience, he should do good work in experimental lines. Any change made, however, should separate him completely from the regular productive organization."

Dr. Blackford reports on No. 1: "He is, however, an undesirable man to be in charge of others. He is far more destructive than constructive, more disorganizing than organizing. He is ultra-conservative, non-progressive, and is not disposed to take on any new methods unless he himself can get the credit for their installation. In disposition he is stubborn and obstinate. He is also reserved and suspicious. Being of the selfish type, he will look after his own interests first in all things. No. 1 lacks straightforwardness and frankness of disposition, so he will be tricky, slippery, and do things in an underhanded way. He has very great dislike of detail and will have a tendency to procrastinate if given an opportunity, I believe he has passed the age limit of mental growth."

Supervisor thus summarizes No. 2: "A well-intentioned, honest and

225

reliable man, lacking absolutely in executive ability. Should have a job as inspector or like, where he would have no one to look after but himself."

Dr. Blackford says of No. 2: "No. 2 is a simple-hearted man of very ordinary ability. He is not systematic or orderly; is very susceptible to criticism; exceedingly emotional, apprehensive, and watchful. No doubt men will like him because he is easy with them. However, he will not be a particularly good executive, because he cannot maintain discipline."

Supervisor thus analyzes No. 3: "Very clannish, lacking absolutely in intelligence, executive ability, frankness; in fact, every attribute that is necessary for a good foreman. Is wholly unfitted for an executive job of any kind. Under very strict supervision, would make a fair workman."

Dr. Blackford reports on No. 3: "He is easily influenced; too undependable and too lax in discipline to make a good executive. He has a keen sense of right and wrong, but will take on the color of his surroundings. If led by an undesirable man, he will be a poor asset, and only a fair one even under good influence."

Supervisor, on No. 4: "An active, honest and frank man; a good boss for a small gang of men. Limited somewhat by lack of education and medium planning ability."

Dr. Blackford, on No. 4: "An energetic, active man of only fair intelligence and capability. He is sympathetic and generous to those he likes, but his strongest quality is a desire to rule. He will enjoy enforcing laws, rules and regulations, and will do this with a degree of energy and watchfulness which probably results in good work on part of those under him. He is a fair executive. Under right influence, might further develop."

Supervisor reports on No. 5: "A capable man, secretive and somewhat clannish; is susceptible, however, to other influences and can be developed. A little quick-tempered in handling help; expects too much at the outset. This man must be removed from the influence of No. 1 or he will make no progress."

Dr. Blackford, on No. 5: "A capable man, secretive in his work; careful, conservative, and conservatively progressive. He is intelligent and industrious. He is also ambitious, and has good artistic sense. He is the type of man that takes pride in doing good work. He will prefer his work to be perfect and finished rather than faulty. In disposition he is usually mild, but has a very destructive temper when aroused; so he is

226

probably a little hot-headed with his workers. He is reserved and secretive, but under encouragement will unfold whatever information he has concerning the work. Perhaps his most negative point is a lack of courage in his convictions, but with encouragement and proper support, he ought to develop into a good executive."

Supervisor says, briefly, of No. 6: "A very loyal, honest and painstaking employee; very sincere and absolutely reliable; lacking somewhat in executive ability to handle a large gang. Very desirable."

Dr. Blackford says, more at length, of No. 6: "Industrious, energetic, watchful, careful, dependable, and conscientious in her work. She is sympathetic, but exacting with her workers. She has fair intelligence, is teachable, and will give considerable thought to improving her work. She is also a good critic and a good judge of values. If not given too large a department or too great responsibility, she ought to be very valuable in an executive position."

Supervisor, on No. 7: "An active, reliable man; a good gang-boss or leader; very susceptible to further training."

Dr. Blackford, on No. 7: "Highest grade and finest-textured of any of the foremen yet considered. He is also intelligent, honest, industrious; has high principles; is careful in his work, and will take very great pride in it. He is naturally artistic and ought to turn out very beautiful work. He is clean morally and physically, thorough, and will always prefer a fine quality of goods and workmanship to coarse quality. He is distinctly a quality man. With training and opportunity he ought to develop into a fine man for greater responsibility than he now carries."

ANALYSES FROM PHOTOGRAPHS

Perhaps, in some ways, an even more convincing evidence of the reliability and practicability of the observational method may be found in the results obtainable by analysis from photographs. A photograph is, in a sense, a purely mechanical product. It is, in graphic form, a record of the subject's physical characteristics, stripped of all of the atmosphere, so to speak, of his personality. A photograph cannot talk, cannot act, cannot reveal the man within by any subtle appeal to what are called the intuitions. Photographs as the basis of analysis are used extensively in employment and vocational work. These analyses are usually written out in detail and stand, in black and white, undeniable records of the analyst's observations and conclusions. The analysis of Sidney Williams appearing on pages 206 to 210 is a sample of the definite and specific manner in which these analyses are made. It has been impossible for us to trace and verify in detail every one of these records. They are being made all the time, and in one form or another, by many of those who are now using this method. But we have traced several hundred of them for purposes of verification and have found amongst them only three which have differed with the facts in the case in any essential particular. In fact, some analysts are far more reliable in making analyses from photographs than in personal interviews. In dealing with the photograph they apply the principles and laws of the science relentlessly and almost mathematically, while, in a personal interview, they are irresistibly influenced by their sympathies, their likes and their dislikes.

As a test, we have had some analyses made without even a photograph as a guide, using simply standard charts of the essential physical characteristics of the subjects. For this test five subjects were chosen, all of them unknown to the analysts. Their physical characteristics were charted by those acquainted with the method and five copies were made of each chart.

In order to give the reader an idea of the nature of the data upon which these analyses were made, we reproduce here, in ordinary language, the information contained in the chart made out for Subject Number One:

Sex--Male. Nationality--Scotch. Occupation--Teacher. Date of Birth--March 19, 1891. Color--Eyes, medium; hair, skin and beard, slightly brunette. Form--Forehead, eyes, mouth and chin, plane; nose, strongly convex. Height--5 ft. 9 1/2 in. Weight--145 lbs. Build--Square-shouldered, bony and muscular; lacking somewhat in adipose. Consistency of Flesh--Hard-elastic. Flexibility of Joints--Rigid-elastic. Long trunk, short legs. Nose section, of face predominates, chin a close second, mouth third. High, wide, long, medium-square head. Middle division of cranium predominates, top second, base third. Crown section of cranium largest; front section, second; back section, third; temporal, fourth. Square forehead, medium wide, more prominent at the brows than above. Expression somewhat grim. Health good; body, clothes, hands and mouth clean and in good condition. Hands square. Fingers medium long, with square tips, well-rounded, sensitive pads and short nails. Thumbs long and set low on hand.

The information as to the other four subjects was similar in character. One of these charts was then sent to Mr. G.C. B----, another to Mr. C.F.R----, another to Miss E.W.R----, another to Mrs. A.W----, and the fifth to Miss M.O.P----, students of this science--two of them having studied it less than one year. Each analyst was asked to make his analysis according to a definite plan, so that the results could be definitely compared. These results are shown in the table on pages 356 and 357.

Herein is the true answer to the serious question with which we opened this chapter. Whether or not reliable analyses can be made by the observation of physical characteristics is no longer debatable.

Such analyses *are being made.*

NOTE--An analysis of the foregoing record shows 82-1/4% of agreement with the record in regard to the subjects' characteristics. This part of the work depends upon an application of principles. In checking the four classifications, Mechanical, Professional, Commercial and Artistic, the element of individual judgment of the analyst entered into the problem; yet here we have an agreement with the record amounting to 65-1/2%. Naturally, choice of exact vocation offers an unusually wide field to the personal equation, especially when the analyst has no data, as in this case, in regard to early environment, education, training, residence, and opportunities. But, even in this case, the students are, in general, in marked agreement with the records. It is impossible to state this agreement in percentages, since each was given a first, second, and third choice, and since some of the vocations suggested are very nearly those indicated in the record, yet not exactly the same. A study of these three columns, however, will impress the reader with the accuracy of the analysts' judgments.

CHAPTER V

IDEAL EMPLOYMENT CONDITIONS

The progress of civilization and enlightment is a good deal like that in the old riddle of the man who had a fox, a goose, and a basket of corn to carry across the river and could carry only one at a time. If you remember, he carried the goose across first, leaving the fox with the corn, since the fox could not eat the corn. Then he went back, leaving the goose, and got the corn; then, when he returned for the fox, he took the goose back with him and left it alone on the bank, while he carried the fox across to keep company with the corn. Then he returned once more and brought the goose over, completing the transfer.

So Civilization carries forward, for a time, one aspect of life. Then she drops this and returns to bring up another. This, in turn, she drops again and goes back once more, and when she goes back she is likely enough to carry the first advance back with her. In the end, however, she finally brings up all of the elements and factors in human life.

For the last fifty years we have made great progress in the invention of machinery, the development of new industries, the organization of great financial and industrial institutions, and the volume of production in nearly all lines. But, in the meantime, in order to make this advance, Civilization has been required to carry back, some hundred of years, the relationship between employer and employed. Now let us hope she is ready to go back and bring this important factor up to date.

ANCIENT AND MODERN EMPLOYMENT CONDITIONS

In the old feudal days, the employee was a serf, bound to the soil of his employer. He received a bare living and shared not at all in the gains of the man whose chattel he was. In the days of transition between ancient feudalism and modern industrialism, Civilization greatly improved the relationship between employer and employee. The proprietor and all his men worked side by side in the same shop, performing the same tasks. Each was proud of his skill. Each took delight in his work. Each understood the other. Oftentimes the employee lived under the same roof with his employer, enjoyed the same recreations, and ate at the same table. The skilful, competent, shrewd employer gathered around him the best men in the trade. He profited greatly and his men shared in his prosperity. The invention of machinery and the great enlargement of industrial units makes such relationship between employer and employee impossible. Yet, when employment conditions are improved to match the improvements in machinery and production, we shall go back to the ancient shop for the fundamental principles upon which the new and better relationship will be built.

MUTUAL INTERESTS OF EMPLOYER AND EMPLOYEE

Observe carefully what these fundamental principles are. First, men who love their work and take pride in it; second, mutuality of interests in that work; third, mutual understanding between employer and employee. By this we mean an understanding by each of the other's point of view, personality, ability, motives, intentions, ambitions, and desires. Already Civilization is groping toward the establishment of a new relation upon this basis. Scientific methods of employment are being adopted in more and more of our industrial and commercial plants. These insure the fitness of the employee for his work and, because of his fitness, his love for it and pride in it. They also insure a better understanding between employer and employee, whose relationship to each other is guided and controlled by a sympathetic and expert corps of men and women especially selected and trained for just such work. Profit sharing, the bonus system, the premium system, study clubs and classes, and many other forms of giving an adequate day's pay for a day's efficient work are all evidences of the desire on the part of the employers and employees to mutualize their interests.

It is true that to-day, perhaps, we have reached the very flood-tide of organization of employees into labor unions and employers into associations, and that these organizations are frequently antagonistic. But these are only evidences of our blind groping toward the ideal. These movements show that we are awake to our needs, that we appreciate the intolerable nature of present conditions and that we have determined to better them. It is inevitable, when such an awakening comes, that we shall eventually learn by our mistakes and direct our effort toward the true solution of our problem.

IDEAL CONDITIONS DIVERSE AS TO DETAIL

Just what would constitute the details of ideal employment conditions it is impossible at this time to say. These will have to be worked out painstakingly, carefully, and with a true appreciation of the fundamental principles involved, by wise and competent employers and employees. It is altogether likely that different conditions will be found to be ideal in different industries and probably in different units of the same industries. One man will maintain ideal conditions by the virtue of his own magnetism and forceful personality, tying his men to himself with the strong bonds of mutual admiration, mutual respect, mutual loyalty, and mutual love. Another will create ideal conditions principally by the magnificent exploits of his organization. It is human nature for a man to like to belong to a winning team, to be proud of his connection with a championship organization. Still, another institution may maintain ideal employment conditions by the good judgment, efficiency, and sincere motives with which it conducts its welfare work. Still another may approach the ideal by means of profit sharing, bonuses, and other such emoluments. We have seen and studied organizations in this country and in Europe which very nearly approached the ideal for each of these reasons. We have also seen some which took advantage of several or all of these.

THE EMPLOYER'S IDEAL

As time goes on, more effective methods of profit sharing will, no doubt, be evolved, methods in which there is greater justice for both employer and employee. New ideas will be developed in welfare work as the result of scientific methods of employment. Employer and employee will learn to understand each other better. The success of all of these methods of organization, when they are adopted, will cause their spread throughout the industrial world, and thus gradually, but surely, we shall approach that ideal organization where every employee is looked upon as a bundle of limitless latent possibilities; where training, education, and development along lines of constructive thought and feeling are held to be of far more importance than the invention of new machinery, the discovery of new methods, or the opening of new markets. This is the reasonable mental attitude. Some obscure employee, thus trained and educated, may invent more wonder-working machinery, discover more efficient methods, and open up wider and more profitable markets than any before dreamed. Even if no such brilliant star arises, the increased efficiency, loyalty, and enthusiasm of the whole mass of employees, lifted by its improved relationships, will yield results far beyond any won by mechanical or commercial exploitation.

THE EMPLOYEE'S IDEAL

The ideal for every employee, therefore, is that he should be employed in that position which he is best fitted to fill, doing work which by natural aptitudes, training, and experience he is best qualified to do, and working under conditions of material environment--tools, rates of pay, hours of labor, and periods of rest, superintendence and management, future prospects, and education--which will develop and make useful to himself and his employer his best and finest latent abilities and capacities.

We have seen that the ideal for the organization is that each man in it shall be so selected, assigned, managed, and educated, that he will express for the organization his highest and best constructive thoughts and feelings.

THE MUTUAL IDEAL--CO-OPERATION

There is one more step. That is, the mutual ideal. It is contained in the other two--and the other two are essentially one. The mutual ideal is the ideal of co-operation. There is no antagonism between these ideals. The old fallacy that the boss must get just as much as possible out of the workman and pay just as little as possible, and that the workman must do just as little as he can and wring from the boss just as much pay as he can for what he does, and that, therefore, their interests are diametrically opposed, has been all but exploded. It was based upon ignorance, upon prejudice, and upon privately interested misrepresentation. The new scientific spirit, working side by side with the new spirit of a broader and deeper humanity, has demonstrated, and is demonstrating, the truth, that in no other union is there such great strength as in the union of those who are working together, creating wealth for themselves and serving humanity. This is the mutual, co-operative ideal in employment.

PART THREE

ANALYZING CHARACTER IN PERSUASION

CHAPTER I

THE PSYCHOLOGY OF PERSUASION

The first act of practically every human being is to cry. This cry, unconscious though it may be, is an eager, insistent demand for attention, an appeal to the minds and the feelings of others, an attempt to persuade others to act. Life itself and all that makes life worth living depends upon the effectiveness of that cry.

From the moment of birth, therefore, you are dependent upon your power to persuade for the provision of all your necessities, the satisfaction of all your desires, and the realization of all your ambitions. The human race produces but few Robinson Crusoes, and even these must have their Fridays. In infancy and early life we persuade our parents to supply our necessities and grant us our privileges and luxuries. Most of us are wise enough to appeal to the powerful sentiments of parental duty, parental love, and parental pride, and, therefore, persuasion is not difficult. As we grow older, we persuade our teachers that we understand our lessons. We persuade our playmates to yield to us a share in their sports, and we persuade our enemies in the boy and girl world to respect us and not to persecute us. As we grow older, we persuade our husbands or our wives to marry us. We persuade our children to grow up in the way they should. We persuade our employers to give us an opportunity to work and to pay us wages. We persuade our neighbors to yield us respect and social privileges. We persuade our servants to render loyalty and efficient service. We persuade dealers to sell us reliable goods at reasonable prices. We persuade our friends to accept our hospitality, to join our clubs, our lodges, and to come and live in our suburbs.

POWER TO PERSUADE ESSENTIAL TO SUCCESS

If we enter some profession, we find ourselves constantly faced by the need of persuading our clients and patients, witnesses, judges, juries, opposing counsel and court officers, our congregations and executive boards of our churches and schools, individual members of our parishes, our partners and assistants, and, in fact, people above us, below us, and all around us. The farmer must sell his produce, the manufacturer his manufactured article, the railroad its transportation service, wholesale and retail distributors their merchandise. Politics consists almost wholly in persuasion. A congressman must persuade first his party leaders and perhaps his competitor in the party; then the voters at the primaries; then the voters at the election; then the speaker of the House; then the members of his committee; then the President and many executives in the administration; then, perhaps, the House itself in assembly; then, in turn, his constituents and, perhaps, the entire nation.

Wealth cannot be gained, social position cannot be attained, honor conies not, power is impossible, authority is not conferred, pleasure cannot be purchased, a happy and harmonious human life cannot be realized, spiritual peace cannot be found, and happiness is forever beyond our reach, except through the power of persuasion. By persuasion in prayer, we attempt to move the very mind and heart of God Himself.

TWO CANONS OF SUCCESS

So all-inclusive is this power that if you will think the matter out clearly, you will see that the answer to the problem of every human being, diverse as these problems are, the gratification of every human desire, the realization of every human ambition, may be summed up in two brief colloquial injunctions, namely: first, have the goods; second, to be able to sell them. Neither one of these is complete without the other. No man can permanently succeed in any truly desirable way unless he has something tangible or intangible, spiritual, intellectual, or material which he can offer to others as compensation for that which he wishes to receive. And no matter how valuable any man's offering, it must lie unnoticed in the world's markets unless he can sell it--in other words, persuade others to exchange for it that which he desires. The thing he wants may be only an opinion or a conviction, may be only of momentary value, or it may be gold and silver coin.

The air-brake is probably one of the most valuable inventions ever applied to the railroad industry, and yet George Westinghouse, its

234

inventor, found it impossible even to give it away to railroad presidents until he had learned how to sell it. The telephone, perhaps the greatest convenience, luxury, and time and money saver of modern times, would have remained a scientific toy unless the most astute and vigorous methods of persuasion had been used to insure its almost universal adoption and use. We have seen that Elias Howe built the first sewing machine so well that its fundamentals have never been improved upon, and yet, despite his most strenuous efforts and the efforts of his friends and associates, it remained a mere mechanical curiosity until he had learned how to persuade others to use it.

MUTUALITY OF ALL HUMAN INTERESTS

A.F. Sheldon has said, "Salesmanship is not conquest, but co-operation." Salesmanship is only the commercial name for persuasion, therefore Mr. Sheldon has uttered a great truth. Human interests do not clash, however much they may appear to. All human interests are mutual. John D. Rockefeller did not amass a fortune by making others poor. On the contrary, in the building up of his hundreds of millions, he increased the wealth of others by billions. The theory that there is not enough wealth to go around, and that if one man has a great deal of money others must therefore have too little, is a vicious and dangerous fallacy. The resources of the universe are infinite. The possibilities of humanity are unlimited. The interests of all lie, fundamentally, in the greater and greater development of the latent possibilities in all men and the more and more efficient exploitation and conservation of the resources of the universe. This is philosophic. It is a generalization. It is a statement of facts so tremendous in their scope and so deep in their significance that it is difficult to make a connection between them and the practical details of every-day life.

PERSUASION REVEALS MUTUALITY OF INTERESTS

The very fact that human intercourse, in every aspect of its activity, rests upon persuasion is an indication that all interests are mutual. The persuader teaches the persuaded that their interest coincide. Take a practical example: Salesmen have declared to us that life insurance policies are the most difficult of all specialties to sell. Yet, in nine cases out of ten, policyholders will agree that their benefits far exceed those derived by the salesmen who persuade them to purchase. The life insurance salesman is not attempting to hoodwink, hypnotize, cajole, or browbeat his client in a case where their interests clash, but simply, by skilful setting forth of facts and appeals to the feelings, to persuade his client to act in his own interest.

235

We have seen in this chapter that all individuals who succeed depend upon their power of persuasion. We have seen, also, that persuasion is not necessarily an attempt to advance the interests of one at the expense of another, but essentially a process by means of which two or more minds reach the conclusion that their interests coincide. Since these two propositions are true, it follows that we shall be justified in laying tribute upon every means within our power to increase our effectiveness in persuasion.

PERSUASION A MENTAL ACT DEPENDING UPON INDIVIDUAL MENTAL RESPONSE

Persuasion has been defined as the meeting of minds. This is an excellent definition, chiefly because it localizes the activities involved. It identifies our problem as a purely mental or psychical one. The reason why any two people disagree as to any truth is because their minds have no common ground upon which to meet. Either the minds do not possess all the facts, have not reasoned in accordance with the facts so as to reach a sound conclusion, or, having the facts and having reached the conclusion, they are actuated by different motives. Or it may be a combination of both of these conditions which prevents their meeting. Granting that it is to a man's interest to buy a life insurance policy, the reason he and the solicitor cannot get together on the proposition is either because he does not know all of the facts involved or because the solicitor has not appealed to motives strong enough to cause his prospective customer to take action. To the insurance solicitor, the facts of the case may be so clear and so easily grasped that he underestimates his prospective client's opposition, and so does not present the facts in a convincing manner or he himself may have such a confused idea of the factors in the case that he cannot state them clearly. The prospective client may have a remarkably quick, keen comprehension of the essential factors of any plan, but may be unable to grasp details, while, on the other hand, the solicitor, not knowing this, may present his proposition in such minute detail as to confuse. Or the situation may be exactly reversed. The client's mind may be very slow in action and demand the presentation of a few essential facts with all of the reasons for them, or it may be very quick in action and demand the presentation of many facts in rapid succession, with no attempt to give reasons for them. It will thus be seen that, even in getting down to a conclusive possession of facts, the persuader and the persuaded may be greatly handicapped by misunderstanding.

THE DIFFERENCE IN MOTIVES

When we proceed from fact to motive, we find even greater possibilities of misunderstanding. To the solicitor the one all-powerful motive for the purchase of a life insurance policy may lie in the fact that it is an excellent investment. Unless, therefore, he understands psychology and his client well enough to do otherwise, he may talk the investment feature and appeal to the investment motive when dealing with a man who cares nothing about the investment, but might respond readily and instantly if his desire to provide for the future of his wife and children were appealed to.

Success in persuading, therefore, depends upon two things: First, knowledge in general as to how the human mind works; how it receives its knowledge; how it proceeds from facts and motives to conclusions; what its ambitions, desires, and other feelings are; how these may be aroused and, finally, how they may provide the motive power and induce favorable action. Second, knowledge as to how each individual human mind works; what it's particular methods are in the obtaining of information, in reasoning upon that information, and forming its conclusions; what its motives are and how these motives finally induce decision and action.

The study of the first of these problems is a study of psychology. Because knowledge in regard to it can be easily obtained in practically all of the standard works of salesmanship, perhaps it is not necessary for us to go into it more deeply here. Those who wish to pursue it further, may find an exceedingly valuable discussion of it in "Influencing Men in Business," by Walter Dill Scott; "The Art of Selling," by Arthur Frederick Sheldon, and "The Science of Business Building," by Arthur Frederick Sheldon.

MANY DOMINATING MOTIVES

As we have already seen, one man gets his information very quickly, another must get it slowly. One demands details, another cannot endure them. But these are not the only differences. One man learns best through his eyes, another through his ears, and still another by his sense of touch. One man gets his facts most easily by reading about them, another must see the actual production, while the third forms the most definite and easily understandable mental picture of them as a result of hearing them described. One man, in buying machinery, wants to examine carefully every detail of its construction, another man wants only to see it in action and examine its product, while still another man demands both.

There is the same diversity in motives. One man's strongest motive is

237

vanity; another's, ambition, love of power; still another's, love of beauty. One man responds most readily to any appeal to his affections, another to an appeal to his pride. So, amongst dominating motives in men, we find also avarice, greed, parsimony, benevolence, progressiveness, love of variety, love of the striking and unusual, love of pleasure, a love of cleanliness, physical appetite, a desire for comfort, love of home, love of family, love of friends, love of country, religion, philanthropy, politics, and many others which will readily occur to the thinking reader.

DIFFICULTY OF DETERMINING MOTIVES

It will readily be seen that no study of psychology in the ordinary acceptance of the term can give us any clue to these variations in individuals. Yet successful persuasion depends upon as accurate a knowledge as possible of these very differences among people. The parsimonious salesman who takes it for granted that every one's motives are the same as his own, and, therefore, talks to every prospect about the money-saving possibilities of his commodity, will most certainly fail in trying to persuade those to purchase who care nothing about saving a few cents, but do care a great deal about the quality, style, and beauty of the commodity. The attorney who makes his plea to the court on the basis of technical justice in every case he pleads will lose many cases in those courts where the presiding judge is rather impatient with technical justice and may, perhaps, decide cases upon their merits or according to his own sympathies. We once knew a learned, able, and conscientious judge who, despite his many years' training in the law, was almost certain to decide a case in favor of the litigant who made the strongest appeal to his sympathies. The parent who knows nothing but the persuasive power of corporal punishment, will have little success in disciplining a child blessed with unusual fighting spirit, independence, and tenacity, just as the parent who appeals only to a love of approval will fail in handling a child who does not care what people think about him.

PERSUASION IN DISCIPLINE OF CHILDREN

We once knew a woman who lived near us who had two little boys. One of them was sensitive, timid, affectionate, and idealistic. Being a healthy, active boy, there was a great deal of mischief in him, and in her attempts to discipline him the mother scolded, berated, and often cuffed and slapped him, occasionally administering a whipping. It was plain that the scoldings and whippings only made the boy more shy, more self-conscious, and less confident of himself, which, in one sense,

238

was the worst thing that could have happened to him. The qualities he most needed were courage and self-confidence. With his ideals, his responsiveness, and his affection, he could have been handled easily and would have developed a splendid intellect and a fine character normally and healthfully.

The other boy, although somewhat younger, was more than a match for his older brother. He was practical, matter-of-fact, shrewd, courageous, too self-confident if anything, always ready for a fight, aggressive and wilful. The mother did not scold or whip this boy for the simple reason that she could not. He was too active and too willing to fight. Being thus deprived of the only means of discipline which seemed to her to be effective, she permitted the boy principally to have his own way, her only appeals being to his reason. Unfortunately, this is the very type of boy who will not listen to reason. In this case, as in the first, she would have been successful if she had appealed to the boy's affections, for he had a very strong love nature and would have responded instantly.

It is plain enough to any thoughtful mind that it is not safe to judge of other people's motives by their conversation. "Language," said Talleyrand, "was invented for the purpose of concealing thought." Many people conceal their real motives under a very alluring curtain of language. It seems to be the most natural thing in the world for the thief and swindler to talk with the greatest apparent earnestness and sincerity and honesty. Pious talk very frequently is the haze in which an avaricious and greedy soul hides itself. Bluff, bluster, and boasting are the sops which the coward throws to his own vanity, while the quietest, sweetest, and gentlest tones often sheath the fierce heart of the born fighter, as a velvet glove is said to clothe a hand of steel.

HOW MOTIVES MAY BE KNOWN

Motives lie at the very foundation of being. They are deeply imbedded in the very cells and fiber of the individual. They shape his thoughts, his habits, and all of his actions. It is, therefore, impossible that they should not show themselves to the practiced eye in every physical characteristic, in the tones of the voice, in the handshake, in gestures, in the walk, and in handwriting, in clothing, in the condition of the body, and in the expression of the face. So the motives of man festoon his personality with flaunting and infallible signs to be known and read by all men who care to take the trouble to learn. Some of them are so plain that there is scarcely any grown person so unobservant as not to have seen them. Others are more elusive, but none the less legible to the practiced eye.

The simpler motives, after they have held sway for years, are easily discernible. Sensuality, arrogance, vanity, coldness, benevolence, sympathy, and others are easily determined. But, in order to be successful in persuasion, you need to be able to trace all of the feelings both permanent and transitory.

THE MENTAL LAW OF SALE

There is a great practical truth in the mental law of sale now generally accepted by business psychologists and by practical men in the business world. This mental law of sale holds true in all kinds of persuasion because it describes the process of the human mind as it proceeds, step by step, from indifference or antagonism to favorable action. It is, therefore, impossible to discuss intelligently the ways and means of successful persuasion, except upon a basis of this law. Here is the law: [10]"Favorable attention properly sustained changes into interest, interest properly intensified changes into desire, desire properly augmented ripens into decision and action."

[Footnote 10: From "The Science of Business Building," by A.F. Sheldon.]

FAVORABLE ATTENTION

Now, it is known to psychologists that certain sensations attract favorable attention in a larger number of cases than others. For example, in an appeal to the eye, rectangular shape in proportion of three to five, that is to say, three units of measurement wide by five units of measurement long is more likely to attract favorable attention than a square. Similarly, any object in motion or having the illusion of motion, is more likely to attract favorable attention than an object at rest. Black letters upon a white background attract more favorable attention than white letters upon a black background. Many such psychological problems have been worked out. They are valuable, but they have no place in this work, since our task here is not to deal with averages, but rather with variations in individuals--how to discern them and how to deal with them.

INTEREST

In a similar way, psychologists have determined that the average individual more quickly becomes interested in that which he can understand than in that which he cannot understand, in that which appeals to something in his own experience than in that which has no such appeal, in that which appeals to his tastes and his feelings than in that which appeals to his judgment. These are rules applicable to the average, but they are very general and are of little use to you unless you add to them specific knowledge of every individual whom you wish to persuade.

DESIRE

Desire, as you will see by the terms of the law of sale, is merely interest intensified. Desire is the main spring of action. It is the real force of every motive. Contradictory as it may seem at first sight, people always do what they want to do even when they act most reluctantly. Their action is inspired by a desire to escape what they believe to be the certain penalty of inaction or of contrary action. The boy who slowly approaches his father to receive a promised whipping, does so because he wants to. And he wants to because he knows he will be whipped so much harder if he runs away. Desire is, therefore, the great citadel toward which all of the campaign of the persuader must be directed. Given a powerful enough desire, decision and action follow as a matter of course.

Psychologists have determined that imagination is the most powerful mental stimulus to desire. Imagination presents to the mind, as it were, a more or less vivid mental picture of the individual enjoying the gratification of his desire--be it physical, intellectual, or spiritual. The longer this picture remains in the mind, the more vivid it becomes, the more it crowds all other thoughts and feelings from the mind, the more powerful and irresistible becomes the desire. It is the task of the persuader, therefore, to stimulate the imagination to the painting of such mental pictures. This we well know, but what we wish to know further is what are the most powerful desires in the particular human mind with which we are dealing. Obviously, the automobile salesman who vividly pictures to the timid person the thrills of speeding around curves would be as far wrong as if he were picturing the sedate, quiet luxury of his car to a speed maniac. What he wants to know and what we all want to know in substance is how to tell, at a glance, which is the timid, sedate person and which the speed maniac.

DECISION AND ACTION

Perhaps the most delicate and most difficult process among all the four steps of persuasion is inducing decision and action. When one reflects upon the multitudinous important decisions made and actions taken every hour, it hardly seems possible that it can be so difficult to induce our fellow-men to make the short step from hesitant desire to definite decision. The truth is, of course, that in the making of almost any important decision there is a stern conflict between conflicting desires. Take, for example, a man buying an automobile. Under the skilful persuasive power of the salesman, he has vividly pictured to himself enjoying possession. But this is not his only mental picture. Perhaps he has a picture of his old age, in which he might enjoy the income from the money which would go into an automobile. There are also in his mind mental pictures of half a dozen to a dozen or more other makes of automobiles. In addition to these, there may be a mental picture of a motor boat, a little cottage by the sea, a new set of furniture for his house, new fittings for his store, an increased advertising appropriation, a new insurance policy, a trip to California and return, and goodness only knows how many other objects of desire. It is no wonder he hesitates and that he must be very skilfully and deftly brought to the point of decision.

WAYS OF INDUCING DECISION AND ACTION

For this reason, experience has shown that many people, perhaps the majority of people, can be induced to decide whether they will have red rubber or gray rubber tires on an automobile they contemplate purchasing far more easily than they can be induced to decide definitely that they will purchase the car. Having decided upon the tires, however, they can be asked to decide upon other minor points, including the terms upon which they intend to pay for the car, and thus eventually go through the entire process of purchasing the car without ever giving their delicate mental mechanism the severe shock and strain of deciding to purchase it at all. As a general rule, such people are surprised and delighted to find that they have made the decision so easily and with so little pain and distress.

But this method will not work with all people. There are some natures so positive, so aggressive, so fond of taking the initiative, so determined to make their own decisions without interference that the wise salesman or persuader apparently permits them to have their own way, at the same time skilfully guiding them in the way he wishes them to go by means of indirect suggestion.

INDUCING A POSITIVE NATURE TO PERSUADE HIMSELF

The story is told of an old-time, domineering railroad official, formerly an army colonel, a great lover of horses, who was intensely prejudiced against the automobile. During the days when carriages were favorite conveyances of the wealthy, this man kept a magnificent stable and boasted that no driver ever passed him on the road. With the coming in of automobiles, he became accustomed to seeing the gasoline-drinking machines flash by. They came up behind him with a honk. They rushed by with a roar and they disappeared in the distance in a cloud of dust. He saw the chauffeurs gripping their steering wheels and glaring intensely along the road.

"Humph!" he scorned, "those fellows work harder than an engineer for their rattlety-bang speed. I had rather sit back and get some pleasure out of riding, as I do behind my bays."

Then one morning he noticed a car slip by him slowly, noiselessly, easily, and with so little evidence of effort that the old man felt that by urging his horses to just a little faster pace he might have kept ahead. The next morning, the same thing happened again. It was the same car, and this time the old man tightened his reins a little and sent his horses speeding ahead. At first he gained a little on the car, but eventually it pulled slowly and easily away from him. The third morning, there was another little brush of speed on the boulevard. By this time the old railroad man had noticed how luxurious the car was, how smoothly it rolled, how deeply upholstered were the seats, how lustrous and satiny the finish.

Finally, one morning, one of the old man's horses cast a shoe and the courteous young driver of the automobile, coming along, kindly offered to take the colonel on downtown. The offer was accepted, the team sent to a horseshoer's in care of the coachman, and the colonel and his new friend drove off still slowly, still quietly, and yet, one by one, they passed other carriages on the road. Finally a trolley car was overtaken and left behind.

"See," said the young man modestly, "just the pressure of a finger on the throttle."

"Oh, do you call that a throttle?" asked the railroader. The word was a familiar one to him, and being distinctly of the mechanical type, he was easily interested in machinery. For the remainder of the journey the young man talked quietly, but interestingly of the mechanism of the car, emphasizing the need of skill, steadiness of eye, steadiness of hand, coolness of nerve necessary to drive it. The colonel was deeply interested and, just as the young man deposited him at his destination, he said, "It is possible your horses may not be ready to come for you this evening. If so, I should be delighted to call for you as I go out your way at about the same time you go." The colonel graciously accepted the invitation and at four o'clock of that same afternoon he was again seated along-side the driver of the car. After they had drawn out of the congested streets onto the wide boulevard, the young man again deftly turned the conversation to the mechanism of the car and the skill necessary for driving it. This was too much for the colonel.

"Pshaw! I do not believe it takes so much skill. With what I know about it, I believe I could drive the car."

After some hesitation, the young man finally permitted the railroad official to take the wheel. At first the colonel drove somewhat clumsily, but this only increased his determination, and within an hour he was sending the car along at a good clip. When finally they drove up to the colonel's country home, the young man scarcely needed to invite his passenger to accompany him to the city on the following morning. Before the end of the week, the old man had purchased a magnificent high-powered car. So skilfully did the young man handle his campaign that his customer did not learn he was an automobile salesman until just a few hours before the deal was consummated.

HANDLING THE INDECISIVE

If there are positive natures which must be permitted to feel that the decision is all their own, there are weak, indecisive natures, also, who are rather grateful than otherwise for having important decisions taken off of their hands. For such people, a direct, positive suggestion is perhaps the most powerful and effective means of securing decision and action. One of the favorite methods of dealing with them is to press a fountain pen into their fingers with the definitely worded command, "Sign your name right here, please."

People are also brought to decide and act by being impressed with the fact that delay may make it altogether too late or may possibly postpone part of the advantage to be gained or may permit some one else to get ahead. Decision oftentimes is also induced by a direct or indirect compliment to the individual's decisiveness, positiveness, and ability to take action when he sees that action is necessary. A very successful salesman often used this method: "You say rightly that you want to think it over. That shows that you are a wise man, because a man who acts without thinking is foolish. On the other hand, the man who thinks without acting is a mere dreamer, and I know you do not belong to that class. You have had the evidence. You have weighed it. You have formed your conclusions, and now, because you are a man of decision and action, you are ready to sign the contract."

NEED FOR CHARACTER ANALYSIS

Here, again, the reader has already seen that we are dealing with generalities. We have, as yet, no way of determining definitely and quickly whether the individual with whom we are dealing will respond best to that treatment which secures his decision upon minor points, or that which permits him to make his own decision guided only by indirect suggestions, or that which makes the decision for him, or that which compliments him upon his decisiveness, or any one of many other methods of closing. And so it is necessary to study humanity to learn to know just what will gain favorable attention of each one individually, just which one of a thousand possible motives to appeal to in order to arouse interest, just what kind of a desire to stimulate in order to intensify it to that point where it becomes irresistible, just what method of closing to use in order to bring about decision and action.

In succeeding chapters of this part of the book, we shall give some attention to these problems.

CHAPTER II

SECURING FAVORABLE ATTENTION

You would find it an interesting study in human nature to stand in front of different shop windows and record the types of people whose favorable attention is drawn by each. Select, for example, a book-store window, a jewelry display, a window full of tools and instruments, an offering of meats and groceries, and a traction engine. You will find a description of various types in the first few chapters of this book. Suppose you took fifty, one hundred, one hundred and fifty, two hundred observations before each display and then analyzed the records to find the percentage of each type whose favorable attention was called to each window.

THE PHYSICALLY FRAIL

These results show that the individual of the physically frail type, as described in Chapter 2 of this book, is chiefly interested in books, in beauty, ideas and ideals, elegance, and luxuries. His favorable attention is caught by that which is beautiful. If the thing offered him has in it or about it any elements of beauty, elegance, luxury, or idealism, this should first be presented, even if the true value of the article lies in its utility. In the same way, this individual will respond most quickly with his favorable attention to that which is intellectual, educational, literary, scientific, or philosophic, unless he is also of the strictly financial type which is sometimes, though not often, true of the physically frail. Then his attention may be readily secured by an apt quotation from a price list.

Because the physically frail man does not like manual labor and cannot do it well, his attention may be gained by any contrivance for saving labor, making life easier physically, and substituting mental work for physical.

"Let the Gold Dust Twins Do Your Work" is a headline which no doubt attracts the favorable attention of many of this class, who might utterly ignore "Let the Gold Dust Twins Save You Money."

THE FAT MAN

The favorable attention of the fat man is very evidently gained most readily by that which appeals to his physical senses and appetites. This is because the keynote of his nature is enjoyment. He is always on the alert for anything which may contribute to his enjoyment. He is not fond of physical or mental work, but he is interested in food products, labor-saving devices, comforts, luxuries, finances, politics, merchandizing, and, in fact, everything which contributes to his enjoyment either directly or indirectly through his ability to command the mental and physical services of others.

He who would gain the favorable attention of a fat man, therefore, might be most successful by beginning with inviting him to luncheon or dinner. In the absence of this, he might begin conversation by a discreet question or comment upon the political situation. The headline, "Let Me Show You How To Make More Money" might appeal to the impractical man, but it is not likely to gain the favorable attention of the fat man. The fat man's natural feeling about a request of that kind is: "If you know how to make more money, why don't you use that knowledge for yourself?" Financially, his favorable attention is much more likely to be secured by asking him whether he believes real estate prices are going to advance or railroad stocks are going to decline or interest rates are going to hold firm. Unless he is of the highly speculative type, he is more than likely to be suspicious of any financial proposition which offers large returns at the outset. He usually has a shrewd way of unearthing propositions which will pay him large returns; but, as a general rule, he would rather unearth them himself than to have some interested party come and offer them to him.

THE MAN OF BONE AND MUSCLE

The favorable attention of the man of bone and muscle is always most quickly gained by something that moves, some piece of mechanism, or, perhaps, by an object suggestive of outdoor sports. Many a salesman has secured the favorable attention and gained his way into the good graces of a man of this type by talking to him about hunting, fishing, golf or baseball. If you take the fat man to luncheon with you, take this man out to play golf or tennis or have a motor ride.

A salesman of our acquaintance once determined to sell a full line of school supplies to the superintendent of schools in a large western city. The contract was a considerable one and meant a large commission to the salesman. As he studied the situation, he learned that one of his competitors had been furnishing all of the supplies for the schools in this city for a number of years and that it was very difficult for the salesmen from other business houses to get a hearing. The superintendent's usual manner of rebuff was to say: "No, I do not care to look at your line. We are being excellently served now, sir, and have no desire to make a change."

This salesman proceeded to the office of the superintendent early in the morning, before that official arrived, and was waiting in the ante-room when his prospective customer came in. Observing the man quickly, as he walked through the ante-room into his private office, the salesman noted that he was tall, square-shouldered, with a square face and jaw, wide forehead and a slow, elastic, graceful stride. In other words, he was distinctly a man of the bony and muscular type. A few minutes later the salesman was ushered into the superintendent's office. He carried with him, instead of a huge sample case--this he left in the ante-room--an ingenious little mechanical pencil sharpener. Stepping up to the superintendent's desk, he set the machine down squarely in front of the official and, without a word, picked up a pencil from the desk and sharpened it.

"How much by the dozen?" asked the superintendent.

"Twenty-five dollars," replied the salesman.

"Send me five dozen," said the superintendent, drawing towards him a requisition blank.

While the superintendent was writing the requisition, the salesman quietly slipped out and brought in his sample case. When he returned, the superintendent was sharpening a pencil for himself with much evident enjoyment.

"What else have you?" said he, without looking up.

Of course that question opened up the salesman's sample case, and when he left the office, he had at least broken down that ancient barrier and had secured an order for considerably more than one-third of the year's supplies.

In our story of the railroad man who was induced to buy an automobile without even suspecting that his patronage was being solicited, observe how skillfully the salesman drew his customer's attention to the mechanical features of the machine. The colonel, being a railroad man, was, of course, of this bony and muscular type.

THE IMPRACTICAL MAN

The impractical man lives in a world of dreams, theories, hypotheses, and philosophies. His favorable attention is immediately attracted to an ingenious idea. If he is of the fine-textured, delicate-featured type, he will give his favorable attention readily to that which is artistic, poetical, musical, dramatic, or literary. Financially, he is far more likely to give attention to a proposition which promises immense returns quickly than to one which is safe, solid and substantial, but promises only small returns. His favorable attention cannot for long be sustained by mere recitation of facts. He does not care much about facts and they are likely to prove dry and uninteresting to him. Give him the theories; show him the philosophy of the thing; appeal to his imagination, his sense of beauty and his ideals, and he is ready to listen further.

THE PRACTICAL MAN

The practical man demands facts. Theories and abstractions worry him. Even if you had his favorable attention and were to try to go too much into the reasons for things, you would probably lose it. He is the kind of man who wants to be shown, who demands that you place the actual object before him, if possible, so that he can see it, taste it, smell it, feel of it. His principal concern about any proposition is not, "Is it reasonable?" or "Is it in accordance with theories?" but rather "Will it work?" "Is it practical?" If you can show him the facts and can convince him by demonstration, if possible, that the thing will work, you will secure his very immediate attention.

THE VAIN

Those who are hungry for fame, who are eager for the limelight, whose ears itch for the sound of applause, are, of course, quickly responsive to flattery. If they are fine-textured and have delicate features, small hands and feet, flattery must be of a refined and delicate nature. If, on the other hand, they are of coarse texture, large, coarse features and big

248

hands and feet, they will, if their vanity be a ruling motive, eagerly swallow the most atrocious and fulsome praises. Look for the extremely short upper lip, for an excess of jewelry, a tendency to over-dress and extreme foppish methods of arranging the hair. Where you find one or more of these indications, you find the easiest road to favorable attention through the appetite of the individual for praise. If he is of the intellectual type, praise him for his smartness. If he is a fat man, praise him for his popularity, his political astuteness, his financial acumen, his artistic ordering of a dinner, for his impartiality. If he is of the bony and muscular type, praise him for his mechanical ability, for his strength, skill and agility, for his love of freedom and independence. If he is of the literary and artistic type, praise him for his art. If he shows a fondness for dress, flatter him on his personal appearance. Watch any man of this type carefully and you will soon discover his pet vanity, and when you have discovered it, you have found an easy road to the citadel of his desires.

THE MATTER-OF-FACT

If an individual has a long, straight upper lip, a keenly practical, matter-of-fact type of forehead, long, severe lines of countenance and a high crown, do not attempt flattery. Such a person is instantly suspicious of anyone who flatters him. He keeps his feelings well under control. He has very decided opinions and convictions of his own and it is difficult to induce him to act except in accordance with them. Such a person gives his favorable attention to fact and, usually, only to facts germane to the proposition in hand. He does not care much for comments upon these facts and is quite likely to refuse to listen to all appeals to his emotions. He has, however, as a general rule, considerable love of power. He likes to dominate, to rule, not so much for material personal advantage as for the sake of imposing his opinions and convictions upon others and the satisfaction of feeling that the power is in his hands. Show him facts that will convince him that your proposition will increase his power and you appeal to one of his strongest motives.

THE SOCIAL AND FRIENDLY

There is a very large class of people who are distinctly friendly and social in type. A leading characteristic of this type is, as we have stated already, the full, round back-head. The best, easiest and quickest way to gain the favorable attention of such people is to develop your relations with them upon a friendly and social basis. Indeed, a capacity for making friends and keeping them is one of the most valuable assets of any human being, no matter what his ambitions and desires. As a general rule, we can more easily persuade those who feel friendly toward us than we can those who are indifferent. Observe the successful salesman and the successful politician, those whose professional success depends upon the power to persuade; they are nearly all of the social, friendly type.

THE VALUE OF FRIENDLINESS

For some men it comes natural to make friends with everyone with whom they come in contact. Others make friends with few, but their friendships are powerful and lasting. Still others are very social; they meet people easily and are fairly successful in dealing with them; but they make few, if any, intimate friends. Still others are neither social nor friendly. They do not particularly care for people but rather enjoy solitude. No matter which type a man may be, he will do well to cultivate true friendliness. Our friends turn business to us. They give us important information at the right time. They influence people in our favor. They warn us of disasters. They come to our rescue in times of trouble and help to protect us against our enemies. Finally, but perhaps most important of all, they give us an opportunity to do all these things for them, and in this service we find our highest and truest pleasure.

COMBINATION TYPES

We have suggested arbitrarily in this chapter a few of the types you will meet and the best ways to gain the favorable attention of each. Naturally, these types may overlap. For example, a man may be a fat man and also of the exceedingly practical type. He is, therefore, approachable upon either one of the two lines suggested or with something which appeals to both elements in his nature at once. Plain, simple, easily recognized facts about a sound financial proposition, for example, would combine the two factors.

There are, of course, many other types and combination types. To treat each one of them exhaustively would require, not a volume, but a library. Yet there are certain fundamental principles by which all of them may be known and in accordance with which each may be successfully persuaded. A thorough scientific study of human nature will reveal them.

CHAPTER III

AROUSING INTEREST AND CREATING DESIRE

Before the days of business psychology, form letters for the purpose of securing business from those addressed used to begin something like this:

"DEAR MR. BLANK:

"We beg to announce that we have on hand a very large stock of bicycles, which we desire to close out as early as possible."

Consciously or unconsciously, the recipient of this letter would say to himself: "What in thunder is that to me? I have no particular interest in this fellow's stock of bicycles. I do not care whether his stock is large or small, nor do I care whether he wants to sell it or not." And the form letter would go into the waste basket. Nowadays, however, we have learned better and our form letter would begin something like this:

"DEAR MR. BLANK:

"What would it be worth to you to have the freedom of movement, the open air, the healthful exercise, and the enjoyment of the beauties of nature which are all placed easily within your reach by the possession of a bicycle?"

The recipient of this letter immediately pictures to himself time saved in going to and from work, in running errands, in paying visits. He also has visions of increased health--perhaps freedom from the headaches that have been troubling him--pictures of long rides upon air-shod wheels over smooth boulevards and through leafy lanes.

Himself!_

Do you get it? The writer of that letter makes the reader think about *himself.* He knows that the latter is more interested in himself than in any other human being in the world and that he is more interested in human beings than he is in anything else. This is the key to the arousing of interest. Make the man think about himself in connection with what you have to offer.

HOW PEOPLE THINK ABOUT THEMSELVES

But different people think about themselves in entirely different ways. The glutton thinks of his stomach; the scholar of his knowledge; the athlete of his prowess, and the seeker after power, of his ambitions. Those who seek to persuade others by scientific means will learn to

251

determine in just what way each individual is most interested in himself. Then his task will be to make every individual whom he seeks to persuade think, as he best likes to think, of himself and, at the same time, in close connection, think of the idea or the article or the proposition offered.

INTERESTING THE INTELLECTUAL MAN

Suppose he were trying to persuade a man of the intellectual type to purchase a life insurance policy. After having gained favorable attention, his further argument might be along these lines: "Your greatest asset is in your mental power. With your intellect you can accomplish what it would take a hundred men a year to accomplish with their hands. In fact, with your intellect you can accomplish what no number of men working throughout eternity could accomplish by the mere toil of their hands. Intellectual power depends upon the ability to concentrate and the freedom and health of your intellectual faculties. Psychologists and physiologists both agree, as you well know, that there is nothing which quite so quickly upsets both your physical and your mental machinery as anxiety and worry. With this policy in force, you are fortified--you are free to concentrate upon your problems, your work, without anxiety as to the future of your wife and children. Whatever happens to you, you know that they will be provided for. Furthermore, if you should live twenty years from now, you will receive ten thousand dollars in one lump sum. That is a provision against the possible day when you may be weary and wish to rest, or it may be just the endowment which you need in order to carry on your researches and investigations and, perhaps, find the solution to some of the intellectual problems on which you have so long been working."

INTERESTING THE FAT MAN

The fat man likes to think of himself enjoying the good things of life as to body and mind, comfort, luxury, a jovial good time with congenial friends, the exercise of executive, financial or political power, or all three. His interest, therefore, is readily aroused if you talk to him about himself in connection with these things. There are many cases, of course, in which this must be done indirectly rather than directly. The effort should be not always to talk directly about the man to himself, but to make him think about himself. It is usually not permissible to talk to the judge on the bench about himself, but it is always permissible to paint the picture in such a way that the judge, if he is a fat man, will almost inevitably think of himself in connection with the matters presented.

252

For example, a lawyer friend of ours often appeared with cases before a corpulent jurist. "If it is at all possible," he told us, "without dragging the thing in too obviously by the ears, I always talk about food in my summing up. If I want to get the sympathy of the judge, I try, somehow or other, to make my client appear before the imagination as suffering from want of nourishment. I can see that the judge always feels those sufferings keenly himself. In one case, where I represented a woman in a divorce case, I told, as graphically as I knew how, the excellence of her cooking. I told about how her roast chicken and her pies tasted, and I could actually see his Honor's mouth water. Of course, in addition to that, I presented a good legal case. But I have always thought it was those imaginary pies and roast chicken that got my client her decision."

INTERESTS OF THE ACTIVE MAN

The man of bone and muscle likes to think of himself in action. Muscular exercise, out-of-doors freedom, skill, agility and strength-- these are the things in which he is interested. You can also interest him in thoughts of himself using tools, building or operating machinery, traveling or, perhaps, working in his garden or amongst his fruit trees. By an easy step in analogy this man is also interested in politics and religion, freedom and reform, and in mechanical principles and construction. Notice how the letter cited at the opening of this chapter makes the man who receives it think of himself in motion, think of himself as enjoying freedom, the outdoor air, exercise, the beauties of nature. All of these things appeal to the man of bone and muscle, who is, by all odds, the most likely purchaser of a bicycle.

THE IMPRACTICAL MAN'S INTEREST

The impractical man usually likes to think of himself as an ideal being, living in an ideal world, surrounded by ideal people, associated together under ideal conditions. In other words, he is a day-dreamer, dreaming of those things which delight him most, without thought as to their foundation in fact, or the possibility of putting them into practice. It is usually easy enough for the eloquent salesman who understands him to persuade such a man. He responds to eloquence. Since he doesn't demand facts, his mind is soon soaring off into realms of fancy upon the wings of the speaker's words. But since interests are all mutual, you will, if you are wise, use your knowledge of this man's impractical nature to help to persuade him to do for himself that which is practicable. Such a man ought to have life insurance, for example, and to have it so protected that he can do nothing visionary and impracticable with it. Make him think of himself, if you can, conferring ideal benefits upon his wife and family. You could never interest him in the bare, trite facts in the case, but when you have gained his interest, see to it that you sell him an entirely practicable life insurance policy for a man of his type. There is never any ultimate advantage gained by using your knowledge of human nature to persuade people to do anything which is not, in the long run, the best thing for them to do.

INTERESTING THE PRACTICAL MAN

The practical man likes to think of himself and others as doing things, as saying things, accomplishing practical things, worth-while things. We shall never forget the intensity with which one of the most practical persons in our acquaintance says over and over again: "I like to see things _done_" If your practical person is also of the financial type, he likes to think of himself as doing things which will result in profit. There is scarcely any proposition of any kind you may ever wish to present to a practical financial person which cannot be presented in such a way as to make that person think of himself as getting something done both practical and profitable. If you can make him think of himself in this way, you will have aroused his interest.

INTERESTS OF THE VAIN

Vain men and women, who live upon the praises, applause and approval of others, like to think of themselves as being admired, courted, favored, appreciated, and even flattered. Such a person once said to us: "I cannot live without flattery. I want people to say nice things about me. I do not care whether they mean them or not, if only they will say them to my face." To interest such a person in himself is really a work of supererogation--because he thinks of nothing else, and usually can talk of nothing else. All you have to do to arouse his interest is to show him the connection between his vanity and the proposition you have to offer, and then heartily join in the applause.

GENERAL APPLICATIONS

In a similar way, the doting mother thinks about herself in connection with her children. Make the devoted husband and father think about himself in connection with his family. Make the social, friendly person think about himself in connection with his acquaintances and friends. Make the detail worker think of himself in connection with little intimate details. Make the generalist think of himself in connection with large movements.

254

The interest a person may feel is not always concerned with that which is immediately and directly connected with himself. Just at present, for example, we are all more or less interested in the war in Europe. We read about it. We discuss and argue about it. We follow its moves of armies and diplomacies. In one sense this interest is impersonal. Yet, psychologically, our interest depends entirely upon our own connection with the results. Through our sympathies we place ourselves either with "the oppressed Belgian people whose homes have been ravished" or with "the great German nation fighting for its existence against an iron ring of enemies who enviously conspired for her downfall." We are also interested in the war because it affects our business, our finances, our means of travel and communication, and a thousand and one other matters which directly concern us. Even a casual observer might be interested in a war between two colonies of ants; but unless the outcome in some way directly concerned him, his interest would be purely intellectual and by no means strong enough to use as a basis for successful persuasion.

UNSELFISHNESS OF SELF-INTEREST

Some may object that in treating the subject of interest, we have made human beings appear far more selfish and self-seeking than they really are. Such is not our intention. The most unselfish acts of heroism that can be performed result from intense personal interest aroused through sympathy, generosity, duty, patriotism, or love. When a person capable of one of these heroic acts thinks of himself, he is likely to think of himself as sympathizing with those who suffer, as being generous to those who are in need, as performing his duty without fear of consequences, as loving his native land, or as pouring out his very soul for the benefit of those who are dear to him.

DESIRE

According to the law of sale, desire is interest intensified. Interest may be purely intellectual. Desire is a feeling. Interest may not even suggest speech or action to the interested person. Desire infallibly suggests speech or action. The woman who stands before a magnificent window display of the latest fashions in evening gowns may be deeply interested in them, but if, perchance, she be a modest, retiring, home-keeping woman with no social ambitions, she doesn't even think of purchasing one. In fact, the chances are that she would not accept it as a gift. She would have no use for it. As a result, her interest in the display begins to wane and soon she passes on. How different is the case of the woman who loves excitement, attends many evening functions, and is ambitious to outshine her friends! She stops before the window. She also is interested. The longer she stands before the window and the more interested she becomes, the more certain is she to begin to think about purchasing one or more of the gowns, or of having one or more made upon these models. If she stands there long enough and her interest continues to increase, she will soon be making definite plans for gaining possession. In other words, her desire for an evening gown has been aroused.

MAKE THEM SEE THEMSELVES ENJOYING POSSESSION

Ask any successful clothing salesman or saleslady what is the best way to arouse desire for a suit, a cloak or a gown. Almost without exception they will answer: "Place the garment on the prospective customer and let him see himself in a good mirror and in a good light." In this way the individual actually sees himself enjoying possession. There is no stronger stimulus to desire than this.

A young man of our acquaintance had a great contempt for spring and fall overcoats, and had never purchased one. One day, after he had ordered a suit from his tailor, the salesman said: "Mr. Jenkins, you ought to have a spring overcoat to wear with that suit."

"A spring overcoat!" scoffed Jenkins. "I never wore a spring overcoat in my life. When it is cold, I wear my winter overcoat. When it is too warm for that, I am perfectly comfortable without an overcoat. Why should I waste my money in a thing which is only ornamental? If I am going to spend any more money on overcoats, I should rather put it into an extra fine winter overcoat."

"Now, here is one of our very latest styles, Mr. Jenkins," went on the salesman, ignoring the protest. "Just slip it on and see how it fits you."

The salesman held the garment invitingly, and, with a grudging warning to the salesman that he was wasting his time, Jenkins slipped it on. The salesman settled it upon his broad shoulders, smoothly folded back the rich, heavy silk facing, and deftly swung a mirror into position.

"Fits as if it were made for you, Mr. Jenkins," he praised. "I tell you, when you walk down the street in that overcoat in the bright, clear sunlight of a spring morning, you look prosperous."

In relating the incident afterward, Jenkins said: "Why, the fellow had me, absolutely. I could see myself walking down Michigan Avenue to business, and the sun shining on the lake, and the little shoots of grass

256

beginning to show in Grant Park. I did feel prosperous. I felt so prosperous that, then and there, I bought that overcoat, the first spring overcoat I ever owned and just exactly one more spring overcoat than I had ever had any intention of owning."

AROUSE THEIR FEELINGS ABOUT THEMSELVES

If interest, therefore, is aroused by making a person think about himself, desire is created by making a person feel about himself and feel about himself in such a way that the feeling impels him to favorable decision and action. The object of the man or woman who would persuade according to scientific principles is to stimulate, through intensified thought, the strongest and most easily aroused feelings of the person to be persuaded. As you have already seen, we have been hammering upon those feelings from the very beginning. In securing favorable attention, we appeal to them. In arousing interest, we do our best to make the person to be persuaded think of himself in connection with these feelings; and now, in creating desire, we simply are going a step further and by every possible means intensifying the excitement of those feelings.

For example, in selling a garment to an exceedingly utilitarian and economical person, we secure his favorable attention, perhaps, by the remark: "Let me show you something that will look as well as the best and wear like iron, at a moderate price." We arouse his interest by showing him the hard, close, wear-resisting weave of cloth, the tenacity with which it holds its shape, and, at the same time, its neatness, attractiveness, finish, and superior workmanship. We create a desire for the possession of the garment by inducing him to put it on, at the same time remarking: "You can see for yourself that this garment is conservative and suitable in style. While not the extreme of fashion, it is not out-of-date nor out of harmony with the prevailing mode. A year from now you will be able to wear it with exactly the same feeling that you are well and neatly dressed, as you feel in wearing it to-day. Furthermore, because it is a standard style and not a novelty, it sells at far below the cost of fancy garments, notwithstanding its superior quality and workmanship. You will be proud to wear this garment when those who have paid twice as much for the more extreme styles have been compelled to discard them and purchase new."

THE PERSUASIVE POWER OF SUGGESTION

In his excellent scientific work, "Influencing Men in Business," Walter Dill Scott says:

257

"In persuading men, logical reasoning is practically never to be used alone. After the arguments have been presented, skillful suggestions should be used as a supplement. This supplement often changes threatened defeat into success. The skillful pleader before a jury, the wise politician, and the successful superintendent of men all alike are compelled to resort to suggestion to supplement their arguments in their attempts to influence men.

"If we should divide all customers into the two classes, professional buyers and the general public, then, in appealing to this latter class, special attention should be given to suggestion. In an advertisement containing both a good suggestion and a good argument, the suggestion is read often and the argument rarely. From infancy, we have been accustomed to respond to suggestions so frequently that we follow this habit in purchasing merchandise, even though we ought to make such purchases only after due deliberation. Deliberation is a process of thought which is very elaborate and very exhausting. The general purchaser--the housewife--does not ordinarily rise to such an undertaking, but contents herself with a process very closely approximating the working of pure suggestion. Even though she begins to deliberate, the process is likely to be cut short by the effect of a clever suggestion.

"The general public responds more readily to suggestions than to arguments; hence, in dealing with this large group, it is usually wise to construct the copy according to this habitual method of response of the general public. Immediate action is more often secured by suggestion than by arguments."

Since this is true, that person is most skillful in persuading who has acquired the most skill in suggestion. He stimulates the imagination to paint vivid and intensely-colored mental pictures of the gratification of desire. Make desire strong enough, and, if you have correctly analyzed the one to be persuaded, the rest follows.

CHAPTER IV

INDUCING DECISION AND ACTION

"I want it," said a gentleman to us, speaking of a piece of property in which he was contemplating investment. "I want it so bad that I can't think of much else. I lie awake nights dreaming of myself in possession of it, and yet, somehow or other, I can't make up my mind to buy it. I have the money and have had the money in the bank for weeks. There is nothing else I want to do with that money half as much as I want to buy that property, but it is an important move and, somehow or other, I just can't make the plunge."

This gentleman's experience illustrates a psychological condition well known to many of our readers, because they have been in substantially the same situation--and well known to every salesman, because he has had to meet and combat just such a situation many a time.

Desire having been created, our law of sale states that desire, properly augmented, ripens into decision and action. This is true. And yet the ripening process is sometimes so slow that the frost of fear or the rot of regret spoils the fruit. It is popularly supposed to be true that if a person really desires to do a thing strongly enough, and it is within the bounds of possibility, he will do it. Nine times out of ten, or perhaps ninety-nine times out of a hundred, this is the case; but there are times when the will simply refuses to respond to desire.

A BALKY WILL

A lady who was of an exceedingly stubborn nature once said to us: "Ordinarily, I consider myself to be quite amenable to persuasion and suggestion. I like to live peaceably with others. Occasionally, however, someone, and perhaps someone whom I love very dearly, says something or does something that makes me stubborn. Then I absolutely balk. Commands, demands, appeals, cajoleries, every means thinkable, are used, but the more people attempt to influence my action, the more stubborn I become. If then I am left alone to think it over for a few hours, very likely I shall begin to think that it would be advisable, from every point of view, for me to yield. My judgment is already convinced that to yield is the best policy. My love for my friends, my desire for peace, my wish to be accommodating and to have their approval all urge me to yield. I want to yield. But, even then--how, I cannot explain--there is something inside which absolutely forbids it. This is so strong that it feels stronger than my judgment and all of my desires taken together. The only possible course for me to pursue is to forget the entire matter for a few days, at the end of which time, perhaps, the stubbornness has seemingly evaporated."

DECISION MAY WAIT UPON AN IRRELEVANT WORD

And so, merely augmenting desire oftentimes is not enough to bring about decision and action, even in cases which are not so extreme as those which we have just cited. The proposition may be of such a nature that it does not admit of arousing desire to any very high pitch.

In all such cases what is needed is some special stimulus to the will. As every chemist knows, sulphuric acid and alcohol, when mingled together in a glass vessel, do not combine. They have an affinity for each other. All of the necessary elements for active combination are present in that glass, and yet they do not combine. But drop in a bit of platinum and instantly the whole mass is boiling with energy let loose. In a similar way, oftentimes, all the elements for decision and action are present in the mind, yet nothing happens. But a word or a little act, seemingly insignificant in itself, oftentimes breaks the spell, as it were, and decision and action follow. In our first chapter of this part we described some of these methods for ripening desire into decision and action. This chapter we shall devote to a consideration of different classes of individuals and the best methods of inducing in them favorable decision and action.

THE IMPULSIVE MAN

The impulsive individual must be rushed. His emotions are very responsive, easily aroused, and, as, a rule, when aroused take a strong hold upon him. It is the impulsive person's tendency always to act quickly and to act in response to his strong feelings. The impulsive man discharges his feelings with speed in action, and they rapidly evaporate. Therefore, desire, when aroused, must be quickly ripened into decision and action or it soon cools, and it is too late. As a general rule, the impulsive person is well supplied with fears, and if he is given time to think the matter over his lack of courage begins to assert itself. Fears of possible or impossible disaster begin to take form until the feelings of fear and apprehension entirely overshadow the desires which have been created.

Mark Twain's story of his attendance at a missionary meeting is typical. After the speaker had been talking for half an hour, Mark was in such hearty sympathy with him and the cause for which he plead that he decided to put one dollar in the collection box when it came around-- but the man kept on talking. At the end of three-quarters of an hour, Mark decided he would give only fifty cents. At the end of an hour, he decided that he would give nothing, and when, at the end of an hour and a half, the collection box finally did come around, Mark took out a dollar to pay himself for his pains.

INDICATIONS OF IMPULSIVENESS

Here are some of the indications of impulsiveness: blonde coloring, especially if accompanied by a florid skin; small, round, retreating chin; small size; fineness of texture; elasticity of consistency; short head; short, smooth fingers, with tapering tips; a keen, alert, intense expression. The impulsive person's movements are also impulsive. He walks with a quick step, sometimes almost jerky. His gestures are quick, and if he is very impulsive, he always has the air of starting to do things before he has properly considered what he is going to do.

THE DELIBERATE MAN

The deliberate individual is the opposite of the impulsive. His feelings may be strong, but he has them well under control. He may think slowly or he may think quickly, but he always acts with deliberation and always after he has thought very carefully. Once he has determined to act, he may act far more energetically, and certainly more persistently, than the impulsive person. The thing to remember about him is that he is constitutionally opposed to hasty decision and action. Even when his mind is made up and his desires are strong, he is very likely to postpone action until his resolution has had an opportunity to harden. Oftentimes these deliberate people are, or seem to be, incorrigible procrastinators. It is useless to try to rush them. Give them time to think and consider.

INDICATIONS OF DELIBERATION

These are some of the indications of deliberation: dark coloring, with an inclination to pallor; a long, strong, prominent chin and well-developed jaw; large size; medium or coarse texture; hard consistency; a long, square head; long, knotty fingers, with square tips; slow, deliberate, rhythmical movements; a calm, poised expression, and either an absence of gesture or gesture of a slow, graceful character.

Looking around amongst your friends and acquaintances, you will readily see that few, if any, have all of the characteristics of impulsiveness in a marked degree, and an equally small number all of the characteristics of deliberation in a marked degree. The majority of people probably have a combination of these characteristics--some indications of impulsiveness and some of deliberation. In such cases, the question is answered by a preponderance of evidence.

OBSTINATE PEOPLE

Some people are remarkably obstinate. If given their own way, they are agreeable and amiable, but when opposed, they are exceedingly difficult to persuade. If such persons are of the positive type and like to feel that they are doing the thing and that no one else is influencing or coercing them, then they must be handled by an adroit suggestion similar in principle to that described in the case of the automobile salesman on page 380. On the other hand, in case these obstinate people are somewhat negative in character, without much initiative or aggressiveness but with a very large degree of stubbornness, then care must be taken not to antagonize them or to oppose them--always gently to lead them and never to try to drive them.

Argument is probably the most useless waste of energy possible in attempting persuasion. Your own experience teaches you that argument only leaves each party to the controversy more strongly convinced than ever that he is right. This is true no matter what the character of the arguers be. It is especially and most emphatically true when either one or the other, or both, who participate in the argument are of the obstinate type.

The obstinate person may be amenable to reason if reasons are stated calmly, tactfully, and without arousing his opposition. His emotions of love, sympathy, generosity, desire for power and authority may be successfully appealed to and he may be gently led to a decision by way of minor and seemingly insignificant points.

INDICATIONS OF OBSTINACY

These are the indications of obstinacy: dark coloring; a prominent chin; a head high in the crown; hard consistency; a rigidity of the joints, especially of the joints in the hands and fingers. Perhaps the most important and most easily recognized indication of a domineering, obstinate, determined will is the length of line from the point of the chin to the crown of the head. When this line greatly exceeds in length that from the nape of the neck to the hair line at the top of the forehead, you have an individual who desires to rule and bitterly resents any attempt on the part of others to rule him.

The indications of a positive, aggressive, dominating will are these: blonde color; prominent chin; a large, bony nose, high in the bridge; high forehead, prominent at the brows and retreating as it rises; medium or small size; medium fine, medium or coarse texture; hard consistency, rigid joints; a head wide just above and also behind the ears and high in the crown; a keen, penetrating, intense expression of the eyes, and positive, decided tones of voice, movements and gestures.

The individual who is negatively stubborn may have a small or sway-back nose; may have a high forehead, flat at the brows and prominent above; may have elastic or soft consistency; may have a head narrow above and behind the ears. Obstinacy will be shown in the length of line from the point of chin to the crown of head and in the rigidity of the joints of the hands and fingers.

THE INDECISIVE

The gentleman mentioned at the opening of this chapter belongs to the indecisive class. They are like those of whom we sing in the old hymn:

"But timorous mortals start and shrink To cross that narrow sea And linger, shivering, on the brink And fear to launch away."

We have often watched boys in swimming. In every crowd there are always a few of these timorous mortals who "shiver on the brink and fear to launch away." As a general rule, some of their companions usually come up behind them and give them a strong push, after which they are pleased and happy enough in the water. We have seen boys who seemed to be waiting for someone to push them in. No doubt they were. Certain it is that grown up men and women who suffer in an agony of indecision usually like to have someone take the matter out of their hands.

In the case of the gentleman to whom we have referred in the opening of this chapter, the real estate agent one day walked into his office, laid a contract down on the desk in front of him, and said, very impressively: "This thing has got to be settled up to-day. Just sign your name right there." And, with a feeling of intense relief and satisfaction, our friend did sign his name "right there." To the best of our knowledge and belief, he has been glad of it ever since.

HOW ONE SALESMAN OVERCAME INDECISION

We once knew a salesman of the positive, domineering type. He was selling an educational work. Now, education is a thing everyone needs but few will take the trouble and find the money to purchase unless they are very strongly persuaded. Men who would readily spend fifty or seventy-five dollars for a night's carousal will hesitate, and find objections, and back and fill for weeks, or even for months, before they spend thirty or forty dollars on a bit of education which they well know they ought to have. Our friend, therefore, was met over and over again with the temporizing excuse: "Well, I will have to think this matter over. I cannot decide it to-day, but you come in and see me again." Almost without exception, this excuse means that the man who makes it knows, deep down in his heart, that he ought to make his decision-- that he will profit by it in many ways. He fully intends to make his decision some time, or else he would not ask the salesman to come back and see him again. But he is a little weak-kneed. He lacks something in decisiveness. Our friend treated practically all of these indecisive prospects of his in the same way.

"I am sorry," he would say, "but I can't come back to see you again. My time is limited. There are plenty of people who want to know about my proposition and who are eager to take it. I must get around and see them. I can't afford to go back on my track and spend time with people to whom I have already explained the whole thing. You want this and you know you want it. You intend to have it, or you would not ask me to come back and see you again. There is no good reason why you should not have it now, and you know there is not. Furthermore, if you do not take it now and I do not come back to see you--and I won't--then you will never take it. That's plain enough. You feel more like taking it right now, to-day, while I am talking to you, than you will later, when you have forgotten half of what I have said. If there is any question you want to ask about this, ask me now and I will answer it. But there isn't any, because I have already answered your questions. You are satisfied. Your mind is made up. There is no reason for delay--just sign your name right there, please." And only about four per cent of those to whom he talked that way refused to sign when he told them to.

The indecisive person wants someone always to decide for him. If you are trying to persuade such a person, then you must decide for him. Do it as tactfully as you can. Sometimes these people want others to decide for them and, at the same time, to make the situation look as if they had decided for themselves. They realize their own indecisiveness. They are ashamed of it, and they do not like to be reminded of it.

INDICATIONS OF INDECISION

These are the indications of indecisiveness: brunette coloring; moderately square and prominent chin--sometimes a long, narrow chin; small, snub or sway-back nose; high forehead, flat at the brows and prominent above; soft consistency; great flexibility of the joints of hands and fingers; a head narrow above and behind the ears and square in the back; a timid, apprehensive expression; rather aimless movements and gestures, and a small thumb, set high on the hand. Rare, indeed, is the person who has all of these indications. So rare, in fact, that he is scarcely a normal being if he has them all in a marked degree.

THE BALANCED TYPE

There are some people of an evenly balanced type. They are neither violently impulsive nor ponderously deliberate. They are interested in facts and pass their judgment upon them, but they are also interested in theories and willing to listen to them. They are practical and matter-of-fact, but they also have ideals. They have clean, powerful emotions, fairly well controlled, and yet, when their judgment has been satisfied, they are perfectly willing to act in response to their feelings. They are neither easy, credulous and impulsive nor suspicious, obstinate and procrastinating. The way to persuade them is first to present the facts and show them the reasons why. Then, by suggestion and word-painting, to stimulate their desire and give them an opportunity to decide and act. Such people are medium in color, with forehead, nose, mouth and chin inclining to the straight line; medium in size; medium in build; fine or medium fine in texture; elastic in consistency; moderately high, wide, long, square head; a pleasant but calm and sensible expression of face and eyes; quiet, well-timed walk and gestures; well-modulated voice.

THE EASY MARK

When the person to be persuaded is indecisive and also has large, wide-open, credulous eyes; a hopeful, optimistic, turned-up nose, and a large, round dome of a head just above the temples, he is the living image of the champion easy mark. What he needs is not so much to be persuaded as to be protected against himself. He, and the greedy, grasping, cunning but short-sighted individual, who is always trying to get something for nothing, constitute that very large class of people of whom it has been said that there is one born every minute.

ADVANTAGE OF PERSUADER'S POSITION

In closing this chapter, we cannot forego the opportunity for a word of counsel to you in your efforts to persuade others. Remember that if you do your work well in securing favorable attention, arousing interest, and creating desire, the person with whom you are dealing is like a man standing on one foot, not quite knowing which way he will go. Even if he is more or less obstinate and should be on both his feet, he is at least standing still and considering which direction he will take. If this is not true, then you have failed to create a desire, or, having created it, have not augmented it until it is strong enough. But, granting that this is true, do you not see what an advantage it gives you? The man who is standing on one foot, undecided, is quickly pulled or pushed in the way you want him to go if you yourself vigorously desire it. Even the man who stands obstinately on both feet is at a disadvantage if he does not know which way to go, and you very decidedly know which way you want him to go.

THE VALUE OF COURAGE

We have seen more sales skillfully brought up to the point of desire and then lost through the indecision, the wavering, the fear, or the hesitation of the salesman than for any other one cause. Of all of the qualities and characteristics which contribute to success in the persuasion of others, there is, perhaps, none more powerful than that courage which gives calmness, surety of touch, decisiveness, and unwavering, unhesitating action.

Some years ago we saw a huge mob surround a building in which a political speaker was trying to talk upon an unpopular subject. The longer the mob remained waiting for their victim to come out, the more violent and the more abusive it became. There was an angry hum, sounding above the occasional cries and shouts, which betokened trouble. Presently a large man scrambled upon the pedestal of a statue in front of the building and began to harangue the crowd. He argued with them, he pleaded with them, he threatened them, he tried to cajole them. But through it all he could scarcely make himself heard and the mob remained solidly packed about the door. Then the police were brought and attempted to force a passageway for the escape of the speaker, whose address inside the building was nearing a close. But the police were powerless and some of them were badly hurt.

Then a quiet little man came down the steps of the building. He was dressed in ordinary clothing and was unarmed. His open hands hung idly at his side. He stood near the bottom step, where he could just look over the heads of the crowd. He stood perfectly still, perfectly calm, and yet with a look of such iron resolution on his countenance as we have seldom seen. Those next him grew strangely quiet. Then the semi-circle of silence spread until the entire mob stood as if holding its breath waiting to see what this man would do.

"Make a passageway there," he said in a matter-of-fact tone of voice; "there is a carriage coming through."

Instantly the crowd parted, a carriage was driven up to the steps, the speaker came down and entered it, and it was driven rapidly away, followed only by a few hisses and cat-calls.

When all is said and done, that is the spirit which secures the decision and action of others.

266

CHAPTER V

EFFICIENT AND SATISFACTORY SERVICE

Marshall Nyall was an excellent workman. He was keen, quick of comprehension, practical in his judgment, and unusually resourceful. He was energetic, industrious, and skillful. Being blessed with considerable idealism, he took pride and pleasure in putting a fine artistic finish on everything he did. He studied his work in all its aspects and was alert in finding ways of saving time, materials, energy, and money. He was, therefore, personally efficient. As an employee of the Swift Motor Company, he rose rapidly until he became superintendent. In that position he made a good record. So valuable was he that the White Rapids Motor Company coveted him and its president and general manager began to lay plans to entice him away. Negotiations were begun and continued over a period of weeks. Larger and larger grew the inducements offered by the White Rapids Motor Company until, finally, Nyall's employers felt that they could not afford to meet them any longer, and this highly efficient man became works manager for the White Rapids Motor Company, at a very greatly increased salary.

Now, the White Rapids Motor Company was larger and wealthier than the Swift Motor Company. The position of works manager was a more important and responsible position than that of superintendent. Nyall was accordingly delighted and had high ambitions as to his career with his new employers.

HOW THE TROUBLE STARTED

"You have a reputation," said the president and general manager to Nyall, "for efficiency. Efficiency is what we want in the works here, and if you can put these factories on as efficient a basis as you did the shops of the Swift Motor Company, your future is assured."

"I can do that all right, Mr. Burton," Nyall replied confidently, "provided I get the right kind of co-operation from the front office."

"Call on us for anything you want, Nyall," returned the president sharply. He was a proud, positive man. He loved power. He had the ability to lead and to rule, and he resented even the slightest imputation that any lack of co-operation on his part might defeat his plans for efficient management.

A few days later Nyall made some changes in the plan of routing the work through the factories. These changes were rather radical and sweeping and necessitated a considerable initial expense. Naturally, Burton was not long in hearing about it. Instantly he summoned his works manager.

"Haven't you begun your work here in a rather drastic manner?" he inquired. "Surely you have not studied this situation carefully enough in a few days to justify you in making such sweeping changes in the system which we have built up here after years of patient study and research. I have given the routing of the work through the factories days and nights of careful study, Nyall, during the years that we have been standardizing it. I believe that it was just as nearly perfect as it can be just as we had it."

"Your system was all wrong, and I can prove it to you," returned Nyall. "Just wait a minute until I bring you in my charts."

RUBBING IT IN

Stepping into his office, he secured a number of charts and also several sheets of tabulated figures. The charts were beautifully executed and in a most admirable manner made graphically clear the sound reasoning upon which Nyall had ordered the changes made. The tabulated figures proved that his reasoning had been correct. He was positive, forceful, and insistent in driving home his argument and in compelling his superior to admit their force and cogency. When it was all admitted and Burton, fighting to the last ditch, had been over-whelmed, Nyall's unconcealed air of triumph was keenly and painfully exasperating to the defeated man.

This was only the first of the clashes between these two positive minds. Ordinarily, perhaps, Burton would have preferred efficiency in the factory to the triumph of his own opinions and ideas, much as it hurt him to be found in error, But Nyall's disposition to wring the last drop of personal triumph out of every victory was more than the good man could endure. With his highly-strung nature, and goaded as he was by intense irritation, the passion to prove Nyall in the wrong overrode all other considerations. Thus he began to "cut off his nose to spite his face," as Nyall expressed it--to conspire against Nyall's success.

If you have ever witnessed a fight for supremacy between two positive, powerful, high-strung natures, with unusual resources of intellect and capacity on both sides, we do not need to describe to you what happened in the White Rapids Motor Company during the months that followed. Nyall simply could not understand why Burton should jeopardize the success, and even the solvency, of his enterprise by plotting against his own works manager. To his friends he confided: "Honestly, I think the old man is going crazy. The things he says and the things he does are not the product of a sane, normal mind." Similarly, Burton could not understand, to save his life, why Nyall should jeopardize the brilliant future which lay before him "by bucking his president and general manager," as he put it. "It is rule or ruin with him," he told his friends. "I never saw a more stubborn man in my life. He is crazy to have his own way. He wants to take the bit in his teeth, and if he were permitted to do it, he would run away and smash himself and everything else."

BOTH BELLIGERENT AND STUBBORN

Why did not Nyall resign or, in default of his resignation, why did not Burton discharge him? Such action was obvious for both men from a mere common sense point of view, under the circumstances. The answer is that both men were so obstinate and so set upon winning the fight upon which they had entered, that neither of them would give up. It all ended when the board of directors finally took a hand and removed Nyall in order to save the institution from shipwreck.

Naturally enough, the word went out that Nyall could not stand prosperity; that when placed in a position of authority and responsibility, he had lost his head and had nearly wrecked the concern for which he worked. He found that he could not go back to his old position with the Swift Motor Company and that his reputation had suffered so seriously that he had to be satisfied for a long time with a minor position in a rather obscure concern.

THE KEY TO THE DIFFICULTY

Nyall was efficient--unusually efficient--but he did not give satisfaction with the White Rapids Motor Company. Perhaps we do not need to point to the moral of this tale. If Nyall had understood his superior and had conducted himself accordingly, he might himself have been president and general manager of the White Rapids Motor Company to-day. He would have known that Burton was not a man to be brow-beaten, not a man to be defied, not a man to be proven in the wrong. With a little tact and diplomacy, he could have effected all of the changes he wished without even the semblance of a clash with his chief. He might even have insisted upon the first ones he advocated without serious trouble if he had done it in the right way and if he had not permitted his feeling of personal triumph to show itself so plainly.

WHAT MIGHT HAVE BEEN

In the first place, if he had known Burton as he should, he would have gone to him before making any changes and said: "Mr. Burton, I understand that you have given a great deal of time and thought to the routing of work through the factories; that you have personally directed the building up of the present system. I usually begin my work by studying the routing, but if you feel satisfied with this routing, as a result of your study; and experience, I will devote my time to something else." Approached in this way, Burton would unquestionably have directed the new works manager to make a complete study of the routing system and to suggest any possible improvements.

This story is typical of many others which we have observed more or less in detail. Nyall was a great success in the Swift Motor Company because the chief executive of that company was a little mild, good-natured, easy-going fellow, who not only needed the spur and stimulus of a positive nature like Nyall's, but was quite frankly delighted with it. If Nyall had approached him with questions and suggestions and a spirit of constant bowing to his authority, he would have been as exasperated in his own quiet way as Burton was with the opposite treatment. His constant injunction to his subordinates was: "Do not come to me with details. Use your own judgment and initiative. Go ahead. Do it in your own way. I hold you responsible only for results."

ALWAYS "SOME OTHER WAY"

In his "Message to Garcia," Elbert Hubbard has the following to say:

"You, reader, put this matter to a test:

"You are sitting now in your office--six clerks are within call. Summon any one of them and make this request: 'Please look in the encyclopedia and make a brief memorandum for me concerning the life of Correggio.'

"Will the clerk quietly say, 'Yes, sir,' and go do the task?

"On your life, he will not. He will look at you out of a fishy eye and ask one or more of the following questions:

"'Who was he?'

"'Which encyclopedia?'

"'Where is the encyclopedia?'

"'Was I hired for that?'

"'Don't you mean Bismarck?'

"'What's the matter with Charlie doing it?'

"'Is he dead?'

"'Is there any hurry?'

"'Shan't I bring you the book and let you look it up yourself?'

"'What do you want to know for?'

"And I will lay you ten to one that after you have answered the questions, and explained why you want it, the clerk will go off and get one of the other clerks to help him try to find Garcia--and then come back and tell you there is no such man. Of course, I may lose my bet, but, according to the Law of Average, I will not."

Now, there are many executives so constituted that they are not only willing, but glad, to explain the why and the wherefore of the orders they give. When they give the order, they are oftentimes willing to listen to suggestions, and oftentimes to adopt them. These are men of the deliberate, calm, reflective, rather mild type, with only a moderate development of the crown of the head which shows a love of authority. Oftentimes, also, they are men of the erratic, impulsive type who realize their impulsiveness and are rather glad than otherwise to be picked up by queries and suggestions from their subordinates. But for the man of the positive, incisive, decided, domineering type these questions and suggestions, this attitude which proposes that something else ought to be done, or that the thing ought to be done in "some other way," are exasperating in the extreme. Since this is the usual type of man to be found in industrial business, it is not strange that so many employees, perhaps efficient enough otherwise, fail to give satisfaction. It is because they seemingly cannot overcome their itch to do the thing "some other way." There is the best of all psychological reasons why every employee should read and take to heart Elbert Hubband's "Message to Garcia."

Over and over again, young men and young women have come to us saying: "I wish you would tell me why I cannot hold a position. I know I do the work well enough, but, somehow or other, I seem to be unfortunate. I have trouble with everyone I work for and cannot remain in any one position for very long." In practically every case the trouble has been that the young man or the young woman did not understand the simple principles of human nature.

HOW TO TAKE DISCIPLINE

Many sensitive souls do not understand that a wide-headed man of the bony and muscular type, with high, retreating forehead, prominent brows, large nose, high in the bridge, prominent teeth and mouth, and somewhat retreating chin, is intensely energetic, practical and impatient--that he wants to see things done--that he demands results and cannot wait for them. He is inclined to be nervous and irritable. When things go wrong, or he thinks they go wrong, he says things, says them with brutal frankness and considerable vigor. He may even use profanity and call names. He is especially impatient with and exasperated by excuses, since his passion is for results. An excuse to him is like a red rag flaunted in a bull's face. His irritation is relieved by speech. Afterward he passes on and probably forgets all about the incident. Certainly he does not hold it against the employee personally.

If, in addition to his other characteristics, this man also has a high crown, he is inclined to be domineering and exacting. Since his whole intention in his sharp speeches is to stimulate his employees to greater efficiency, and since the farthest thing from his thoughts or his intentions is to hurt their personal feelings, there is probably nothing that will so quickly and thoroughly arouse his resentment as any expression, word or act of wounded pride on the part of his employee.

Most employees make the serious mistake of taking criticism or censure as a personal matter. They should reflect that their employer has no interest in hurting their feelings--that what he wants is efficient service, profitable not only to himself but to the employee, and that, according to his type and his knowledge, he is taking the best possible means to secure it.

When an employee enters an organization, he becomes an integral part of a complicated service-rendering and profit-making machine. If he has any tender personal feelings, he should wrap them up carefully in an envelope of indifference and lock them away safely in the strong box of ambition. Then he is perfectly willing to let his employer call him a blockhead, provided the result is increased efficiency and profit.

TOO MUCH DIGNITY

A young man of our acquaintance once went to work as assistant to the manager of an insurance company. This young man was quiet, hard-working, dependable, and efficient. With his self-effacing modesty and the remarkable accuracy and care with which he attended to every detail of his work, he would have made an ideal assistant to most employers. The manager of this insurance company, however, was jovial, friendly, social, witty, and companionable. At first he was delighted with his new assistant. As time went on, however, the young man's solemnity, his taciturnity, and the quiet, dignified way in which he permitted all attempts at sociability and jocularity to pass over his head, as it were, unnoticed, began to get on his employer's nerves.

"If I don't get that young man out of the office, I will either murder him or commit suicide," he told us. "Efficient? Lord, yes! I never knew anybody so damnably efficient. Dependable? He is so dependable that he is uncanny. I would rather have a human being around who is willing to smoke a cigar with me once in a while, to crack a joke, or at least to laugh at my jokes. Just to break the monotony, I would be perfectly willing to have him make a few mistakes, to forget something. I have lots of faults--too many, I guess, to be comfortable around such a paragon of perfection as that boy."

Now, the truth of the matter was, as we well knew, that this young man, while serious-minded and efficient, had a keen sense of humor, appreciated a good joke, and was at times very merry with his own companions. He had in his mind, however, a certain ideal conduct for a business man. And to the best of his ability, he lived up to this ideal, no matter what the personality of his employer.

"FAMILIARITY BREEDS CONTEMPT"

Many employees make the mistake of attempting familiarity with employers whose dignity is largely developed and whose sociability and sense of humor are only moderate or even deficient. The man whose head shows its longest line from point of chin to crown, who has a long face with long, vertical lines, whose lips are rather thin, whose forehead is rather narrow and somewhat retreating, and whose back-head is only moderately developed or even deficient, is not a man to slap on the back. He will resent any familiarity or any jocular attempt to draw him down on a plane of equality with his employees. If such a man is also fine-textured, he is very sensitive and must be treated with deference and respect. If he has a short upper lip, he is amenable to flattery, but the flattery must be delicate and deferential.

Even when these characteristics are not extreme and the habitual attitude of an employer is one of geniality, with a certain amount of jocularity, employees should be on their guard, especially if the executive has a square head behind. Such a man, like Cousin Egbert, in Harry Leon Wilson's story, "Ruggles of Red Gap," "can be pushed just so far." It is dangerous to try to push him any further. He has a very true and proper sense of dignity and, while he is perfectly willing to be sociable and to live with his employees upon terms of friendliness, he knows well how to check any exuberance which tends to trench upon familiarity.

THE "NAPOLEONIC" EXECUTIVE

There is a type of employer who has a high, well-rounded, long head; his head is also wide above the ears, but rather narrow back of the ears. He is usually light in complexion, fine textured--a good combination of the bony and muscular type and the fat man type. This man's eyes are the neither round, wide-open eyes of simple credulity nor the long, narrow, somewhat oblique slits of secretiveness, avarice, shrewdness and suspicion. His face tends to roundness, curves and dimples, and his lips are rather full. His head is especially high and dome-shaped just above the temples and behind the hair line. His chin may be fairly well formed or it may be narrow and retreating. If it is of the narrow and retreating variety, then some of the characteristics are accentuated.

This man is a man of intense enthusiasm, great energy, a desire to accomplish things and to be the head of whatever he undertakes. He is eager, responsive, emotional, ambitious, and erratic. He is often brilliant, nearly always resourceful, conceives large projects, attempts big things, makes friends with important people, and often secures a very enviable reputation, at least for a time. But this man has his faults. He is emotional and enthusiastic. He throws himself intensely into the accomplishment of one ambitious plan after another. He has not the calmness of dispassionate judgment and the deliberateness necessary to be a good judge of men. He lacks real courage and therefore attempts to cover up his deficiency by bluff and bluster. Because of his poor judgment in regard to human nature, he frequently selects employees on the impulse of the moment, absolutely without reference to their fitness for the work he wants them to do. The ruling emotion which prompts him in selection may be any one of a dozen. We have seen men like this select important lieutenants because of their personal attractiveness, because someone else wanted them, because of similarity of tastes in matters wholly irrelevant, because the fellows knew how to flatter, out of sympathy for their families, and, in one pathetic case, because the young man thus chosen had painstakingly read through an immense set of books supposed to be representative of the world's best literature.

INJUSTICE TO EMPLOYEES

In many cases, enthusiasm and optimism on the part of such executives have placed men in positions far beyond their capacity and loaded them with responsibilities for which they had no aptitudes. Oftentimes such rapid promotion and such sudden increase of income have utterly turned the head of the victim, setting him back years in his normal development and his pursuit of success.

Because the sudden infatuations of such executives are based upon emotion and not judgment, they flicker out as quickly as the emotion evaporates. Then ensues a period of suspicion, oftentimes wholly unjust. Because the executive lacks real courage, every word and every act of the employee makes him afraid that there is something sinister and dangerous behind it. This is accentuated by the fact that, deep down in his own heart, the executive knows that he does not understand men. When this condition of affairs arises, both the executive and his employee are utterly miserable unless the employee, being a man of judgment, and understanding the situation in its essence, has the good sense either to bring the executive willy-nilly to a complete readjustment of their relations or to resign. Oftentimes, however, the employee has a larger salary than he ever received before--he also feels certain that if he resigns, he cannot secure so large a salary in any other place--and so he hangs on, hoping against hope that the attitude of his superior will change. The executive, on his part, feels that he ought to discharge the employee. He is not satisfied with him. He is suspicious of him. He is afraid of him. He realizes that he has used bad judgment in selecting him. But he lacks the courage to discharge the man and oftentimes, for this reason, resorts to a series of petty persecutions in an attempt to make him resign.

HOW TO STEER A DIFFICULT COURSE

The employee who is suddenly taken up, flattered, and offered an unusually good position by a man of this type would do well to hesitate long before accepting. If he does accept, he should take care that he does not attempt anything beyond his powers and that he does not accept a larger salary than he is able to earn. Once in his position, he should be modest, efficient, and do his best to keep out of cliques and inside politics. At the same time, he should take great care not to offend those who are powerful. The employees of every "Napoleonic" executive are, by the very nature of the organization, forced into politics. Tenure of office, promotion, and increase in pay all depend, not upon real service--although real service counts; not upon efficiency and merit--although these also count; but primarily upon the whims and caprices of an employer of this type. Every employee of any importance, therefore, does his best, first, to keep his own relations to his employer on a frank, easy, confidential basis; second, in so far as in him lies, to be at peace with all his fellow employees. We have seen

275

some of the most valuable men of their kind we have ever met suddenly discharged without a word of explanation by employers of this type. The trouble was that someone who could get a hearing carried a bit of scandal, perhaps without the slightest foundation in fact, to the ever-suspicious ears of the boss. The boss, because he lacked the courage to admit that he had listened to such gossip, removed a man who had served him satisfactorily for years without a word of warning, and without a hearing.

Unless you understand human nature, and if you are at all responsive to appreciation, there is probably no greater pleasure than to work for such a man as we have described, so long as the sunshine of his favor falls upon you. But, as a general rule, we find their employees anything but happy. Almost without exception they feel that their tenure of office hangs by the slenderest of threads and that it is necessary to regard all of their fellow employees with suspicion. Some men enjoy working in this fevered atmosphere. If you are one of them, there are excellent opportunities for you in the employ of a man of this type. But you will do well always to have a good safe place prepared in which to land if you should suddenly be dropped.

THE BLUFFER

In all of your dealings with the man who lacks real courage, remember that his blustering and show of bravery is only an assumption to cover up his deficiencies and that if you yourself have the courage to face him and, in the language of the street, "to call his bluff," he will quiet down and be perfectly amenable to reason. But be sure to observe your man carefully and accurately before trying to call his bluff.

SUCCESS AS AN EMPLOYEE

The ultimate success of every employee depends, first of all, upon his selection of the kind of work for which he is pre-eminently fitted; second, his selection, so far as possible, of the kind of employer and superior executive under whom he can do his best work; third, upon his study and mastery of every possible resource of knowledge and training connected with the technical and practical aspects of his work; fourth, upon his careful and scientific development of all of the best and most valuable assets in his character; fifth, upon a thorough understanding and application of the principles of personal efficiency; sixth, upon an accurate knowledge of the character, disposition and personal peculiarities of his employer or employers and superior executives;

276

seventh, upon an intelligent and diplomatic adjustment of his methods of work, his personal appearance, his personal behavior, his relationship with his fellow employees and with his employers, to the end of building up and maintaining permanently the highest possible degree of confidence in him and satisfaction with his service.

PART FOUR

PRINCIPLES AND PRACTICE OF CHARACTER ANALYSIS

CHAPTER I

THE SCIENTIFIC BASIS OF CHARACTER ANALYSIS

A few years ago we were content to guess, to follow tradition, and to charge up to the caprices of fate or an all-wise Providence the failures we experienced as a result of our ignorance. Then someone, less bound by tradition than the average, discovered that exact knowledge was obtainable about most subjects. Scientific research took the place of guess-work or mere haphazard leaps in the dark. We began to observe, classify, measure, weigh, test, and record, instead of guess. Thus science was born.

As far back as human records go men have made observations upon others, have formed certain conclusions as a result of these observations, and have recorded them. Some were accurate and valuable; others merely ludicrous and misleading. Tens of thousands of men and women have attempted to analyze human character, but most of them became lost in a maze of apparent contradictions and gave up in despair, content to follow impression and intuition. Though they became discouraged and abandoned the field, each of these workers contributed something of value to the subject, and to-day we have a science of character analysis exact enough to add very greatly to our wisdom in dealing with humanity and its problems.

LIMITATIONS OF THE SCIENCE

We do not wish you to misunderstand our claims for the science. Character analysis is not a science in the mathematical sense. As we said in our introduction, we cannot place a man on the scales and determine that he has so many milligrams of industry, or apply measurements and prove that he has so many centimeters of talent for salesmanship. Nor can we, using the method of the chemist, apply the litmus to his stream of consciousness and get his psychical reaction in a demonstrable way. We are glad we cannot, else humanity might lose the fine arts of coquetry and conquest. Perhaps we never shall be able to do these things, but that is small cause for discouragement. What we do claim for the science of character analysis is that it is classified knowledge based upon sound principles; that it is as accurate as the science of medicine; that it can be imparted to others; and, best of all, that anyone can test it for himself beyond any question of doubt.

TESTS SHOW UNTRAINED JUDGMENT UNRELIABLE

"Oh, I'm a pretty good judge of men," people say to us. We have heard this declaration thousands of times in the last seventeen years. Occasionally it was, no doubt, true, but more often not, even when the statement was made in the greatest sincerity. So we determined to test the ability of the public to analyze men. The first test appeared in a number of magazines, giving a profile and full-face view, showing the hands of a young man. A few simple questions were asked concerning him, such as these:

"Would you employ this man?

"If so, would you employ him as salesman, executive, cashier, clerk, chemist, mechanic?

"Is he healthy, honest, industrious, aggressive?

"Would you choose him as a friend?"

Of 5,000 replies but 4.1 per cent were right or nearly right. Some of the replies were astounding. One manager of a big business wrote: "This man would be an exceptionally honest and trustworthy cashier or treasurer." One sales manager replied: "I would like to have this man on my sales force. He would make a hummer of a salesman, if I am any judge of men. His hands are identical with my own," etc., etc. But the climax was reached with this letter from a young lady: "He would be a devoted husband and father. I would like him as a friend."

Our own analysis of this man, from photographs on a test, was as follows:

"We would not employ this man.

"He is not healthy.

"He is intelligent.

"He is not honest.

"He is not industrious.

"He is aggressive in a disagreeable way.

"We would not choose him as a friend.

"John Doe is a natural mechanic who has had very little training in that line of work. Being exceedingly keen and intelligent, without right moral principles, he has used his natural mechanical ability in illegitimate lines."

Here is a brief sketch of John Doe, furnished by a gentleman who befriended him and has followed his career for years:

"John is thirty-one years of age and has just been released from a term in Sing Sing Prison. The crime for which he served sentence was burglary. He made a skeleton key with which he gained access to a loft where were stored valuable goods. He stole three thousand dollars worth of these from his employer. He admits that he has committed other crimes of forgery and theft. Perhaps the cleverest of these was forgery which was never discovered. He is exceedingly friendly and makes friends easily. He is, however, very erratic and irritable in disposition and often quarrelsome. He is a fair example of a common type which has intelligence and skill but has not learned to direct his activities along constructive lines."

A more complicated advertisement followed this first one, giving the portraits of nine men, each successful in his chosen work because well fitted for it by natural aptitude as well as by training. People were asked to state the vocation of each. Out of 4,876 replies but three were correct.

SOME FUNDAMENTAL TRUTHS

Surely, when the untrained judgment of intelligent people goes so wide of the mark, it is worth while to inquire whether or not science can come to the rescue. Perhaps a brief examination of some well-established truths about human beings will aid in finding an answer to our query.

The science of character analysis by the observational method is based upon three very simple scientific truths:

First, man's body is the product of evolution through countless ages, and is what it is to-day as the result of the combined effect upon it of heredity and environment.

Second, man's mind is also the product of evolution through countless ages, and is what it is to-day as the result of the effect upon it of the same heredity and the same environment as have affected his body.

Third, man's body and man's mind profoundly affect each other in all of their actions and reactions and have affected each other through all the centuries of their simultaneous evolution.

EVOLUTION OF BLONDES AND BRUNETTES

Men's bodies differ from one another in many ways. A little scientific investigation soon proves to us that these differences are the result of differences in heredity and environment. Men's minds differ from one another in countless ways. Scientific investigation also proves that these mental differences, or differences in character, are also the result of differences in heredity and environment.

For example, people whose ancestors, through countless ages, lived in the bright sunlight and tropical luxuriance of the warmer climes, have dark eyes, dark hair, and dark skin because nature found it necessary to supply an abundance of pigmentation in order to protect the delicate tissues of the body from injury by the actinic rays of the sun. The same soft luxuriance of their environment has made these people slow, easy-going, hateful of change, introspective, philosophical and religious. On the other hand, people whose ancestors dwelt for centuries in the cold, dark, cloudy and foggy climate of Northwestern Europe have less need for pigmentation and are, therefore, flaxen-haired, blue-eyed and white-skinned.

The hardships and rigors of this Northern climate made these people aggressive, active, restless, fond of variety, and, because of their fierce struggle for existence, exceedingly practical, matter-of-fact, and material.

WHY NOSES DIFFER IN SIZE AND SHAPE

Another example illustrates this truth clearly: The type of human nose evolved in warm, humid climates is low and flat, with large, short passageways directly to the lungs. People living in such a climate have little need for great energy and activity, since there is food in abundance all around them. On the other hand, the type of nose evolved in a cold, dry climate is high in the bridge, with thin nostrils, so that the air may be both warmed and moistened before reaching the lungs. People living in such a climate have great need for activity, both in order to secure the means of subsistence and in order to keep themselves warm. Thus we find that the low, flat nose is everywhere the nose of indolence and passivity, while the large nose, high in the bridge, is everywhere an indication of energy and aggressiveness.

WHY SOME HEADS ARE HARD, OTHERS SOFT

In brief, then, darkness of color is not the cause of deliberation and conservatism, but both darkness of color and conservatism are results of the same causes, namely, a heredity and environment which produce these characteristics. Blonde coloring is not a cause of restless activity, but both the color and the activity are the result of evolution in a cold, dark, rigorous climate.

A striking example of the working out of the three truths which we have given is seen in the consistency of the body. Hard hands, hard muscles, and, in general, a dense, compact, unyielding consistency of fiber, are both inherited and acquired as the result of hard physical labor and the enduring of hardships. As is well known, those who spend their lives in grinding toil in the midst of hard conditions care little for the finer sentiments and sympathies of life. They have no time for them, no energy left for them. By the very necessities of their lot they are compelled to be hostile to change, free from all extravagance, and largely impervious to new ideas. Therefore, wherever we find hardness of consistency we find a tendency to narrowness, parsimony, conservatism, and lack of sympathy. Looking at this fact from a little different angle, we see that, since the body affects the mind and the mind the body so profoundly, the body of hard fiber, being impervious to physical impressions, will yield but slowly and meagerly to those molecular changes which naturally accompany emotional response and intellectual receptivity.

These are but a few examples of the truths upon which the science of character analysis by the observational method is based. Many others may occur to you. Many others have been observed, traced and verified in our work upon this science.

A BRIEF RECAPITULATION

Briefly recapitulating, we see that for every physical difference between men there is a corresponding mental difference, because both the physical differences and the mental differences are the result of the same heredity and environment. We see, further, that these physical and mental differences are not only results of the same environment affecting the individual through his remote ancestry, but that they are tied together by cause and effect in the individual as he stands to-day.

BASIS OF CLASSIFICATION

We have told you that the science of character analysis is classified knowledge. It is clear to you by this time that the knowledge which lies at the basis of this science is knowledge concerning physical and mental differences and their correspondences. In this science, therefore, since we are to observe physical differences and from them to determine differences in intellect, in disposition, in natural talents, in character in general, our first classification must deal with these physical differences.

Men differ from one another in nine fundamental ways These ways are: color, form, size, structure, texture, consistency, proportion, expression, and condition. Let us consider each of them briefly.

COLOR

Color is, perhaps, the most striking variable. You instantly observe whether a person is white or black, brown or yellow. Indeed, so striking are these variations that they were formerly the basis upon which humanity was divided into races.

We have already briefly touched upon the cause for pigmentation and the indications of differences in color. For many years anthropologists were at a loss to understand exactly why some men were black and others white. About twenty years ago, however, Von Schmaedel propounded the theory that pigmentation in the hair, eyes and skin was Nature's way of protecting the tissues from injury by the actinic or ultra-violet rays of the sun, which destroy protoplasm. Following the enunciation of Von Schmaedel's theory, prolonged experimentation was made by many anthropologists, chief among whom was our own late Major Charles E. Woodruff, of the U.S. Army. In Major Woodruff's book, "The Effects of Tropical Light Upon White Men," are to be found, set forth in a most fascinating way, evidences amounting almost to proof of the correctness of Von Schmaedel's theory.

Since Major Woodruff's book appeared, many other anthropologists have declared their acceptance of the theory, so that to-day we may assert with confidence that the black man is black because of the excessive sunlight of his environment, and that the white man is white because he and his ancestors did not need protection from the sun. Mountain climbers cover their faces and hands with a mixture of grease and lamp-black in order to prevent sunburn. When in India we wore actinic underwear, dark glasses, and solar topees to protect us from the excessive light.

282

DIFFERENCES BETWEEN BLONDES AND BRUNETTES

Now, in regard to differences in character between the dark races and the white races, you have only to consider the languorous air of the tropics and sub-tropics, the abundance of food, the small need for fuel, clothing and shelter--in general, everything in the environment which tends to make man indolent and to give him plenty of time for introspection, philosophy, theology, and the occult.

The dweller in Northern climes has had to wrestle with rapid changes, demands for food, clothing, shelter and fuel, relative scarcity of all these and difficulty of securing them--in short, nearly every possible element in his surroundings which would compel him to get out and hustle, to take an active interest in material things, to be constantly on the alert both mentally and physically--in a word, to master and conquer his environment.

These are some of the differences between the dark and the white races. We find the same differences in proportion between blondes and brunettes in the white races.

HAVELOCK ELLIS ON BLONDES AND BRUNETTES

The noted anthropologist Havelock Ellis says, in regard to this:

"It is clear that a high index of pigmentation, or an excess of fairness, prevails among the men of restless and ambitious temperament; the sanguine, energetic men; the men who easily dominate their fellows and who get on in life, and the men who recruit the aristocracy and who doubtless largely form the plutocracy. It is significant that the group of low-class men--artisans and peasants--and the men of religion, whose mission in life it is to preach resignation to a higher will, are both notably of dark complexion; while the men of action thus tend to be fair, men of thought, it seems to me, show some tendency to be dark."

The practical application of this truth is seen in the fact that the white races of the earth seem to have a genius for government, for conquest, for exploration, and for progress; while the dark races of the earth seem to have a genius for art, for literature, for religion, and for conservatism. Not long ago we read the conclusions of several anthropologists on this subject. One declared that the first men were undoubtedly brunette, and that the blonde was an abnormality and rapidly becoming extinct. Another was equally sure that the pure white blonde was a special creation but little lower than the angels, and that all the dark races were so colored by their sins. This is a matter upon which we hesitate to speculate. It would, however, be of some interest to know the respective coloring of these two investigators.

PRACTICAL APPLICATION OF LAW OF COLOR

Color has its commercial application. The active, restless, aggressive, variety-loving blonde is found in large proportions amongst speculators, promoters, organizers, advertising men, traveling salesmen; while the more stable and constant brunette predominates amongst the plodders, the planners, the scientists, the administrators, and the conservators. Even the poets bring out the difference. They sing of the fickle, light-hearted coquette with golden hair and azure eyes, and of the faithful, constant, true, undying affection of the lady with soft, brown eyes.

FORM

The second variable--Form--refers to form of face and features as seen in profile. The sharp face, with the long, pointed nose, prominent eyes, retreating forehead, prominent teeth and retreating chin, is the extreme convex form. The hammock-shaped face, with high, prominent forehead, flat brows, deep-set eyes, small snubbed or sway-back nose, retreating teeth and long, prominent chin, is the extreme concave in form of profile.

It would involve much dry, technical writing to explain in detail the scientific reasons why the extreme convex in profile indicates extreme energy, quickness, impatience, impulsiveness, keenness and alertness of intellect, and great rapidity in action. The large nose, high in the bridge, however, indicating, as you have already seen, great energy, is one of the scientific reasons for this. In a similar way it would take me too long to tell in detail why the extreme concave of profile indicates just the opposite qualities.

It is a scientific fact that that which is sharp is penetrating and moves quickly; that which is blunt is non-penetrating and of necessity moves slowly. The needle darts through the cloth more quickly than the bodkin. The greyhound is swifter than the bulldog. The stiletto does quicker work than the bludgeon. This, of course, is only a symbolism which may make vivid the truth that the convex man works more rapidly than the concave.

In commercial work, the man who is successful in positions requiring quick decision and quick action has a convex profile, while the man whose duties call for patience, deliberation, reflection, and the ability to plod should have some modification of the concave form of profile.

284

SIZE

It is an old saying that large bodies move slowly. It would be more scientifically correct to say that large bodies get under way slowly. Difference in physical size between men is important in many ways. If, as William James says, "the causes of emotion are indubitably physiological," then the smaller the physical bulk which must be affected in order to have an intense emotion, the more quickly and easily is that intense emotion aroused.

Other things being equal, the small man is more excitable and becomes angry more easily than the large man. He also cools down more quickly. When the huge bulk of the big man becomes thoroughly aroused, thoroughly wrought up, it is time to get out of the way and stand from under.

STRUCTURE

Hall Caine, the novelist, has an immense head, a slender jaw, and a small, fragile body. James J. Jeffries, the pugilist, has a comparatively small head, a large jaw, and huge bones and muscles. Ex-President Taft has a comparatively small head, round face, round body, round arms and legs. These are differences in structure.

Hall Caine is of the mental type. He is by nature unfitted to be either a pugilist, a hammer-thrower, an explorer, a banker, or a judge. He is, however, pre-eminently fitted to dream dreams of truth and beauty, to construct those dreams into stories and plays. James J. Jeffries is by nature and physique fitted for the trade of boiler-maker, for the sport of pugilism, and for physical and manual accomplishment in general. Ex-President Taft is by nature and physique fitted to sit quietly in a big chair and direct the work of others, to administer affairs, to sit upon the bench and weigh impartially causes of dispute between his fellow men. As you see, these three are our old friends, the physically frail, the man of bone and muscle, and the fat man.

The assignment of vocation according to structure is but common sense. The dreamer has too slender a body for manual labor and is both too nervous and too impatient of confinement to sit in an easy chair or on the bench. The big, corpulent man enjoys the good things of life. He is well nourished and free from anxiety. He is, therefore, especially well fitted to judge calmly, deliberately and impartially. The man of bone and muscle is too busy with his physical activities for dreams and too impatient of confinement to sit in an easy chair or on the bench.

TEXTURE

Men also differ from one another very markedly in texture. This is easily observable in the texture of hair, skin, features, general body build, hands and feet. According to Prof. Ernst Haeckel, the skin is the first and oldest sense organ. Indeed, all the other sense organs and the nervous system and brain which have evolved in the use of them, are simply inturned and specialized skin cells. This being true, the texture of the entire organism, and especially the brain and nervous system, is accurately indicated by the texture of the skin and its appendages, the hair and nails.

Even the most casual observer notes the differences between the man with coarse hair, coarse skin, rugged features, large, loosely-built limbs, hands and feet, and the man with fine skin, silky hair, delicate, regular features, slender limbs, and finely moulded hands and feet. The individual of fine texture is sensitive and naturally refined. He loves beauty. He does his best work when he is creating something or handling something which is fine and beautiful. The coarse-textured individual is strong, vigorous, virile, and enduring. He can do hard, unpleasant work, can go through hardships, and can remain cheerful even in the midst of grimy, unpleasant and unlovely surroundings. For these reasons, fine-textured people do their best work in such lines as art, literature, music, jewelry, dry goods, millinery, and fine, delicate tools, machinery and materials; while we must rely upon coarse-textured people to do the heavy, hard, rough, pioneering and constructive work of the world. Even in art and literature coarse-textured people produce that which is either vigorous and virile or gruesome and horrible.

Because of their refined sensibilities, fine-textured people usually sympathize with the classes, the aristocracy; the coarse-textured people with the masses. It is a remarkable fact that practically all of our great liberators, radicals and revolutionists have been and are men of coarse texture. There is a great scientific truth underlying the saying amongst the people that certain ideas or books are "too fine-haired" for them.

PROPORTION

One of the most important of all the nine fundamental variables is proportion. This refers to proportion of one part of the body to another, of one part of the head to another. Each part of the body and of the head has its own particular function. Nature is orderly and systematic in all her work. She does not, therefore, try to digest food with the feet or pump blood with the hands. She does not try to use our stomachs as means of locomotion. Neither does she try to make us think with the

286

backs of our heads.

No one needs to be told that the long, slender, wiry legs of the deer were made for swiftness, or that the huge, square, powerful jaw of the bulldog was made to shut down with a vise-like grip that death itself can scarcely relax. These are crude examples of proportion. In our study and research we have learned to associate many fine gradations of differences in proportion with their corresponding differences in mental aptitudes and character.

EXPRESSION

Everything about a man indicates his character. Color, form, size, structure, texture, consistency, and proportion indicate almost entirely the man's inherent qualities. It is important for us to determine, however, in sizing up men, what they have done with their natural qualifications. This we do by observing Expression and Condition.

The cruder, simpler emotions are so frankly expressed that even a child or an animal can tell instantly whether a man is happy or loving, grieved or angry. These emotions show themselves in the voice, in the eyes, in the expression of the mouth, in the very way the man stands or sits or walks, in his gestures--in fact, in everything he does. In the same way, all of the finer and more elusive thoughts and emotions express themselves in everything a man says or does. Even when he does his best to mask his feelings, he finds that, while he is controlling his eyes and his voice, his posture, gestures, and even handwriting are giving him away. No living man can give attention to all of the modes of expression at once, and the trained observer quickly learns to discriminate between those which are assumed for the purpose of deception and those which are perfectly natural.

Transient emotions have transient expression, but the prevailing modes of thought and feeling leave their unmistakable impress just as surely as does a prevailing wind mould the form of all the trees growing in its path. The man who is sly, furtive, secretive, and fundamentally dishonest need not deceive you with his carefully manufactured expression of open-eyed frankness and honesty. If you have ever been "taken in" by a confidence man or a swindler, you either gave very slight attention to his expression or, what is more likely, suspected him but hoped to "beat him at his own game."

CONDITION

Discriminating employers long ago learned to observe carefully the condition of every applicant. It is now a pretty well accepted fact that the accountant who neglects his finger nails will probably also neglect his entries; that the clerk who is slovenly about his clothes will also be slovenly about his desk and his papers; that the man who cannot be relied upon to keep his shoes shined and his collar clean is a very weak and broken reed upon which to lean for anything requiring accuracy and dependability.

HOW THE SCIENCE IS VERIFIED

We have presented to you, in a brief way, the fundamental principles of the science of character analysis and the nine fundamental variables in man to which those principles apply. Are we not justified in saying that a body of knowledge which has been so classified and organized that the main fundamental facts of it can be presented in a few pages, is, indeed, a science? Add to this the fact that every conclusion is not only based upon these fundamental scientific principles, but has been carefully verified by investigation and observation in not only hundreds but thousands of cases, and has been used daily for years under the trying conditions of actual commercial practice, and this science has passed out of the merely experimental stage.

CHAPTER II

HOW TO LEARN AND APPLY THE SCIENCE OF CHARACTER ANALYSIS

There are two ways to learn any science.

The first is to begin by collecting all possible facts, recording them and verifying them under all possible conditions, until they are as thoroughly established as any facts can be in our imperfect human understanding. The collection of facts in this way requires the most painstaking research, oftentimes including many thousands of observations. When all the facts have been thus collected and verified, they are classified. Then they are carefully analyzed and an effort is made to find some of the laws which underlie them. Perhaps, instead of a definite law, all that can be at first advanced is a hypothesis or theory. This hypothesis or theory having been formulated, many thousands of observations are taken in an effort to establish it as a definite law or a principle. Oftentimes whole new realms have to be explored before this can be determined. Sometimes, after a theory is advanced, perhaps seems to be approaching complete establishment, some fact or set of facts is discovered which compels the setting aside of all old theories and the formulation of a new one. When a theory has been definitely established as a law, other laws are sought in the same way until, finally, there are enough laws established to form the basis of a general principle. Then more laws and more principles are added in the same way until, finally, the body of knowledge has become sufficiently accurate, sufficiently definite and sufficiently organized and classified to be called a science.

HOW SCIENCE SLOWLY EVOLVES

This is the way in which all of the sciences known to man were first learned; that is to say, they were learned by their formulators coincident with the process of their formulation. This is a slow and laborious process of learning. Few, if any, sciences have ever been thus mastered by any one individual. Indeed, the certain establishment of a very few facts, or, perhaps, only one important fact, the formulation of a theory, or the final statement of a law is usually the limit of the contribution of any one person to any science.

No science is independent. The science of physics, for example, could never have reached its present-day state of development if it had not laid heavy tribute upon the sciences of mathematics, astronomy, chemistry, geography, mechanics, optics, and others. In a similar way, the science of character analysis has derived many of its facts, laws, and even principles, from the sciences of physics, chemistry, biology, anthropology, ethnology, geography, geology, anatomy, physiology, histology, embryology, psychology, and others. Since this is true, it is obvious that the work of collecting, verifying, classifying, analyzing, and organizing the facts upon which the science of character analysis is based has been going on from the very dawn of civilization. Many investigators, students and scholars, in many branches of knowledge, have labored, added their little mite to the sum total, and passed on. The net result of all their work, all their thousands of years of research, investigation, study and thought, can now be gathered together and presented in so simple a form that it can be learned by anyone of intelligence in a few months. It took humanity untold thousands of years to learn the scientific truth that the earth is an oblate spheroid. Many men gave their lives to establish the truth. As a result, to-day every schoolboy learns and understands the fact within a very few days after his first opening of a text book on geography. Thousands of scholars have been working on the science of physics from the dawn of human intelligence down to the present date. Now a high school student learns all of its essentials and fundamentals in a short term of fourteen weeks.

A SHORT CUT TO KNOWLEDGE

The second method of learning a science, therefore, is to take advantage of all that has been done and, instead of beginning with facts and working up to principles, begin with principles and work down to a practical application amongst facts.

There are many ways of learning principles. One may memorize them from books, or have them set forth and explained by an instructor or lecturer, or stumble upon them in general reading, or work out a series of carefully prescribed experiments in a laboratory, leading up to an enunciation of the principles or, through its intelligent application in the world of work, establish it in one's consciousness.

The student who learns his laws and principles out of books may have a very clear and definite understanding of them. He may be able to add to them or to teach them. But he has little skill in their practical application as compared with the student who learns them in a laboratory. Furthermore, the laboratory student is at a disadvantage, probably, as compared with the man who makes intelligent application of the laws and principles to his daily work. So well recognized by educators is this truth that no attempt is made in our colleges and universities and, for the most part, even in our high schools, to teach sciences involving observation, logical reasoning and sound judgment purely out of books. Medicine, surgery, agriculture, horticulture, mechanics and other such sciences are now taught almost entirely by a combination of text books and actual practice. This rule also applies to the science of character analysis.

LEARN THE PRINCIPLES

The first step in the mastery and practical use of the science of character analysis is to learn the principles and the laws which underlie them. These principles and laws are comparatively few in number and comparatively simple. They are all classified under and grouped around the nine fundamental variables, a list of which was given in the preceding chapter.

The best way to learn a principle is not to memorize it, but to understand it. Learn, if possible, the reason for its existence, at least in a general way; the laws which underlie it, and the facts upon which it is based. The student who memorizes the words, "all bodies attract one another directly in proportion to their mass and inversely in proportion to the square of the distance between them," knows little or nothing about the law of gravitation, while the student who understands just what those words mean, whether he is able to repeat them correctly or not, does know the law of gravitation, and, if necessary, can probably apply it. The boy who learns that any object weighs less on a mountaintop than at the sea level learns an interesting and perhaps valuable fact. The man who learns that the law involved in this fact is the law of gravitation has learned something which he may be able to apply in a thousand ways. The man who, in the future, may learn *why* the law of gravitation operates as it does, may open untapped reservoirs of power for himself, for all humanity, and for all future generations. Therefore, in learning a principle, learn not only to understand it, but, if possible, *why*.

DEMONSTRATE AND VERIFY

Having gained as complete as possible an understanding of the laws and principles of the science of character analysis, the next step is to demonstrate to your own satisfaction that they are sound. This process will also enable you to understand them even more definitely and specifically than before.

When you learn, for example, that a blonde is more volatile, more fond of change and variety, more inclined to pioneering and government, than the brunette, you have learned an important law. When you study carefully the history of the evolution of the blonde and brunette races, you know why the law is as it is. But when you have gone out and observed several hundred blondes and several hundred brunettes and have seen them manifest dispositions, aptitudes and characteristics in accordance with the law, you have not only demonstrated the law to your own satisfaction, but you understand it even better than before. Furthermore, you are far better able than ever to determine the characteristics of the people you meet, as indicated by their color.

ANALYZE YOURSELF

There are many good reasons why the very first application of the knowledge of the principles and laws of character analysis should be to yourself. While, in one sense, you know your own thoughts and feelings and innermost desires and ambitions better than anyone else does, in another and very important sense, your friends and relatives probably understand you far better than you understand yourself. If you need any demonstration of this truth, look for it amongst your relatives and friends. You may have a relative, for example, who is very modest, retiring and diffident, who lacks self-confidence, who imagines that he is unattractive, unintelligent, and below the average in ability. You and all the rest of his friends, on the other hand, know that he has genuine talent, that he has an unusually attractive personality once his self-consciousness has been laid aside, that he is intelligent and far above the average in ability. Contrariwise, you may know someone who vastly over-estimates himself, whose own opinion of himself is at least fifty per cent higher than that of his relatives and immediate acquaintances. If other people, therefore, do not understand themselves, is it not at least probable that you do not understand yourself? So universal is this lack of self-under standing that the poet expressed a real human longing when he said:

"Oh, wad some power the giftie gie us To see oursels as others see us! It wad frae mony a blunder free us And foolish notion: What airs in dress and gait wad lea'e us And even devotion!"

Careful analysis of yourself, however, with your own intimate knowledge of the depths of your being will do more than give you an understanding of your own character. It will give you a better understanding of some, at least, of the laws and principles of character analysis. For this reason, it will also give you a far more intimate understanding of others.

COMPARE INDICATIONS AND CHARACTERISTICS

When you have learned what certain physical characteristics indicate, practise observing these indications amongst the people whom you know well. Try your skill at making the connection between the indication and the characteristics which, according to the science, it indicates. For example, go over in your mind all of the blondes you know and trace in their dispositions and characters, as you know them, the evidences of volatility, love of variety, eagerness, exuberance, positiveness, and other such characteristics. Take careful note as to how these qualities manifest themselves; observe differences in degrees of blondness, and corresponding differences in the degrees in which the characteristics indicated show themselves. Observe, also, how the various characteristics manifest themselves in combination. For example, note the difference between a blonde with a big nose and a blonde with a small nose.

ANALYZE, CHECK UP AND VERIFY

When you have analyzed yourself and your relatives, friends and acquaintances, you will be ready to begin on the analysis of people previously unknown to you. You will find them everywhere--in street-cars, in stores, on the streets, in churches and theaters, on athletic fields, in offices, in factories, in schools and in colleges. When you have analyzed them as carefully as you can and, if possible, have written down a brief outline of your analysis of them, check up and verify; find out how far you have been right. If, in any case, you find that you have been mistaken, find out why--study the case further. You have already demonstrated and verified your principles; therefore, either you have made an error in your observation or you have reasoned illogically in drawing your conclusions. Find out which it is and correct your analyses--then verify them.

This is a practice which, if you are at all interested in human nature, you will find intensely fascinating. It is one which you can pursue for years and not find it monotonous. Not a day will pass, if you are diligent in this practice, in which you will not learn something new, something interesting, something valuable. Those who have studied and practised this science for many years are, almost without exception, the ones who are most eager and enthusiastic about making these observations, analyses and verifications.

STUDY TYPES

Perhaps one of the most interesting and valuable forms of exercise in the practical application of this science is the study of types and their variations. Anyone who has observed humanity knows that, while no two persons are exactly alike, practically all human beings can be classified satisfactorily into comparatively a few general types. We have considered some of these types at length in earlier chapters of this book. It is by a study and comparison of people belonging to these general types, the careful noting of resemblances and differences, that the science of character analysis becomes almost as easy as the reading of a book. If you see a man for the first time who resembles in many important particulars of appearance some man you know well, study him to see whether he will not manifest in much the same way the same characteristics as your friend. This kind of observation, intelligently made, is the basis of accuracy and swiftness in making analyses.

KEEP ACCURATE AND ADEQUATE RECORDS

The human mind is an excellent storehouse of knowledge, but it should not be over-burdened. One of the first principles of efficiency as enunciated by Mr. Harrington Emerson is: "If you would find the best, easiest and quickest ways to the desirable things of life, keep and use immediate, reliable, adequate, and permanent records."

The complete record of an analysis should show the name, address, sex, exact age, height, weight, and all other essential physical characteristics of the person analyzed, classified under the head of the nine fundamental variables. It should show your conclusions as to his ability, disposition, aptitudes and character in general. It should also show the result of any further observations for the purpose of verifying your conclusions, and should be so kept that, if, at any time in the future, the individual should speak or act in any way which is either a striking verification of the analysis or in striking disparity with it, these incidents may be recorded and their relationship to what has gone before on the record studied.

Such records as these are valuable in many ways. When you have collected a large number of them, they become the basis of statistics, averages, and other interesting and important collections of facts.

STICK TO THE PRINCIPLES

It has been our universal experience amongst practitioners of this science that those who adhere most closely and most faithfully to its principles are most successful. There is always a strong inclination, especially on the part of those who are just beginning and those who are unusually emotional and sympathetic, to make exceptions. It is very difficult for some people of exceedingly sympathetic and responsive natures to analyze correctly. The personality of the individual being analyzed appeals to them either favorably or unfavorably. Perhaps his words make a strong impression upon them. All these things cloud the analyst's judgment and, instead of applying the principles rigidly, he falls back upon the old, unreliable method of analyzing by means of his "intuitions."

The laws and principles of the science of character analysis are based upon scientific truths regarding the development, evolution, history, anatomy and psychology of the human race. They have been verified by hundreds of thousands of careful observations. They have stood the test of years of practical use in the business world. They are now being successfully applied in commerce, in industry, in education, and in the professions, by thousands of people. They can be relied upon, therefore, to give you an intimate knowledge of the ability, disposition, aptitudes, and character in general of every human being who comes under your careful observation.

CHAPTER III

USES OF CHARACTER ANALYSIS

The old-time farmer planted his potatoes "in the dark of the moon." He probably took good care not to plant them on Friday, never planted a field of thirteen rows, and would have been horrified at putting them into the ground on the same day when he has spilled salt or broken a mirror. By taking all of this superstitious care to insure a good crop, he probably counted himself lucky if he got 100 bushels to the acre. Eugene Grubb, out in Wyoming, by throwing superstition to the four winds and depending, instead, upon exact scientific knowledge, leaves luck out of the question and knows that he will net 1,000 bushels to the acre.

One thousand years ago or more, our educational methods stiffened and set in the rigid moulds of tradition. For nine hundred years civilization and progress stood still. Then here and there men began to break the moulds with hammers of scientific knowledge. Education, instead of blindly following traditional forms, began to shape itself more and more to exact knowledge of the child nature and its needs--very slowly, cautiously and tentatively at first, but, as knowledge grew, with more and more boldness and freedom. This is one of the reasons why the last one hundred years has seen greater progress toward our dominion over the earth than all of the thousand years before it.

For more than four thousand years--perhaps more than five thousand-- men have been constructing buildings with bricks. Brick-laying was a trade, a skilled occupation, almost a profession, but its methods were based upon traditions handed down from father to son, from journeyman to apprentice, unbroken throughout that entire four-thousand-year period.

Then a bricklayer and his wife defied the heavens to fall, threw aside traditions and began to apply exact knowledge to brick-laying. As a result, they learned how to lay bricks three times as rapidly as the best workman had ever been able to before--and with less fatigue.

SCIENCE TAKES THE PLACE OF GUESSWORK

Fifty years ago, the merchant and the manufacturer guessed at their costs and fixed their prices with shrewd estimates as to their probable profits. They also guessed as to which departments of their business paid the most profit, how much and what kind of material they should buy, where the best markets were to be found, what would be the best location for their stores and factories, and many other important factors of profitable enterprise. Some of these old worthies were good guessers. They built up fairly large business institutions and made some very comfortable fortunes.

The business men of to-day--who are, indeed, of to-day and not a relic of yesterday and the day before yesterday--have an exact and detailed knowledge of their costs, determine prices scientifically, know definitely where are the best markets and what are the best locations for their factories, forecast with a reasonable degree of accuracy their need for materials, determine in a laboratory just which materials will best supply their needs, and in many other ways walk upon solid highways of exact information rather than upon the quaking bog of guesswork. Partly because of this, they have built up a multitude of institutions, each of them far larger than the largest of the olden days and have made fortunes which make the big accumulations of other days seem like mere pocket money. In making these fortunes for themselves, they have enabled millions not only to enjoy far larger incomes than people of their class and situation ever received before, but to enjoy conveniences and luxuries beyond even the dreams of the rich men and kings of olden days.

RANDOM METHODS YIELD TO SCIENTIFIC

In the old-time factories the various departments of work, machinery and equipment in each of the departments were arranged almost at random. Even a few years ago we sometimes saw factories in which the materials worked upon were moved upstairs, then downstairs, then back upstairs, hither and yon, until a diagram of their wanderings looked like a tangle of yarn. Even in offices, desks were placed at random and letters, orders, memoranda, and other documents and papers were moved about with all of the orderliness and method of a school-girl playing "pussy wants a corner." Modern scientific management, horrified at the waste of time and energy, makes accurate knowledge take the place of this random, helter-skelter, hit-or-miss basis of action and multiplies profits.

If the old-time farmer rotated his crops at all, he did it at random. He was, therefore, a little more likely than not, perhaps, to put a crop into a field which had been exhausted of the very elements that crop most needed. By this method and by other superstitious, guesswork, traditional, random, and neglectful methods, he struggled along on an average of about twenty bushels of corn to the acre, proudly defying anybody to teach him anything about farming out of books, or any white-collared dude from an agricultural college to show him anything about raising corn. Hadn't he been raising corn for nigh on forty years? How could there, then, be anything more for him to learn about its production?

But a little twelve-year-old boy down in what had always been supposed to be the poor corn lands of Alabama, by the painstaking application of a little simple knowledge, produced 232 and a fraction bushels of corn on one acre of land. Other boys in all parts of the South and of the corn belt began producing from 100 to 200 bushels of corn to the acre in the same way.

SCIENCE TAKES THE PLACE OF SUPERSTITION

Because man has lacked accurate knowledge about the world around him, he has been the credulous victim of countless generations of swindlers, fakers, fortune-tellers, mountebanks, and others experienced in chicanery. Speculators used to consult clairvoyants, crystal gazers, astrologists and card-readers for a forecast of business conditions. To-day, through accurate knowledge based upon statistics relative to fundamental factors in the business situation, they forecast the future with remarkable accuracy.

The practice of medicine was once a combination of superstition, incantation, ignorance and chicanery. In those days people were swept into eternity by the millions on account of plague, cholera, and other pestilences. To-day medical practice is based upon knowledge, and people who are willing to order their lives in accordance with that knowledge not only recover from their illnesses, but are scarcely ever ill. The ignorant man pays $1.00 for a small bottle of colored alcohol and water which some mountebank has convinced him is a panacea for all ills. In his blindness he hopes to drink health out of that bottle. The man who knows eats moderately, drinks moderately--if at all--smokes moderately--if at all--does work for which he is fitted and in which he can be happy, secures recreation and exercise according to his own particular needs, and almost never thinks of medicine. Should he need treatment, however, he goes to a man who has scientific knowledge of diagnosis and materia medica. The first man, in all likelihood, goes to an early grave, "stricken down by the hand of a mysterious Providence." The second man lives to a ripe old age and enjoys life more at eighty than he did at eight or eighteen.

Fifty years ago, mothers relied upon tradition and maternal instinct in the care of their babies. More than one-half of all the babies born died before they were five years old. The wise mother of to-day knows what

297

she is doing, and, as a result, infant mortality amongst the babies in her hands becomes an almost negligible quantity.

NEGLECT YIELDS TO SCIENCE

Because we did not know how to take care of them, we neglected our forests until they became well nigh extinct. To-day, by means of the science of forestry, we are slowly winning back the priceless heritage we almost threw away. Because of our ignorance, we neglected the by-products of our fields, our mines, and our industries, and no one can compute the fortunes we lost. Through scientific knowledge, we have begun to utilize these by-products. Some of the greatest of modern industries, and the fortunes which have grown out of them, are the result.

Selling and advertising used to be done partly by tradition and partly by instinct, so called. To-day, while they have, perhaps, not been reduced to exact sciences, they are based more and more upon exact knowledge, so that merchandizing has become less and less a gamble and more and more a satisfaction.

Since, through scientific knowledge, man has wrought such miracles in agriculture, construction, education, commerce, industry, finance, medicine, war, mining, and practically all of his other activities, it is time he applied the same scientific methods to that without which all these wonderful things would never have been executed, namely, his mind and soul.

SCIENTIFIC KNOWLEDGE OF SELF

In Part One of this book we have attempted to show the benefits which follow upon self-knowledge as to vocation. But this is only one phase, after all, of your life and activity. Obedience to the injunction, "know thyself," will help, also, to solve many of the hard problems you meet in education, social life, religion, morality, and family relations. The man who, through character analysis, has a scientific knowledge of himself, has therein a valuable guide to self-development and self-improvement. He knows which qualities to cultivate and which to restrain. He knows what situations and associations to avoid so that his frailties and weaknesses will handicap him as little as possible.

SCIENTIFIC KNOWLEDGE IN EMPLOYMENT

In Part Two we have shown briefly the application of knowledge of human nature to the selection, assignment and management of employees. In common with so many other important matters, this has been left in the past very largely to superstitious traditions, guesswork, random, hit-or-miss methods, chicanery, and so-called intuition. Now, for the sake of his profits, and also for the sake of the fellow human beings with whom he deals, the wise employer is seeking for and, in many cases, using exact knowledge.

SCIENTIFIC KNOWLEDGE IN PERSUASION

In Part Three we have referred to the use of character analysis in persuasion. Without this knowledge, it is the most natural thing in the world for the man who seeks to persuade others to present to them the arguments and suggestions which would appeal to him. Long ago some wise man said: "If you would persuade another, put yourself in his place; look at the matter through his eyes." 'Twas easier said than done. You cannot put yourself in another's place or see things from his point of view unless you know him accurately, which is possible only through the science of character analysis. We have often found people who have lived together for a lifetime who neither knew nor understood each other.

SCIENTIFIC KNOWLEDGE IN SOCIAL RELATIONS

Man's fundamental needs are food, drink, clothing, shelter, work, companionship, and rest. If one of man's fundamental needs is companionship, then he needs to know how to be successful socially. Most people deeply feel this need. One of the most frequent questions we are called upon to answer is: "How can I be a greater social success?" Social success depends upon personal attractiveness in the broadest sense of that term and upon a desire to make the most of that attractiveness. Many people have great social ambitions but, for some reason or other, are so unattractive that they are social failures. There are others who have pleasant personalities but who, because of other interests, neglect their social opportunities.

Personal attractiveness depends, first, upon the development of those elements which are pleasing to others, such as intelligence, judgment, reason, memory, sympathy, kindliness, courtesy, tactfulness, refinement, a sense of humor, decision, adaptability, self-confidence, proper personal pride, dignity, and perhaps others; second, upon a knowledge of each individual with whom one comes in contact, so that one knows best how to gain that person's favorable attention, to arouse his interest, and to give him pleasure.

Many people are shy, diffident, self-conscious, and painfully embarassed in the presence of strangers. They feel these deficiencies keenly. They long, perhaps with an intensity which the naturally self-possessed person will never know, for that social ease which they so greatly admire. Their self-consciousness, diffidence and timidity in the presence of others is very largely the result, first, of a lack of knowledge of themselves and how to make the most of their own good qualities socially; second, of a lack of knowledge of other people. It is a human trait deeply ingrained and going back to the very beginning of life to be afraid of that which we do not understand. Courage, self-confidence, and self-possession always come with complete understanding. Therefore, these timid, bashful ones may find, and many of them have found, greater social ease through a knowledge of themselves and of others, gained through a study of character analysis.

LOVE AND MARRIAGE

We shall probably not be disputed when we state that, aside from religion, at least, the most momentous problem in the life of every man and woman is that of love and marriage.

Says Edward Carpenter: "That there should exist one other person in the world toward whom all openness of interchange should establish itself, from whom there should be no concealment; whose body should be as dear to one, in every part, as one's own; with whom there should be no sense of Mine or Thine, in property or possession; into whose mind one's thoughts should naturally flow, as it were, to know themselves and to receive a new illumination; and between whom and one's self there should be a spontaneous rebound of sympathy in all the joys and sorrows and experiences of life; such is, perhaps, one of the dearest wishes of the soul. For such a union Love must lay the foundation, but patience and gentle consideration and self-control must work unremittingly to perfect the structure. At length, each lover comes to know the complexion of the other's mind; the wants, bodily and mental; the needs; the regrets; the satisfactions of the other, almost as his or her own--and without prejudice in favor of self rather than in favor of the other; above all, both parties come to know, in course of time, and after, perhaps, some doubts and trials, that the great want, the great need, which holds them together is not going to fade away into thin air, but is going to become stronger and more indefeasible as the years go on. There falls a sweet, an irresistible trust over their relation to each other, which consecrates, as it were, the double life, making both feel that nothing can now divide; and robbing each of all desire to remain when death has, indeed (or at least in outer semblance) removed the other.

"So perfect and gracious a union--even if not always realized--is still, I say, the bona fide desire of most of those who have ever thought about such matters."

A HEAVEN ON EARTH

In such a union as the author quoted has here described men and women find life's deepest and truest joys and satisfactions. In it there is solace for every sorrow, balm for every wound, renewal of life for every weariness, comfort for every affliction, a multiplication of every joy, a doubling of every triumph, encouragement for every fond ambition, and an inspiration for every struggle. Those who are thus mated and married have found a true heaven on earth. But such a mating and such a marriage is not, as many fondly suppose, based solely upon the incident of "falling in love." If we have no other advice to give the young man or the young woman than that which has so often been given, "let your heart decide," we have, indeed, little to offer.

MARRIAGE A PRACTICAL PARTNERSHIP

The marriage relationship is not wholly, or even chiefly, a romantic and ethereal social union far above and unaffected by material and practical considerations. While this spiritual union is an essential part of every true marriage, it cannot exist unless there is also a true union upon intellectual and physical planes. Marriage is, in one sense, a business partnership. In another sense, it is an intellectual companionship, and in still another sense, it is a friendly, social relationship.

A man and a woman are, therefore, mated in the true sense of the word, not alone by a mysterious and intangible spiritual identity, but by mutual beliefs, mutual ideas and ideals, mutual or harmonious tastes, mutual physical attractiveness, and mutual respect and admiration each for the other's talents, disposition, aptitudes, and character in general. One of the reasons why there are so many unhappy marriages is because a blind instinct, which may be purely physical or purely intellectual or purely psychical, which may be a mere passing fancy, which oftentimes is based upon the flimsiest and shallowest possible knowledge of each other's characteristics, is mistaken for love. Many marriages, of course, are consummated without even the existence of an imagined love--marriages for convenience, marriages because of pique, marriages arranged by parents or others. When such a marriage is a happy one, it is, indeed, by virtue of great good fortune, a happy accident.

KNOWLEDGE THE BASIS OF CHOICE

Since a true marriage, therefore, must encircle with its golden band and harmonize all of the psychical, intellectual and physical qualities, activities and interests of two people, it follows that it must be based upon knowledge as well as intuition. He who would choose a mate must, first of all, understand himself, so that he may know what qualities will be most agreeable to him. This may seem unnecessary, but, unfortunately, it is not. Any man who will compare his youthful tastes and judgment in regard to women with his mature inclinations will see the truth.

Second, he ought to know before he reaches the point of falling in love, the disposition and character of those to whom his fancy turns. When propinquity and mere physical attraction have aroused the emotions of a young couple, the ardor of their excitement so obscures observation and judgment that any careful analysis of each other's characteristics is impossible. Even if such an analysis were possible, one could not be intelligently made by a mere observation of behavior and conversation, even under the most advantageous circumstances. As a general rule, young people associate together in their "company clothes and company manners." Every possible endeavor is made to show forth that which is considered to be most desirable and to conceal, so far as possible, that which may be undesirable. Even traits and tendencies which do manifest themselves do so under disguise, as it were, and their full seriousness is not recognized. In fact, many a young man and young woman have found the very characteristics which appeared most charming in a lover or sweetheart the ugly rock upon which marital happiness was wrecked.

"CHARMS" WHICH PROVE DEADLY

For example, many girls admire rather fast young men. But few wives find happiness with drunken, gambling, unfaithful husbands. Many young women experience a delightful thrill of interest in the young man who is inclined to be somewhat authoritative. But few wives submit with pleasure to the exactions of a domineering husband. Some young women find a gay, careless irresponsibility charming in a lover but bitterly resent having to shoulder all the burdens of financing and maintaining a home.

In a similar way, some men admire dimpled, pouting girls, but they cordially detest whimpering, whining wives. Most men are flattered by an air of helpless dependence in a sweetheart, but they soon grow tired of a wife who cannot think and act for herself and who is, perhaps, an imaginary or real invalid.

These characteristics in both men and women may be mere affectations and mannerisms, assumed for the purpose of imagined allurement and charm. Or they may be bedded deep in the character. Only a scientific knowledge of human nature will reveal the truth.

KNOWLEDGE IN MARITAL RELATIONS

No matter how truly mated a man and woman may be, life-long happiness in the marriage relation depends upon mutual understanding. Many a noble ship of matrimony has been wrecked hopelessly upon the jagged rocks of misunderstanding. Character analysis opens the eyes, reveals tendencies and motives and offers true knowledge as a guide to the making of one's self truly lovable, and the finding and bringing out in the other of lovable qualities.

An intelligent woman of thirty once said to us: "I could never get along with my father. As soon as I began to have a mind of my own, he and I clashed, notwithstanding the fact that I loved him and he idolized me. After I had married and left home, my love for him frequently drew me back under his roof for a visit. But before I had been there a week we had somehow managed to have a bitter quarrel and separated in anger. After I learned to apply the principles of character analysis, I returned home on a visit and the first thing I did was to analyze father. For the first time in my life I understood him. Since that time we have never clashed, and my visits with him are a great joy to me as well as to him."

We have in our files a sheaf of letters from both men and women telling of the regaining of a lost paradise through mutual knowledge and mutual understanding.

THE SCIENCE OF CHARACTER ANALYSIS NOT A CURE-ALL

We do not offer the science of character analysis as a panacea. We have already emphasized the fact that mere knowledge of one's true vocation is not enough for an unqualified success in it. We do not believe that character analysis alone will solve the age-long problem of capital and labor, nor do we hold forth the promise that a scientific knowledge of human nature will enable every individual who obtains it to be uniformly successful in selling, advertising, public speaking legal practice, and other forms of persuasion. The serious and intricate puzzles of social life will find no golden key which unlocks them all in the science of character analysis. The supreme problems of love, marriage, marital relations, divorce, and family life are far beyond the limited scope of character analysis for their complete solution. Human life; human efficiency; human mental, moral, and physical development; human civilization in all of its aspects, are a matter of slow evolution, with many a slip backward. He is either self-deceived or a charlatan who claims to have found that which will enable the race to arrive at perfection in a single bound.

On the other hand, just so far as even one spark of true knowledge is a light on the way, to the degree in which one little adjustment helps men to harmonize with nature and her eternal forces, and in the measure in which one solid step adds to the causeway which man is building out of the mire of ignorance to the heights of wisdom--in so much is the science of character analysis an aid to man and his striving toward perfection and happiness.